CHRISTIANITY

"Hill offers a delightfully fresh telling for religious and non-religious readers alike. Balanced and engaging, Hill's clean and easy style makes the messy business of emerging Christianity a riveting read for experts and novices alike."

Kristin M. Swenson
Virginia Commonwealth University
Author of *Bible Babel*

CHRISTIANITY

HOW A DESPISED SECT

FROM A MINORITY RELIGION

CAME TO DOMINATE THE ROMAN EMPIRE

JONATHAN HILL

FORTRESS PRESS
MINNEAPOLIS

CHRISTIANITY
How a Despised Sect of a Minority Religion
Came to Dominate the Roman Empire

Fortress Press edition: 2011.
Copyright © 2010 Jonathan Hill
This edition copyright © 2010 Lion Hudson

Cover image © Werner Forman/CORBIS
Cover design: Nicole Summers

Library of Congress Cataloging-in-Publication Data available
978-0-8006-9777-8

Manufactured in China
16   15   14   13   12   11   1   2   3   4   5   6   7   8   9   10

Contents

Introduction

Christianity was founded by a group of fishermen and peasants from Galilee, a rural backwater in an unimportant region of the Roman empire. They were the followers of a relatively minor wandering prophet who had died as a condemned criminal. When their movement came to the attention of the Roman authorities, it was brutally suppressed. Yet little more than three centuries later, the Christian religion had become the faith of the empire itself. Christian bishops had combined Christian theology with classical philosophy to create an intellectual and spiritual synthesis that would endure for over a thousand years, while Christian emperors were busy dismantling the ancient religion of Rome itself and supplanting it with the official teachings of a triumphant church. How did this happen? How did this unregarded Jewish cult come to displace the traditional religion of the empire and go on to become the largest religion in the world?

In this book we trace the first four centuries of Christianity. These centuries were the most tumultuous and important in the religion's history. They saw Christianity not only being founded but being refined and defined as it faced a series of potentially crippling challenges, both internal and external. These forced Christians to reflect on their faith and what it meant. By the end of this period, Christians possessed official declarations of doctrine and practice, holy writings, and ecclesiastical and monastic structures that were capable of enforcing orthodoxy. None of these things existed in the days of the first disciples of Jesus. So the first four centuries were truly a crucible for Christianity. It began rather rough and ill-defined, caught between a disapproving Jewish leadership and a hostile Roman state. It endured centuries of proscription, persecution, and massacres in both the Roman and the Persian empires. It emerged stronger than ever – but had

it been refined by the experience, or changed out of all recognition?

Throughout, our focus is on what the Christian religion really meant to its adherents. How did they live and what did they believe? Why did they believe these things? To understand these, we must place the early church in its social and cultural context, and see how the early Christians interacted with the world around them. For the crucible of the first four centuries did not simply refine and transform the Christian religion: it did the same thing to the pagan and Jewish religions, and to society as a whole.

This book is divided into three main sections. The first three chapters tell the story of the founding of Christianity and its first century, roughly the period in which the New Testament was written. Since this period is relatively well known and covered, these chapters are relatively brief. Chapters 4–7 then cover the next two centuries. In them we find out how Christianity developed and spread within Roman society and beyond during this period, and how it reacted to the increasingly violent persecutions against it. We also find out how Christians began to construct notions of orthodoxy and heresy, and how they distinguished between them. Finally, the last four chapters of the book cover the fourth Christian century. We see how Christianity was decriminalized, promoted, and finally made the official religion of Rome, and how the traditional Roman religion was increasingly marginalized and forbidden. But we also see how Christianity was riven by its greatest internal divisions yet, and how it forged a new understanding of its doctrinal and spiritual heritage.

Jesus and the First Christians

Christianity was, and still is, unusual among the major religions in that its founder is also its message. Christians do not simply believe things that Jesus taught – they believe things *about* Jesus. So who was Jesus? What do we know about him? How did his followers come to believe such remarkable things about him?

Judaism

Both Jesus himself and the first generation of Christians can be understood only in the context of the Jewish religion. Judaism in the first century was enormously complex and is still only imperfectly understood. A proper discussion of Judaism and the various parties and sects that composed it is beyond the scope of this book. Here we shall just indicate some of the most important and relevant elements.

All Jews believed that they belonged to a special people, descended from Abraham. All Jewish boys were circumcised on the eighth day after their birth as a sign of this covenant, and all Jews sought to keep the Law. This was part of a sacred covenant between God and his people. God, for his part, had promised to Israel – the Jewish people – that they would occupy the land of Palestine. Perhaps the greatest event in the sacred history of Israel was the exodus, described in the book of that name in the Old Testament, when God had rescued his people from slavery in Egypt and brought them to the Promised Land. He had given the Law to Moses and Israel had promised to keep it. The holiest festival in the Jewish religion was therefore Passover, when Jews ate a sacred meal in remembrance of the meal that their ancestors had shared on the eve of their departure from Egypt.

Modern-day ultra-Orthodox Jewish men say the Passover prayers at the Western Wall in Jerusalem's Old City.

At the heart of the Jewish religion was the Temple, which had originally been built by King Solomon in Jerusalem centuries before and had been recently restored and rebuilt by Herod the Great. This immense building and its precincts surrounded an inner chamber, known as the Holy of Holies, which could be entered only by the high priest, once a year. The Pentateuch prescribed a complex system of sacrifices which were all offered here, and it employed around 20,000 priests and lower clergy, known as Levites. The number was so high because they all worked only part time at the Temple, spending most of their time in other jobs all over Palestine. This meant that although there was only one Temple, there were priests in every community.

Although the Temple was central to Judaism, most Jews did not live in Jerusalem and could not visit it often. The central focus of most Jewish communities was the synagogue. Synagogues at this time were places not of worship or sacrifice, but of prayer and study of the Scriptures. In most synagogues, a meeting would have involved readings from the Scriptures, as well as prayers, and the recitation of passages from the Scriptures. These Scriptures were also central to the Jewish faith, although it had not yet been officially decided which texts were 'scriptural' and which were not; the notion of a 'canon' of Scripture distinct from all other writings had not yet developed. The most important texts, however, were those contained in the Torah, also known as the Pentateuch, consisting of the first five books of what Christians call the Old Testament. These books contained the story of the creation, God's covenant with Abraham and the other ancestors of the Jews, the exodus from Egypt, and the Law which he gave to Moses. The attempt to follow this law in all aspects of life was one of the major elements of Judaism as a religion, and one of the major ways in which Jews as a people distinguished themselves from others.

The Jewish Sukkot holiday is celebrated by the Premishlan congregation in Bnei Brak, Israel. The *rebbe* (rabbi) is seen with his hassids who are carrying the Four Species.

Jesus' Palestine

It is often thought that the Palestine in which Jesus lived was an occupied territory. His people was a conquered people, living in fear of the Roman forces who taxed them mercilessly or treated them like slaves, an image which has been reinforced by Hollywood in films such as *Ben Hur* and parodied by Monty Python's *Life of Brian*. In fact the truth was much more complex. Rather than rule the area directly, the Romans preferred to appoint a suitable local ruler. At the time of Jesus' birth, this was Herod the Great, who had been in power for over thirty years. Herod ruled mostly independently, although he was required to send tribute to Rome and follow Roman foreign policy.

When Herod died in 4 BC, his territory was divided between his sons. However, the son who governed Judea – the most important part, where Jerusalem was – proved ineffective and unpopular. In AD 6, the Roman emperor Augustus removed him from power and replaced him with a Roman official, the prefect, who would govern this area directly. But the prefect did not do much day-to-day governing. He left that to the Jewish high priest of the Temple in Jerusalem.

Jesus came from Galilee, in the north, and apparently spent most of his life there. It was a largely rural, agricultural area noted for the fertility of its soil and the excellent fishing in the large lake known as the Sea of Galilee. So he lived in an area that was technically part of the Roman empire but which was effectively self-governing. He would have seen Roman-style civilization in the Hellenized towns of the region, especially Sepphoris – just a few miles from Nazareth – and Tiberias. But scholars disagree over how 'Roman' life was in these towns, which seem to have had largely Jewish populations, and how much they might have allowed someone like Jesus to become familiar with Roman culture.

Map of Palestine in Jesus' time, showing the division of Herod the Great's territory between his four sons.

Sidon

Tyre

PHOENICIA

Caesarea Philippi

GAULANTIS
TRACHONITIS

Chorazin
Jordan
BATANAEA

Magdala
Capernam
Sea of Galilee

GALILEE
Tiberias
AURANITIS

Sepphoris
Nazareth
Gadara

DECAPOLIS

Caesarea

Scythopolis

Plain of Sharon

Gerasa

SAMARIA

Jordan

PERAEA

Lydda

Jericho

Jerusalem
Qumran

Bethlehem
Bethany

Ascalon

JUDEA
Dead Sea
Machaerus

Masada

IDUMEA

— border of Herod's realm

to Archelaus

to Herod Antipas

to Philip

to Province of Syria

Salome's portion

0   60 km
0   40 miles

Because the Law was so central to Jewish life, interpreting it properly was a key concern of many Jews. There were many points where the Torah was not exactly clear, and these sparked debates among Jewish scholars about what exactly it meant. Scholars would issue pronouncements which would be treated by their followers as definitive, and which would become rather like legal precedents. These pronouncements were known as *halakah*, and they would eventually find their way into a vast corpus of literature known as the Mishnah, which was compiled over the following couple of centuries. However, different scholars often interpreted things differently.

In many ways, then, Judaism was very uniform. But there was also considerable variety within it. By Jesus' day there were more Jews outside Palestine than in it, mostly spread throughout the Roman and Persian empires. Every city contained a Jewish community with its own synagogue. Inevitably, the Judaism of the Diaspora tended to be less focused upon the Temple than Judaism in Palestine. Members of these communities might be influenced by local religious or philosophical traditions.

Even in Palestine itself there were different groups within Judaism. One of the most important in the first century were the Pharisees, who were mostly laymen, although a few were also priests. The Pharisees had no official status or authority within Jewish society or religion; they were simply a group of dedicated Jews who were particularly interested in trying to understand the Law and apply it to their lives. In pursuit of this aim they developed a number of *halakah*, although these were intended for their own use, and were not meant to be normative for other people. However, the Pharisees were extremely popular; even those who did not belong to this party liked them because they were trying to preserve and apply their people's traditions and cultures.

There was also a strong current among some Jewish groups of eschatology, or interest in the end times. Many believed that God would, at some point, make a massive personal intervention in history, when all wrongs would be righted; this would effectively be the end of the world and the beginning of something new and better. This way of thinking had its roots in various passages from the prophetic writings, some of which predicted that a new King David (one of the great heroes of Jewish history) would emerge in the end times. But there were different versions of this hope. Some were political in nature: people hoped that God would appear and remove the Romans, restoring Israel to full independence. Others were more global in scope: people hoped that God would appear and sweep away the whole earthly system, making a far more radical change than just a different government. There were also different versions of the new David, although most eschatologists (scholars of the end times) agreed that he would be a human descendant of the ancient king. Some texts refer to him as 'Messiah', a term meaning 'anointed'. It is important to note that this title did not imply that he would be anything more than a normal human being, although he would be specially blessed and ordained by God.

These various eschatological hopes sometimes coalesced around individual figures. There were, in fact, many charismatic teachers and others around at the time. Some were regarded as miracle-workers. One of the most famous was Honi the Circle Drawer, who was active a few decades before the birth of Jesus. He would draw a circle on the ground and stand in it praying to God. He had a particular reputation for being able to pray for rain. Another well-known miracle-worker was Hanina ben Dosa, who was probably a younger contemporary of Jesus and came from Gabara, just a few miles from Nazareth. He could also apparently pray for rain, but, like Jesus, he was especially famous for his healing miracles.

The earliest known fragment of the New Testament is *P52*. Dating from c. AD 125, it contains text from John 18.

Jesus

More books have been written about Jesus than about any other figure from history. Today, scholarly interest in the historical Jesus is intense, and the literature on the subject is vast, offering a dizzying array of interpretations of the evidence. Once again, a proper survey of the information is well outside the scope of this book. We can, however, offer a brief outline of what we can know, with a reasonable degree of confidence, about Jesus.

The sources for Jesus

The sources for Jesus' life fall into three main groups. First, there are non-Christian sources. The early ones are extremely patchy and tell us nothing except that Christians followed him, while the later ones either depend upon Christian sources or seem unreliable. Second, there are Christian sources outside the New Testament, such as Gospels that purport to describe Jesus' life or teachings, but which never made it into the Christian Bible. Most scholars agree that almost all of them give us no reliable information about the real Jesus. Most were written relatively late (from the second century AD onwards) and contain material that is obviously legendary or written simply to support the doctrines of the groups who produced them. The only major exception to this is the Gospel of Thomas, but scholars do not agree whether the author of this Gospel had access to authentic sources apart from the canonical Gospels.

The third group of sources is by far the most important: the New Testament, that is, the documents from the early church which, by the end of the fourth century AD, were accepted throughout the church as Scripture. The most important part of the New Testament for our knowledge of Jesus is the four Gospels, which are named after the people who are traditionally supposed to have written them, Matthew, Mark, Luke, and John. Matthew and John were disciples of Jesus, while Mark and Luke were followers of Peter and Paul respectively. However, the texts themselves include no authors' names, and most scholars today think it unlikely that these people really wrote the Gospels. But it is usual to use the traditional names to refer to both the Gospels themselves and their authors, for convenience's sake. Matthew, Luke, and Mark are known as the 'Synoptic Gospels', meaning that they have a similar viewpoint; there is much repetition between them and it is likely that Matthew and Luke both took material from Mark. John has different material and is different in tone from the others. Many scholars believe that John is less historically reliable than the Synoptics, but some disagree.

As this suggests, no one is quite sure how reliable the Gospels are as sources for Jesus himself. Most of the material in them seems to be based upon earlier, oral traditions, mainly fairly short stories about Jesus. These were originally stories which Christians told each other about Jesus: the authors of the Gospels collected these and wrote them down. The order in which they appear in the Gospels therefore seems to be entirely the invention of the authors, but the stories themselves were not, at least for the most part.

This means that the Gospels are very complex documents. When we read one of these books, we are not simply reading a single text that a single author sat down and wrote – either as a form of fiction or as an honest memoir. Each Gospel contains a number of voices. First, there is whatever Jesus himself actually said or did. Second, there are the innumerable Christians who, later on, remembered the event and told it to one another, perhaps changing elements here and there. And third, there is the author of the Gospel, who wrote down the story as he heard it and perhaps changed it himself, or created a context for it, to make it serve his purpose.

This is not to say that trying to isolate the first of these layers – Jesus himself – from the others is a hopeless task. Both the oral tradition and the writers could be quite conservative and reluctant to alter important elements. A good modern analogy might be jokes. When a joke is told and retold, it tends to change as each teller gives it his or her own spin – but the basic 'point' of the joke, the situation it describes, and the punchline tend to remain the same. If they didn't, the joke would lose its value. Similarly, we can imagine that stories about Jesus were moulded as they were transmitted, but that the 'point' would tend to remain roughly intact.

The ministry of Jesus

Jesus was actually called Yeshua ('Jesus' is a Latinization). It was a fairly common Jewish name at the time and also appears in another form as 'Joshua'. He was probably born in around 4 BC in Palestine and apparently worked in Galilee as an artisan, perhaps (although not certainly) a carpenter. At some point he became attached to the movement associated with John the Baptist, a popular preacher, and was baptized. He then set out as a preacher

The titles of Jesus

In John's Gospel, Jesus hardly ever talks about the kingdom of God or gives ethical teaching, but instead talks about himself most of the time. In this teaching, which is delivered openly, he calls himself 'the Son', and he speaks of his relationship to 'the Father', that is, God. But the Synoptics offer a completely different picture. There, Jesus' teaching is dominated by moral questions and the kingdom of God; he talks about himself very rarely. When he does, he does not talk of 'the Son' or offer 'I am' statements. Instead, by far the most common phrase he uses is 'Son of man'. But it is not clear whether this is an oblique way of referring to his own mortality and humanity (the phrase has this meaning in the book of Ezekiel) or a way of claiming to be a heavenly herald of the eschaton (the end times) (it has this meaning in the book of Daniel, chapter 7).

Other titles for Jesus appear in the Gospels, with two in particular being of interest. The first is 'Son of God'. In later centuries, Christians came to believe that Jesus had two natures: he was fully divine and fully human at the same time. Later theologians often used the two titles – 'Son of God' and 'Son of man' – to express these two natures. The implication was that the title 'Son of God' indicated Jesus' divinity just as 'Son of man' indicated his humanity. However, this is not what it would have meant to first-century Jews. The title 'Son of God' appears at various points in the Jewish Scriptures, where it is applied to different people, generally meaning that they are especially dear to God. For example, Psalm 2:7 applies it to

the king of Israel. In the Gospels, Jesus never calls himself by this title; it is always suggested by other people, although he usually does not deny it. In fact the most common appearance of the term in the Gospels is in exorcisms, when demons use it to address Jesus. So the question whether Jesus believed himself to be 'the' Son of God, which is sometimes asked today, is rather misleading. Whether Jesus himself used that actual title of himself or not, he did at least believe himself to be close to God and favoured by him; and that is all that the title would have meant to him and his contemporaries. It certainly would not have meant that he was *literally* God's biological offspring.

Finally, there is the title 'Messiah'. It is surprising, given how important the title 'Christ' (the Greek version of 'Messiah') would later be for Christians, how rarely this title appears in the Gospels. Jesus is almost never represented as applying it to himself. Indeed, the remarkable paucity of material portraying Jesus as claiming to be the Messiah, when the authors of the Gospels were convinced that he *was* the Messiah, indicates how reluctant they were to invent material of their own. If the authors of the Gospels were more interested in glorifying Jesus and confirming the beliefs that they and their readers had about him than they were in the historical truth, we might expect them to have simply invented a few sayings of their own in which Jesus told everyone he was the Messiah. The fact that they did not do this shows that they were quite conservative in their handling of the material.

in his own right and acquired a reputation as a miracle-worker, as well as a group of disciples. In around AD 30, he was put to death near Jerusalem on the orders of the Roman prefect of Judea, Pontius Pilate. But within a few days, his disciples were convinced that he had been raised from the dead, and began preaching that he was the long-awaited Messiah.

Details are harder to fill in. As with other ancient figures from lowly backgrounds, we probably know most about the end of Jesus' life and least about its beginning. All four Gospels portray Jesus as being initially involved with John the Baptist in some way, but he soon left John the Baptist and started preaching in his own right. According to the Synoptic Gospels, Jesus preached almost exclusively in Galilee, and then made one fateful journey to Jerusalem, which ended in his death. According to John, however, Jesus preached all over Palestine, and visited Jerusalem on a number of occasions. Nevertheless, all the sources agree that Jesus preached, that he healed people, and that he worked non-healing miracles too. It seems certain that, at the very least, Jesus had a reputation for all of these things within his lifetime or very soon afterwards. This in itself was unusual. There were various holy men with reputations for working miracles, and there were preachers who taught their followers how to live, but we know of no one who did both to the extent that Jesus seems to have done.

The Presentation of Christ Before the People, c. 1500, painted by Hieronymus Bosch (c.1450–1516).

Opposition and death

The Gospels tell us that Jesus clashed repeatedly with various individuals and groups during his ministry, clashes that ultimately led to his death. Much of the controversy described in the Gospels concerns Jesus' attitude to the Law. For example, a series of stories from Mark 2:1 to 3:6 shows the Pharisees objecting to Jesus' behaviour: he tells people their sins are forgiven; he eats with sinners; he does not fast; his disciples pick grain on the Sabbath; and he heals someone on the Sabbath. Most of these actions would probably not have been offensive or law-breaking. For example, telling someone that their sins were forgiven would have been a normal way of stating that God forgave them, while healing someone simply by speaking did not break any rules about the Sabbath at all. Moreover, Jewish religious experts themselves disagreed about how to interpret and apply the Law. Jesus' actions and sayings on the matter seem to fit well into that tradition, which makes it hard to see how they could have brought about the kind of opposition that the Gospels report. The rabbinical literature tells us of Jewish teachers who deliberately flouted the Law altogether without being murdered for it. It seems likely, then, that these accounts of conflicts with Pharisees and others over the Law reflect the later situation of Christians rather than of Jesus himself. They were written at a time when many Christians were facing great opposition from many Jews, and they make it seem as if Jesus faced the same kind of opposition.

Moreover, the Gospels suggest that the hostility that Jesus aroused was so great that it led to his death. It seems intrinsically unlikely that such extreme hostility could have come from these kinds of disputes; Jewish teachers disagreed with one another all the time about such things without plotting to kill one another. It may, then, be more likely that Jesus' death was caused by more immediate factors associated with his presence in Jerusalem during Passover, rather than by long-term factors that had been building up over the course of his ministry.

It is virtually certain that Jesus was indeed crucified on the orders of Pontius Pilate, probably in around AD 30. No official record of the sentence exists, but enormous numbers of people were executed in this fashion and no official records survive for any of them. But we can be confident that the Gospels are correct in saying that Jesus was crucified, because the later Christians would not have made it up. As we shall see in chapter 3, increasingly hostile relations with the Jewish authorities led the Christians to tend to try to 'blame' them for Jesus' death, and exonerate the Romans and especially Pilate. But crucifixion was a Roman punishment. If the Christians had invented the details of Jesus' death, they would probably have said he had been stoned to death, a more Jewish method of execution. As it is, the authors of the Gospels have to take considerable pains to 'show' that although Pilate ordered Jesus' death, he did so very reluctantly and only because the Jewish leaders forced him to. It seems that we can safely conclude that Jesus really did die in this way.

To suffer Roman execution Jesus must have committed some crime against the Roman state. According to the Gospels, Pilate ordered his men to attach a mocking sign to Jesus' cross, reading 'This is the king of the Jews'. If Jesus had made such a claim it would have been a treasonous rejection of the authority of Rome, and this would explain why Rome had him executed. According to the Gospels, the high priest of the Temple in Jerusalem had handed Jesus over to Pilate for punishment. The high priest was responsible for keeping public order, but he could not authorize executions.

Why, then, did the high priest arrest Jesus in the first place? He may simply have seen Jesus as a troublemaker. This preacher had arrived in Jerusalem during Passover, when the city was packed with pilgrims and tensions were high, and the Roman prefect and his men were in residence to try to keep things calm. He had entered the city in a sort of 'triumph' on a donkey, gone around preaching about the kingdom of God and predicting that the Temple would be destroyed, and caused some kind of disturbance in the Temple itself. That would probably have been quite enough for the high priest to want to remove Jesus from the scene before anything got out of hand.

The first Christians

The followers of Jesus

Even during his own lifetime, Jesus was not an isolated figure but the focal point of a movement. Jesus is the main character of the Gospels, but they feature a strong supporting cast of disciples. Jesus' disciples were not simply hangers-on who decided they might learn something from him; he actively went out and commanded at least some of them to follow him. The Gospels agree that this was one of the first things he did, almost immediately after his baptism. Two sets of brothers – Simon and Andrew, and James and John – were the most important. In the Synoptic Gospels, Andrew falls into the background, leaving James and John and above all Simon (whom Jesus renames Peter) as the leading disciples. These three were part of a group known as 'the Twelve'. The Twelve are named at various points in the Gospels, but the names do not all add up to exactly twelve. However, we can explain this apparent discrepancy easily if we bear in mind that 'the Twelve' was actually the name of the group, and not simply the number of its members. Twelve was a very significant number in antiquity, and it was especially significant to Jews, being the number of the sons of Jacob and of the tribes descended from him. But the twelve tribes had been scattered and most of them lost. If Jesus chose an inner circle of disciples called 'the Twelve', then he did so to make a symbolic point: this was to be the beginning of the renewal of Israel and its twelve tribes. And if this is so, then there needn't actually have been precisely twelve of them. The name was what mattered. This would explain why, if one adds up all the disciples named as members of the Twelve in the Gospels, one comes up with rather too many.

Certainly the most prominent of the Twelve was Peter, who acts more or less as the spokesman for the disciples in the Synoptics. Close behind him come James and John; these three are present at Jesus' transfiguration in Mark 9:2–8, and he takes them with him to pray just before his arrest in Mark 14:33. In John's Gospel, however,

James and John are not even mentioned, except obliquely in 21:2, and Peter is rivalled by an unnamed 'beloved disciple'. Traditionally, this disciple has been thought to be John (and the author of the Gospel, hence the name). A flaw with that explanation is that if he were John one would expect him to be accompanied by James, but James doesn't appear at all. Perhaps this disciple *is* John or one of the others, who had founded the community that read the Gospel, and therefore did not need to be named; or perhaps the character is simply a literary device of the author's and cannot be identified with any historical figure at all.

There were many other disciples too – Paul mentions a group of over 500 of them in 1 Corinthians 15:6. The Twelve appear to have all been men, but many women are mentioned in the Gospels as quite dedicated disciples. By far the most famous female disciple is Mary Magdalene. However, contrary to some popular accounts, virtually nothing is known about her, like most of the other named disciples in the Gospels. Later stories that she was a reformed prostitute, or that she was in love with Jesus and even bore his child, have no basis in any reliable evidence.

These disciples formed the core of what would later become the church. To any observer at the time of Jesus' arrest, this might not have seemed very likely. The Gospels tell us that even before Jesus had been executed, his disciples scattered in fear. When bystanders asked Peter if he was one of Jesus' followers, he denied that he even knew him. After his death, Jesus' body was taken down and buried in a grave donated by a supporter, Joseph of Arimathea, but the burial was done quickly because it was Friday afternoon and the Sabbath was about to begin. It was not permissible to handle a dead body on the Sabbath. Apart from Joseph, who according to Mark 15:46 actually took Jesus' body down from the cross and wrapped it, the only disciples left on the scene were some of the women, notably Mary Magdalene. Perhaps the male disciples had given up and run away entirely.

The resurrection

All four Gospels tell us that on the Sunday morning, with the Sabbath over, the women returned to Jesus' tomb to finish preparing his body properly. But they found the tomb – a cave with a large stone in front of the entrance – empty. Mark's Gospel ends there, with the women leaving the tomb fearfully and telling no one. Later editors seem to have found this unsatisfactory and tacked on two alternative endings to the Gospel, which tell us that in fact the women went and told the other disciples, and that Jesus himself appeared to them. This is exactly what happens in the other Gospels: they all agree that the first people to encounter the risen Jesus were the women, that the women returned to the male disciples and told them what had happened, and that Jesus appeared to all of them.

People have proposed all sorts of theories about what 'really' happened – everything from Jesus not really being dead at all, and waking up and walking off, to someone hiding the body as a practical joke. Many others argue that the best explanation is that Jesus really did rise from the dead and appear to his followers. One of the central issues here is how reasonable it is to accept a 'miraculous' explanation of events such as this. It is not the place of this book to try to answer questions of this kind. We can, however, at least point to another problem in interpreting the resurrection stories, which is quite distinct from metaphysical or theological issues. This is that the evidence is so fragmentary. The Gospels agree on some key points, such as that it was Jesus' female followers who first went to the tomb on Sunday morning and realized that something dramatic had happened. But they disagree on which women it was and whether they saw the risen Jesus themselves. They also disagree on who saw Jesus after this, and under what circumstances. They even disagree on what form the risen Jesus took. Some stories describe him as apparently a normal, physical person who could eat and drink; others have him passing through locked doors or changing his appearance in the blink of an eye. In 1 Corinthians 15:8, Paul – who never met Jesus in his lifetime, and who does not explicitly mention the story of the empty tomb – lists himself as one of those who saw the risen Jesus. But the description of this event in Acts 9 suggests that all he saw was a bright light, not a physical person at all. Later, in 1 Corinthians 15, Paul speaks of the future resurrection of all believers, of which he regards Jesus' resurrection as a sort of prototype. He tells his readers that they will be raised with a 'spiritual body', the meaning of which is hard to determine.

There can be no reasonable doubt that the disciples believed that Jesus had been raised from the dead and that he had appeared to his followers. All the early Christian sources agree on that fundamental claim, at least, and the subsequent history of the first years of the Christian church confirms the certainty with which the disciples continued to believe it. But it is less certain what these first disciples thought that 'raised from the dead' meant, exactly, or what they experienced that led them to hold this belief with such devotion. This means that it seems very hard to state with any certainty – from a historical point of view – what actually happened.

The Acts of the Apostles

In dealing with the Christian movement in the first two decades after Jesus' death, we are reliant almost entirely upon a single document: the book known as the Acts of the Apostles, or just Acts.

This book, which appears in the New Testament after the Gospel of John, was almost certainly written by the same person who wrote the Gospel of Luke – scholars sometimes refer to 'Luke-Acts', as if it were a single work in two volumes. It is traditionally thought to have been written by Luke, one of Paul's companions, because in some passages it slips into the first person, suggesting that it was written by somebody who was actually there. However, scholars disagree over how these passages should be interpreted, and they may well be just a literary device.

Acts probably dates from around the 80s of the first century – some decades after the events it describes. Some scholars are very dubious about the value of Acts as a historical document, partly because the sections of it that deal with Paul seem to contradict Paul's own letters on a number of points. For example, Acts 9:26–30 describes Paul's first visit to the Jerusalem church and tells us that he met the apostles, argued with some members of the church, and was taken away by others. But Paul's own account of the same occasion in Galatians 1:18–20 specifies that the only Christians he met there were Peter and James. Where there are such discrepancies, scholars usually think it more reasonable to trust Paul (who was certainly there) rather than the anonymous author of Acts. However, that does not mean that the general outline of Acts is not reliable. In the example of Paul's visit to Jerusalem, Luke disagrees with Paul over who he met there, but he agrees that this visit occurred. If Luke is shaky over (some) details, there is no reason to distrust him when it comes to the general course of events. For the most part, Acts is virtually all we have to go on for our information about the church before Paul started writing twenty years after Jesus' death, in the early 50s. So we are very reliant upon it for our knowledge of this critical period, whether we like it or not.

Pentecost

According to Acts, the key events during this period all took place in Jerusalem. The disciples here seem to regard themselves as a definable group, able to plan for the future and organize themselves; they are in fact a 'church'. The Greek term that Luke uses literally means 'assembly'.

The major event during this time, as Acts describes it, occurred during the festival of Pentecost. Jesus had been executed during Passover, and Pentecost occurred on the fiftieth day after Passover. Luke tells us that, during this festival, 'they' (just the Twelve, or all of the disciples?) were gathered together in one house when the Holy Spirit came upon them like a rushing wind and a fire. They all acquired the ability to speak many languages and the urge to preach in them. Peter took the lead, standing before the crowd and preaching to them that Jesus was the Messiah, that he had been put to death by Israel but raised by God, and that the outpouring of the Holy Spirit which had just occurred was a sign of the last days, as foretold by the prophet Joel. This emphasis on the Holy Spirit is very typical of Luke: in both his Gospel and Acts he mentions the Spirit more frequently than other New Testament authors, and in Acts he often talks about people becoming filled with the Holy Spirit or led by the Holy Spirit to go to particular places or do particular things. Clearly, he wants to stress that the history of the early church was being directed by God himself.

The first days of the church

According to Luke, the disciples' preaching on the day of Pentecost led to 3,000 people joining the movement. If the resurrection experiences mark the beginning of the distinctive faith of the Christian church, then the first conversions of Pentecost mark the beginning of its existence as a social movement. For the first time, people had joined the movement who had never met Jesus, but who put their faith in him through the testimonies of others. Luke gives us the following description of their lifestyle:

A late 10th-century manuscript in the pontifical of Westminster portrays the events of Pentecost.

> They devoted themselves to the apostles' teaching and fellowship, to the breaking of bread and the prayers. Awe came upon everyone, because many wonders and signs were being done by the apostles. All who believed were together and had all things in common; they would sell their possessions and goods and distribute the proceeds to all, as any had need. Day by day, as they spent much time together in the temple, they broke bread at home and ate their food with glad and generous hearts, praising God and having the goodwill of all the people. And day by day the Lord added to their number those who were being saved.

Acts 2:42–47

Some commentators regard this as something of an idealization. If we remember that Luke was writing perhaps fifty years later, it is easy to imagine that he might look back upon those early days through rose-tinted spectacles. In Acts 12:12, for example, we hear of a Christian named Mary who owned her own house, suggesting that they didn't really own everything in common.

However, some elements of Luke's account stand out as particularly interesting. He tells us that the community was rapidly growing, which seems intrinsically highly likely given how widespread it had become within a couple of decades of this period. He also tells us that 'the apostles' were effectively the leaders of the community. Who were these? One might think that they were simply the Twelve, but in 1 Corinthians 15:5–7 Paul distinguishes between these two groups, implying that 'the apostles' are a larger group than 'the Twelve'. We should perhaps understand 'the apostles' to be those people who had been Jesus' disciples during his lifetime, including but not restricted to the Twelve. Again, it is very reasonable to suppose that these original disciples would take the lead, just as it is reasonable to suppose that Peter – according to the Gospels Jesus' closest friend – would be pre-eminent among them.

Finally, it seems from Luke's account that the followers of Jesus existed quite happily within Judaism. They had 'the goodwill of all the people', so there were no conflicts with the religious authorities; and they frequented the Temple. Indeed, the next verse after this passage – Acts 3:1 – tells us of an incident that took place as Peter and John were going to the Temple at the hour of prayer. There seems, then, to have been no sense among the community at this time that they were founding a new religion. They remained what the apostles had been during Jesus' lifetime: Jews who were followers of Jesus.

The faith of the first Christians

What message did the apostles preach that led so many to join them in those early days? This first Christian message is sometimes known as the primitive *kerygma*, meaning 'preaching' or 'proclamation'. What did it consist of?

Given that we have no Christian writings until the letters of Paul – written twenty years after the primitive *kerygma* was first proclaimed, and containing Paul's own much more developed and personal understanding of the Christian message – one might think it a hopeless task to try to reconstruct the preaching of the very first Christians. But in fact we can have quite a good idea of this preaching, for two main reasons. The first is that the New Testament authors, and especially Paul, incorporate older material into their work at certain places. In fact there are a number of passages in Paul's letters where he is evidently working older formulations of faith into his text, but here we can mention two in particular:

For I handed on to you as of first importance what I in turn had received: that Christ died for our sins in accordance with the scriptures, and that he was buried, and that he was raised on the third day in accordance with the scriptures, and that he appeared to Cephas, then to the twelve.

1 Corinthians 15:3–5

[God's] son... was descended from David according to the flesh and was declared to be Son of God with power according to the spirit of holiness by resurrection from the dead, Jesus Christ our Lord.

Romans 1:3–4

Taken together, these two passages contain much of the core of the original Christian message. Jesus was the Christ or Messiah, and he died, but God then raised him from the dead. There are two particular points of importance. In the 1 Corinthians passage, Paul states that Christ died 'for our sins' – he didn't simply die; he died to save people, in some way. And in the Romans passage, Paul states that Jesus' resurrection was not simply a resuscitation – it was a powerful, dramatic event which actually made Jesus the Son of God and Lord.

We find much of this reflected in our second main source for the primitive *kerygma*, the book of Acts. Despite the doubts that some scholars have about the historical reliability of this book, the preaching which Luke attributes to the apostles does seem to match what other sources tell us about the primitive *kerygma*. Consider the speech that, according to Luke, Peter made to the crowds on the day of Pentecost:

Jesus of Nazareth, a man attested to you by God with deeds of power, wonders, and signs that God did through him among you, as you yourselves know – this man, handed over to you according to the definite plan and foreknowledge of God, you crucified and killed by the hands of those outside the law. But God raised him up, having freed him from death, because it was impossible for him to be held in its power... Being therefore exalted at the right hand of God, and having received from the Father the promise of the Holy Spirit, he has poured out this that you both see and hear... Therefore let the entire house of Israel know with certainty that God has made him both Lord and Messiah, this Jesus whom you crucified.

Acts 2:22–24, 33, 36

Here again we have the notion that God raised Jesus in a way that transformed him: he actually became Lord and Messiah through his resurrection. Another element which is found in other speeches in Acts is the claim that Jesus was going to return very soon. This is also attested to in other sources. Jesus seems to have taught that the kingdom of God was coming soon, and the first Christians believed the same thing. Paul's first surviving letter, 1 Thessalonians, devotes some space to assuring its readers that those who have died will not miss out on the coming kingdom. Evidently, the Thessalonian Christians had assumed that the kingdom would come within their own lifetimes, and had been unprepared for the prospect of any of them dying. In 4:15–17 Paul assumes that he and at least most of his readers will still be alive when Jesus returns, and he even specifies that this comes from 'the word of the Lord', that is, the teaching of Jesus himself. Clearly, the imminent return of Jesus was an element central to the primitive *kerygma*.

So we can summarize the very first Christian message quite simply. Jesus was a holy man, who performed great miracles by the power of God; but he was despised and executed. But God raised him from the dead, as a result of which he is now Lord and Messiah. Right now, those who believe in him can be saved from sin. And very soon, he will return in power, bringing the kingdom of God.

The first persecutions

However, Acts suggests that not everyone was pleased to hear this message. According to Acts 4, the priests and the Sadducees (an aristocratic group within Palestinian Judaism associated with the priests) objected to the preaching of Peter and John and had them brought before the high priest and the Jewish council. The council told them not to preach about Jesus, but no further action was taken and the apostles were released. The next chapter tells us that the high priest actually arrested the apostles and imprisoned them, but they escaped and had to be arrested once more. At the urging of Gamaliel, a prominent Pharisee, the council decided to wait and see what happened to the new movement. The apostles were scourged and then released.

Finally, Acts 6–7 tells of the arrest of Stephen, not one of the apostles but a prominent member of the church, who was arrested for blasphemy. Ordered to explain himself, Stephen gives a long speech to the council about the patriarchs and prophets, concluding that the Jews have always persecuted those

In *St Stephen Before the High Council*, Vittore Carpaccio (c. 1455/65–1526) shows Stephen defending himself against the council.

whom God sent, and describing the building of the Temple itself as a sign of the rejection of God by Solomon, for God cannot be located in a physical building. Such a claim would certainly have been incredibly offensive to most Jews of the time, since, as we have seen, the Jewish religion revolved around the Temple. The claim also sits very uneasily with the notion that the apostles were in the habit of going to the Temple to pray. There are several possibilities to explain this. Perhaps Luke has exaggerated the degree to which the early church conformed to Jewish behaviour, and they didn't really pray at the Temple. Alternatively, perhaps Stephen did not really hold views like those Luke attributes to him: perhaps this is an anachronistic speech, written to make Stephen seem to hold the views of later Christians about Judaism in general and the Temple in particular. Another alternative is that Stephen did hold these views, and other Christians did pray at the Temple, and there was enormous disagreement within the early church about these matters. Finally, perhaps Luke has done some telescoping: perhaps Stephen's trial occurred quite some time after the period when members of the church prayed at the Temple.

The story of Stephen's trial in Acts ends with Stephen stating that he can see the Son of man standing at the right hand of God. Enraged, the council drag him out of Jerusalem and stone him to death. Luke tells us that immediately following this, persecution broke out against the church, and many members fled Jerusalem.

The spread of the church

Luke portrays this persecution as the catalyst that led to the movement spreading beyond Jerusalem, where it had been confined until this point. In fact it may have existed in other locations already. According to Matthew and John, Jesus' disciples went straight back to Galilee after his resurrection. If some did do this, we know nothing about what they did or how their faith developed while they were isolated from the other disciples. In any case, the narrative of Acts from chapter 8 onwards changes into what is effectively a long description of missionary activities on the part of the apostles. Initially, they travel through Palestine preaching about Jesus, but they do not restrict their preaching to Jews: in Acts 8:26–39, Philip preaches to a visiting official from Nubia (he is described as an 'Ethiopian', but this term was often used in antiquity to mean someone from anywhere south of Egypt).

In chapter 11, however, we first hear of the church outside Palestine – in Phoenicia, in Cyprus, and above all in Antioch, the major city of Syria. Antioch had been founded some three centuries earlier by Seleucus Nicator, one of the heirs to the empire of Alexander the Great, as a shining beacon of Greek civilization in the east. It became famous as a centre of learning, before the

Romans conquered it in 64 BC. The city quickly became one of the most important in the Roman empire, helped by a programme of major building works. 'Golden Antioch', as it was sometimes called, lay between Mount Silpius – where the city's citadel was located – and the River Orontes, and consisted of four walled quarters which together made up the 'Tetrapolis' or 'four cities' of Antioch. The city had many parks and gardens, including a park dedicated to Daphne which contained a large temple to Apollo; another temple to Jupiter had recently been built on Mount Silpius. With a varied and cosmopolitan population of a couple of hundred thousand at the end of the first century AD, it was the third largest city in the empire, after Rome and Alexandria, and it was also a very important military base. There was a particularly thriving Jewish community here, and the city was relatively tolerant of new or unusual religious groups, so it is perhaps unsurprising that this is the first place where we hear of Christianity taking root outside Palestine itself.

According to Acts 11:26, Antioch was the first place where members of the church were called 'Christians'. Antioch also played two further critical roles in the development of the early church. First, it was the scene of crucial conflicts over the relationship between Christianity to both Judaism and paganism. And second, it was one of the major bases of operations of the man who would become the first and most influential of the great Christian theologians, Paul of Tarsus.

Paul

Paul is without doubt the most forceful and dominant personality of the New Testament outside the Gospels. Indeed, he looms so large that many people have regarded him as the true founder of Christianity. On this view, Paul hijacked the movement started by Jesus and changed its message, creating a new religion of his own

A Roman street of ruins in Pisidian Antioch, modern-day Turkey. Acts 13 tells how Paul and Barnabas visited the city on their first missionary journey.

which eventually smothered the original faith. But is there any truth to this? Who was Paul really?

We do not know when Paul was born, although it is often supposed that he was probably born at around the same time as Jesus. Fortunately we know some details about his early life from his own writings. According to his own account of who he was before he became a Christian, Paul was 'circumcised on the eighth day, a member of the people of Israel, of the tribe of Benjamin, a Hebrew born of Hebrews; as to the law, a Pharisee; as to zeal, a persecutor of the church; as to righteousness under the law, blameless' (Philippians 3:5–6). Paul deliberately emphasizes his Jewish credentials in that passage as part of the argument he is making, but it is still clear that he was not only a Jew but a very devout one – not only a Pharisee, but one who believed that he upheld the Law perfectly. 'Paul' was the Greek version of his name, which was 'Saul' in Hebrew. Acts 13:9 states that he was known by both names, although Luke's habit of calling him 'Saul' before this point and 'Paul' afterwards creates the impression that Paul actually changed his name after he became a Christian. In fact it seems more reasonable to suppose that he used whichever form was more appropriate in the linguistic or cultural context in which he found himself. Finally, like all Jewish men of the time, Paul knew a trade and mentions in his letters that he supported himself by his own labour during his career as a missionary. According to Acts 18:3, that trade was tent-making.

This stone slab from the sepulchre of a child, Amellus, depicts the apostles Peter and Paul and dates from c. AD 313.

This remarkably zealous Pharisee first appears in Acts in chapter 7, as an approving witness to the stoning of Stephen. He then visits Christian houses in Jerusalem to arrest any Christians he can find, before travelling to Damascus with the intention of doing the same thing there. Paul mentions his period as a persecutor of Christians several times in his letters (most notably Galatians 1:13 and Philippians 3:6), but the fact that the Christians in Judea did not know what he looked like (Galatians 1:22) suggests that in fact the persecutions he carried out did not take place in Jerusalem. However, neither Acts nor Paul himself tells us why he persecuted the Christians, and it is perhaps striking that in his surviving letters he never shows any remorse for it. The closest he comes is 1 Corinthians 15:9, where he says that his career as a persecutor makes him unfit to be called an apostle, but he still doesn't express any wish that he had not done it. The anguished, guilty self-accusations of some later Christian theologians, such as Augustine or Martin Luther, find no parallel in Paul's letters.

According to Acts 9, while Paul was travelling to Damascus he was thrown to the ground by a flash of light and heard the voice of Jesus telling him to enter the city. Miraculously blinded, he was led into the city, where a Christian named Ananias met him, tended to him, and cured the blindness; Paul then began preaching about Jesus in the synagogues. Paul himself tells us only that God revealed Jesus to him (Galatians 1:16) and that Jesus revealed the true faith to him (Galatians 1:11–12). He also gives no indication

The map below illustrates the Christian diaspora c. AD 70.

First century church

0   600 km

0   400 miles

that he regarded this event as a conversion from one religion to another. Nowhere in his writings does Paul suggest that by becoming a Christian he stopped being a Jew, or even that he stopped being a Pharisee.

This would have happened in around AD 34, within the first few years of Christianity's existence. Paul tells us in Galatians that immediately after his conversion he travelled to Arabia before returning to Damascus and staying there for three years. Then he travelled to Jerusalem and stayed for a fortnight with Peter, also meeting James, before going to Syria (presumably Antioch) and Cilicia. Paul had already settled upon his new career, that of missionary, and this is how he spent the rest of his life. The next two decades saw him travelling throughout the eastern Mediterranean – especially in Asia Minor and the Greek peninsula – preaching the Christian message. This ended in AD 57 when the Jewish authorities arrested Paul in Jerusalem and imprisoned him in Caesarea for two years. He was taken to Rome to be tried – since he was a Roman citizen – and, probably, he was executed there some time in the early to mid 60s. Paul had hoped to travel to Rome as a free man and then continue west to Spain, and some have argued that he was released from prison and did make it to Spain after all, but it is unlikely.

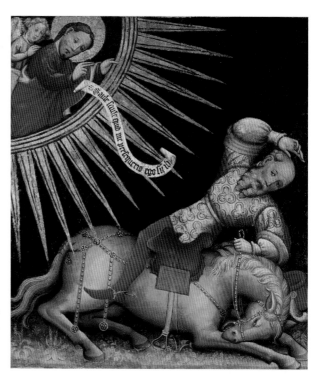

Hildesheim's 15th-century *Conversion of St Paul* depicts the story, told in Acts 9, of Jesus appearing in a vision on the road to Damascus.

Everywhere he went, Paul founded new churches. How exactly did he go about this? Acts generally portrays him as visiting the synagogue first of all and preaching there. This may seem implausible given that, according to his own account, Paul's mission was only to the Gentiles and he agreed to leave it to missionaries working for Peter and James to preach to Jews. But there would have been Gentiles at many synagogues; plenty of non-Jews were interested in Judaism, and Paul might well have thought that such people were good prospective converts to Christianity. Thus Acts 17:4, describing Paul's preaching in Thessalonica, mentions that many 'devout Greeks' joined him after hearing him talk at a synagogue. It is also likely that Paul used his manual labour as means of spreading the word. In 1 Corinthians 4:12 he mentions supporting himself by this work while preaching, so he must have set up a tent-making stall or shop in the towns that he visited. No doubt he would preach to customers or passers-by while working. If Paul ever stood in the middle of town squares and preached to the crowds, as Acts 17 represents him doing in Athens, it is unlikely that he did it very often; he acknowledges in more than one place that he was a poor speaker. He would probably have built up the Christian community in each city a few individuals at a time, speaking to small groups. Little wonder that he thought of his converts as 'beloved children' (1 Corinthians 4:14) – he probably forged close personal bonds with most of them individually.

Paul's letters

While he was travelling, Paul wrote letters to the churches he had set up, to encourage them, to remind them of what he had taught them, and to tackle problems that he had heard about. These letters are the earliest Christian writings which survive – indeed, perhaps the earliest ever written. The first, 1 Thessalonians, was probably written in about AD 50 to the church at Thessalonica; the latest, Philippians and Philemon, were written in around AD 59 while Paul was in prison in Caesarea.

There are thirteen books in the New Testament which appear to be letters by Paul. However, the situation is not as simple as that. The practice of passing off one's own writing as the work of some great figure of the past was common in antiquity. Many people must have thought that the best way to ensure that their work was read was to write it under the name of somebody famous. The inauthenticity of such texts is often easy to spot. Sometimes, however, people wrote very good imitations. Their purpose was to fill in gaps in the great author's work: they wrote what they thought he *would* have written, had he addressed that particular problem or lived longer. They wrote in tribute to the great author, not simply in order to trade off his name. Pseudonymous writings of this kind can be harder to recognize, because they were written

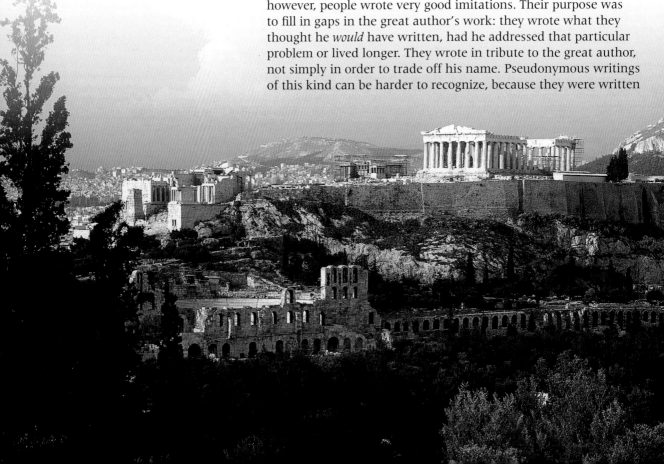

The Acropolis, Athens, Greece. Paul visited Athens on his second missionary journey.

by people who were more familiar with the real work of the supposed author.

What of the Pauline letters? Today, in addressing questions of authenticity, scholars usually consider three main criteria. The first is language. If the text being studied uses different terminology from a text which is known to be authentic, then this might well indicate that it was written by somebody else. A second criterion is theology. If the text in question contains ideas that are hard to reconcile with those in a text which is known to be authentic, this too could be a sign that it was written by another author. And the final major criterion is the historical context that the disputed text implies. If it seems anachronistic in some way, it may be the work of a later writer.

Each of these criteria, taken by itself, might not prove very much. But for many scholars, when all three of these hints appear in the same text, the cumulative evidence means at least that we cannot be confident that the text is authentic. On these grounds, Paul's letters can be divided into several groups, according to how much doubt exists about their authenticity. The core of letters that are almost entirely undisputed are Romans, 1 Corinthians, 2 Corinthians, Galatians, Philippians, 1 Thessalonians, and Philemon. Next, we have 2 Thessalonians and Colossians, which some scholars believe are not by Paul. However, many others think they are. If they are really not by Paul, their authors did a great job imitating Paul's style. Ephesians is less likely to be authentic. It matches Paul's style in many ways, but is quite unusual in others, and seems to develop his thought significantly in some areas. Some scholars believe that this text was written by someone who greatly admired Paul and wanted to write a sort of up-to-date summary of his theology. Finally, there are 1 Timothy, 2 Timothy, and Titus (known collectively as the Pastoral Epistles). Most scholars believe that the great differences between these three texts and the certainly genuine Pauline letters make it extremely unlikely that Paul wrote them – indeed, their author may not have understood the real Paul very well, although he certainly admired him.

Paul's Christian message

Paul's theology is one of the hardest bodies of thought to come to grips with. Unlike the theology of the very first Christians, there is far more evidence for it: seven letters of undisputed authenticity, which together form the theological centre of gravity of the entire New Testament. No other first-century Christian figure, let alone one *so* early, left such an extensive body of work. But none of these texts is a simple 'what I believe' statement. Paul wrote his letters to address particular problems or situations that he could not deal with in person. All, apart from Romans, presuppose that the readers already know Paul personally and are familiar with his teaching. Each therefore gives a different angle on Paul's thought, which means we must do reconstruction work to describe it as a whole. But worse – Paul's argument often seems to meander and change track as he writes: he does not work out his position in every detail before writing, but thinks on the go. Finally, there is good reason to think that Paul changed his mind on key questions as time went on and circumstances changed, and perhaps even that he might have been quite capable of believing contradictory things at the same time.

All of these things mean that there is enormous scholarly controversy over almost every aspect of Paul's thought. All we can do here is indicate some of the main outlines of his theology. Like the other early Christians, Paul was convinced that Jesus was the Christ or Messiah, the fulfilment of the Jewish Scriptures, and he almost invariably referred to Jesus as 'Christ', as if it were his name. He believed that Christ's resurrection was the first sign of the coming kingdom, the eschaton, which would be marked by a general resurrection of the dead.

But there were more distinctive elements to Paul's teaching as well. Some of them seem to have arisen as a response both to Paul's own personal situation and to the changing circumstances of the Christian movement itself, especially in relation to Judaism, in the two decades between Jesus' death and the period when Paul was writing. For example, he grappled extensively with problems raised by the Jewish law. The main texts in which Paul discusses the Law are Galatians and Romans, but they do not say the same thing. In Galatians, Paul is addressing a particular problem that had arisen among the Galatian Christians. It seems that some people had been telling the Galatian Christians – who had been pagans

Paul's missionary journeys.

before Paul arrived and converted them to Christianity – that they had to become Jews and be circumcised in order to be Christians. In response, Paul insists that the Law does not save anyone, and implies that God gave it only as a sort of temporary stopgap until Christ came along.

By the time Paul wrote his letter to the Romans, a few years later, the situation had changed. The controversy over the Law had moved on. Some people now claimed that Paul's teaching about the Law led to laxism and immorality and actually encouraged people to sin. His concern in this letter, then, is to show that the Law does have a positive function, although it still does not save. In some passages, such as Romans 7:1–6, the Law is represented as an oppressive captor from which people need to be liberated, but Paul also insists that the Law is not itself sinful.

The problem of the Law is closely connected to that of the Jews. As a Pharisee, Paul believed that the Jews were a special people, beloved of God. But as a Christian, he had to accept that no one got saved simply by being Jewish, because salvation comes through Christ, not the Law. He also had to face the fact that most Jews had rejected Christianity. How could he reconcile these beliefs? In Romans 4 he argues that to say people are saved by faith – and that circumcision is useless – is actually part of the Jewish law itself, because Abraham had faith in God, and God considered him righteous, even before the Law was given and before Abraham was circumcised. Therefore, the real descendants of Abraham are those who have faith, not those who are physically descended from him or those who are circumcised.

In chapter 9 Paul turns to an emotional discussion about the Jews, speaking eloquently of his despair that they do not have faith in Christ. Initially it had seemed to Paul, and to other Christians, that the message of salvation in Christ would come to the Jews first and then to the Gentiles (Romans 2:9). But events had forced Paul to rethink this. He concluded that the order was reversed. God had caused the Jews not to believe, and this had given the Gentiles time to believe. Salvation had thus come to the Gentiles first. But the unbelief of the Jews was only temporary; God would bring belief and salvation to them in turn, as the example of the Gentiles spurred them on. Thus the Jews were still central to God's plan, although not in the way that anyone might have guessed.

One of the most striking features of Paul's letters is his emphasis upon union between Christ and the believer. This is brought out by his constant use of the phrase 'in Christ'. This has become such a common phrase in Christian circles that it is easy not to realize how odd it actually sounds. But there is nothing like it in the Gospels or Acts, or in the letter to the Hebrews, or the letters of James and John. It is peculiarly Pauline. In Galatians 3:26–29, for example, Paul tells his readers that all Christians are one 'in Christ' and that they have been baptized 'into Christ'. But what does that mean? The idea seems to be that of some kind of mystic union. Just as mystics through the ages report an experience of union with the divine, so too the Christian is united to Christ so closely that he can say he is 'in' Christ. In fact, the person who is 'in Christ' seems to take on the characteristics of Christ, to such an extent that Paul can reverse the phrase and speak of Christ being 'in' the Christian as well.

Precisely what Paul meant by this language remains unclear. But there are two particularly important elements. The first is that it shows that Christians are not simply people who believe in the Christian message and hope that Jesus will return soon. They are people who have an active and very intimate relationship with Jesus right now. To be a Christian is to be transformed; it is to have one's inner nature renewed no matter what one's external circumstances (2 Corinthians 4:16). And second, the 'in Christ' language is always communal. The Christian does not simply enjoy union with Christ; he or she enjoys union with all Christians, with the church as a whole. In Romans 12 and 1 Corinthians 12, Paul uses the image of a body with many limbs; Christ is the body, but Christians are the parts of the body. In some sense, if one takes the metaphor really seriously, Christ is the sum total of all Christians – Christ *is* the church.

This sense of unity and identity also underlies Paul's understanding of salvation. In fact, Paul's writings, more than any other part of the New Testament, emphasize the death of Christ. Paul stresses that this was the means by which God gives his grace to believers. He has a number of ways of expressing this. One image is that of sacrifice: Christ was a sacrifice to God, which allowed God to forgive people's sins and make them righteous (Romans 3:21–26). This idea is found in other early Christian writings, most notably the letter to the Hebrews. A more distinctively Pauline approach to Christ's death is closely linked to his theme of being 'in Christ'. It is also linked to his distinctive understanding of sin. In many passages, especially Romans chapter 7, Paul talks about 'sin' not as actions that people take but as a force that oppresses them. Sin brings death; yet death is also an escape from sin. In Romans 7:1–3 Paul points out that legal contracts such as marriage are binding upon people only while they are alive; in the same way, when one dies, one escapes from the Law and from sin too. And this leads to the central point – it is possible to escape from sin without actually dying, because Christ has already died. Those who are 'in Christ' share in his death and escape from sin in that way:

> *Do you not know that all of us who have been baptized into Christ Jesus were baptized into his death? Therefore we have been buried with him by baptism into death, so that, just as Christ was raised from the dead by the glory of the Father, so we too might walk in newness of life... We know that our old self was crucified with him so that the body of sin might be destroyed, and we might no longer be enslaved to sin. For whoever has died is freed from sin.*

Romans 6:3–7

It is a true escape from sin because Christ did not simply die; he rose from the dead. Paul does not say that Christians have already risen from the dead – for him, the resurrection of Christians lies in the future. But Christians will be raised from the dead because, being 'in Christ', they share in Christ's resurrection. And they enjoy the benefits of that resurrection – freedom from sin – right now in the present:

> *For if we have been united with him in a death like his, we will certainly be united with him in a resurrection like his ... if we have died with Christ, we believe that we will also live with him. We know that Christ, being raised from the dead, will never die again; death no longer has dominion over him. The death he died, he died to sin, once for all; but the life he lives, he lives to God. So you also must consider yourselves dead to sin and alive to God in Christ Jesus.*

Romans 6:5–11

Members of the Elim Evangelical Pentecostal church pray during a group baptism in the Ilopango lake, 15 km (9 miles) east of San Salvador, El Salvador.

From One Generation to the Next

The apostles were rural Galileans, and their leaders, Peter and James, were fishermen. But Christianity very quickly moved away from these rural roots. It seems to have developed first in Jerusalem and then in Antioch, and Paul travelled between the great cities of the eastern Mediterranean. To read first the Gospels and then the letters of the New Testament is to move from a landscape of fields and small villages to one of bustling, cosmopolitan cities.

The Christian communities

There is evidence that many of the people who responded to the Christian message in this new environment were from what would have been considered the lower classes. Paul wrote to the Corinthians:

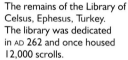

The remains of the Library of Celsus, Ephesus, Turkey. The library was dedicated in AD 262 and once housed 12,000 scrolls.

Consider your own call, brothers and sisters: not many of you were wise by human standards, not many were powerful, not many were of noble birth. But God chose what is foolish in the world to shame the wise; God chose what is weak in the world to shame the strong; God chose what is low and despised in the world, things that are not, to reduce to nothing things that are, so that no one might boast in the presence of God.

1 Corinthians 1:26–29

As Paul implies, not *all* Christians were lower class and uneducated. Paul himself is an obvious counter example, as are the authors of other parts of the New Testament. Clearly, the Christians could consider some of their number to be educated elite. However, it is highly unlikely that any Christians at this time belonged to the true social elite in the ancient sense. Such people were nobles or wealthy individuals who owned estates outside the city and led prominent public lives within the city. Simply being educated – or being wealthy – did not make someone elite in the Roman sense. Social rankings in antiquity tended to revolve around who you knew, what you did, and what groups you moved in. These were determined, to a large extent, by birth. Someone who was not born a noble could not hope to become one, and someone who was born a noble would always remain one no matter what happened.

The importance of social groups for people's social identity tells us much about how people became Christians in the first place. It is intrinsically very likely that people generally became Christians because they had close friends or relations who were Christians: that is, the religion spread through already existing personal ties. People identified themselves on the basis of the social group to which they belonged, so if Christianity became a major feature of that group, other members were more likely to become Christians. This is how minority-interest religions and cults typically spread. Very few people join them because missionaries have knocked on their door or because they have read some recruitment literature; most converts are friends or relations of people who are already members.

The New Testament confirms this picture, especially in the role that households play in the picture of the early church that it offers. In antiquity, a 'household' might consist of an extended family rather than just a couple and their children. In Mark 1:29–31, for example, we learn that Peter lived with his brother and his mother-in-law. Presumably Peter's wife and children, and perhaps his brother's wife and children, were also there. In the Roman empire, a household might well also have slaves; Ephesians 5:22–6:9 presents us with the picture of a Christian household of husband, wife, children, and slaves. And other people could also be considered members of a 'household': close friends and guests,

A reconstruction of the living quarters in the old Jewish settlement in Katzrin, 13 km (8 miles) northeast of the Sea of Galilee.

even people who did not actually live in the same building but who were considered 'family'. These families were close social groups, and when some members joined a new religion, the other members might have been very likely to do so as well. And so, in Acts, we find stories of entire households being converted and baptized together. Paul's letters also testify to the importance of pre-existing social bonds, and especially the household, among Christians. The people he greets by name frequently seem to be clustered into families. Romans 16 alone gives us Prisca and Aquila, Tryphaena and Tryphosa, Rufus and his mother, Nereus and his sister, Christians in the household of Aristobulus, others in the household of Narcissus, and so on. We also encounter Andronicus, Junia, and Herodian, relatives of Paul himself.

As we saw in chapter 1, Paul and those like him probably worked, to a large extent, by networking; he would have spoken to customers at his tent stall or mingled with pagans who were already visiting synagogues and were interested in Judaism. Where Acts represents Paul as converting strangers, it is generally in the context of a personal, one-to-one encounter or conversation; when Paul stands in the middle of a town and makes a speech to the crowd, as at Athens in Acts 17, he has relatively little success. And when Paul converts strangers, what usually happens next is that they run off and convert their families too. We can reasonably suppose that this pattern of new converts introducing their families to the movement was a common one, although no doubt it would normally take longer than the few minutes implied in Acts.

But if the church spread by using pre-existent social and kinship ties, it created new ones as well. When somebody became a Christian, he or she probably knew some – perhaps many – members of the local Christian group already; but unless it was a really tiny group there would probably be some that he or she did not know. To join the church was to shift one's social centre of gravity. Moreover, the geographical spread of the Christian movement meant that a convert to Christianity became involved in something much wider than just a small circle of friends with a shared faith. If a Christian travelled to another city, he or she could find a welcome with the Christians there. And many Christians did travel around, seeking new converts or encouraging the churches, which meant that social ties were forged between the groups. Again, the greetings at the end of Paul's letter to the Romans illustrate this: Paul could consider so many people 'beloved' to him in a city he had never visited.

From oral traditions to the written word

Christianity initially spread entirely by word of mouth. When Paul visited synagogues, or chatted to customers at his tent-making stall, he did not have some holy book to preach out of. Perhaps he used the Jewish Scriptures when talking to Jews or to Gentiles interested in Judaism, and told them that Jesus was the fulfilment of the prophecies found in those Scriptures, but he did not have any *Christian* writings. The message he brought them was one that he himself had been taught by the first disciples of Jesus. Memories of Jesus and his teachings were obviously central to this message. For example, in 1 Corinthians 7:10–12, on the question of divorce, Paul first tells his readers what Jesus commanded, and then describes his own views, distinguishing carefully between them. The teaching attributed to Jesus here corresponds with that given in Mark 10:1–12, making this a valuable witness to Jesus' own teaching, but the passage also shows how the oral tradition was working at this time. Those who had known Jesus in his lifetime had remembered his teachings and told later converts about them. These converts, such as Paul, might then pass on the teachings or other stories about Jesus, adding their own opinions, but still distinguishing between the views of Jesus and their own views.

However, by the 50s of the first century AD, Christianity had become sufficiently widespread for oral communication to be no longer sufficient. The existence of Paul's own letters is testament to that, as we saw in the previous chapter. But although written to address particular, immediate problems, these letters were quickly recognized – even within his own lifetime – as significant writings in their own right. In 2 Corinthians 10:10, Paul mentions critics who attack his speaking ability but have to admit that his letters are 'weighty and strong'. At some point, Paul's letters were collected together and circulated throughout the church. Exactly when this happened is uncertain, but it must have marked a significant moment in the development of Christianity: a moment when Christians realized not only that written accounts of what they believed would be useful, but that they already possessed such an account, and a remarkable one at that.

In his letters, Paul had effectively invented a new literary genre – the Christian letter – and others imitated it. Among the most important are the letter to the Hebrews, and the Johannine letters (1 John, 2 John, and 3 John). Although the latter are traditionally ascribed to the apostle John, the letters themselves are anonymous. Of particular interest are the letters of James and 1 Peter, which are apparently written by the two major leaders of the first generation of Christians. Are they authentic? The problem here is that, unlike the situation with Paul, we have nothing to compare them to, so there is more guesswork involved. Most scholars think that 1 Peter is not really by Peter.

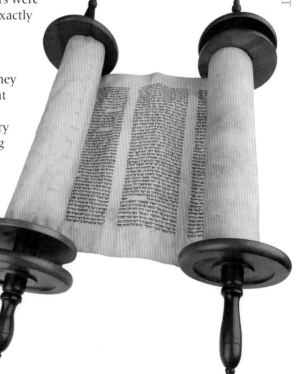

Example of a scroll on wooden spools.

There is less agreement about the letter of James. There is nothing about the letter that seems particularly to disqualify it from being a genuine work of Jesus' brother, while equally there is nothing other than its attribution to indicate that it is one. A majority of scholars believe that the letter dates from after James's death and so is not by him, but there is no consensus on the matter.

And the most important group of writings, other than Paul's letters, are the Gospels themselves. We saw earlier how they came to be written, by authors who used the oral tradition to create accounts of Jesus' ministry, death, and resurrection. The Gospels were almost certainly all written after Paul's death, although not necessarily before his letters were widely available. It is generally thought that Mark's Gospel was written probably in the late 60s or perhaps the early 70s of the first century. The Gospels of Matthew and Luke were written later (since they probably used Mark as a source); these Gospels are often dated to the mid 80s or thereabouts. Finally, John is usually dated to the mid 90s, although a few scholars have argued for a much earlier date, perhaps as early as the 40s. Others argue that all four Gospels were written much later, perhaps in the second century AD, but this is a minority view.

The time of the composition of the Gospels marks another turning point in the history of Christianity. By the 60s and 70s, times had changed. Many of the first generation of Christians had died, and a new generation of Christians had emerged. Jesus was not such an immediate memory any more – he was a figure of the past, and so too were most of those who had actually known him. It is little wonder that some Christians therefore sought to preserve the memories that remained by writing Gospels describing Jesus' deeds and recording his teachings. The passage of time was transforming Christianity from a group of disciples who remembered their charismatic master and their converts into a religion; but by writing the Gospels, Christians hoped to ensure that the church remained true to the memory of the master, or at least true to the version of him that *they* remembered.

Living as a Christian

What sort of lifestyle did the early Christians live? There is reason to think that different Christian groups in the early decades lived in quite different ways. The Synoptic Gospels, for example, seem to be written with a relatively impoverished lifestyle in mind. In Matthew 10:5–15, Jesus sends out the Twelve with instructions to carry no belongings or money with them. Some scholars have seen in this material, and other sections like it in the Synoptics, a reflection of the lifestyle of some of the early Christians. If that is so, then some of the material in the Synoptic Gospels was passed down by Christians who regarded themselves as directed by Jesus to wander from place to place, preaching, with no secure means of sustenance. Such Christians might also have told one another how Jesus instructed his followers not to worry about tomorrow (Matthew 6:25–34), and have reminded each other that Jesus himself had no permanent home (Matthew 8:20).

The Pauline churches, however, offer a different picture. Paul reports a tradition perhaps akin to that of the Synoptics, that Jesus told his disciples to make their living from the Gospel (1 Corinthians 9:14), but states that he did not take advantage of it, choosing instead to work by his own hands. And 2 Thessalonians 3:6–12 clearly instructs its readers that everyone in the church must work: anyone who doesn't work doesn't eat. The Pauline churches seem to have been founded, right from the start, as groups of people within normal society, quite unlike the wandering Christian prophets who, if they really emulated the homelessness of Jesus and his first disciples, would have existed on the fringes of society. In 1 Corinthians 11:33–34, we hear of Christians leaving their own homes to come together to eat – so the Corinthian Christians, at least, lived in their own homes and did not wander from place to place. The rules for Christian households in Ephesians 5:22 – 6:9 suggest a similar picture.

Christian morality

When it came to ethical views, the early Christians seem to have adopted fairly standard Jewish attitudes. Paul gives lists of virtues and vices at various points in his letters, most of which are quite standard Jewish lists. For example, he speaks of pagans like this:

Full of envy, murder, strife, deceit, craftiness, they are gossips, slanderers, God-haters, insolent, haughty, boastful, inventors of evil, rebellious towards parents, foolish, faithless, heartless, ruthless.

Romans 1:29–31

In 1 Corinthians 5:1, lambasting his readers for permitting sexual immorality, he comments that it is of a kind that 'even' pagans do not engage in. For Paul, paganism is a byword for immorality. He contrasts it with the kind of qualities that Christians should embody:

By contrast, the fruit of the Spirit is love, joy, peace, patience, kindness, generosity, faithfulness, gentleness, and self-control.

Galatians 5:22–23

An Egyptian man uses traditional methods to decorate a tent.

Despite giving traditional lists of this kind, however, Paul also stresses that the characteristic Christian behaviour stems from the basic principle of loving one another. Indeed, in Galatians 5:14 he repeats Jesus' claim that the whole law comes down to the commandment to love one another. This was a common sentiment among Jewish teachers of the day, and one that Paul, as a Pharisee, would certainly have been familiar with. We find similar ideas in the Johannine letters. There, 'the Elder' writes:

> God is love, and those who abide in love abide in God, and God abides in them... There is no fear in love, but perfect love casts out fear; for fear has to do with punishment, and whoever fears has not reached perfection in love. We love because he first loved us. Those who say, 'I love God,' and hate their brothers or sisters, are liars; for those who do not love a brother or sister whom they have seen, cannot love God whom they have not seen.

1 John 4:16–20

For these theologians, at least, the moral behaviour of Christians stemmed not from adherence to an ethical code or list of precepts but from a fundamental principle of love for each other. Little wonder that Paul was so appalled when he heard that the Corinthian Christians were taking one another to court.

The Roman ruins of Sufetula include an early Christian baptismal bath in a basilica converted from a Roman temple. The remains are located near the town of Sbeitla, in north-central Tunisia.

The first liturgies

The word 'liturgy' comes from a Greek term meaning 'work of/for the people', and it originally meant work that was done to benefit the community. In Judaism, however, it came to mean the worship of God (the most important 'work' one could do). It came to have this meaning in Christianity too. 'Liturgy' is therefore what happens in religious services: the prayers and rituals that are performed. Right from the start, there were several major elements to Christian liturgy.

Baptism

One of the most prominent and distinctively Christian things that the characters in Acts do is baptize people. In fact, ritual washing was a common element in ancient religions. Jesus had begun his career as a follower of John the Baptist, who acquired his nickname from the fact that he would baptize large numbers of people in the River Jordan. Jesus was among them, and according to John 3:22, Jesus continued to baptize people himself after leaving John. Precisely where John got the practice, however, is uncertain. He may have been inspired by references to God washing believers in Isaiah 1:16–17 and Ezekiel 36:25–28. We do not know to what extent baptism, or practices like it, were performed in early first-century Judaism. The practice of baptizing converts to Judaism seems to have been introduced to the religion later in the first century AD, but that was probably an imitation of Christian baptism.

Whatever its origins, the practice remained important within Christianity. When someone professed faith in Jesus, he or she was ritually washed. A practice like this had two main functions. First, it symbolized the removal of the person's sins and their new life. John the Baptist seems to have regarded baptism as a sign of repentance in the face of the coming kingdom. The Christians shared this view, but extended it. We saw in the previous chapter how Paul, in particular, interpreted baptism as a sharing of Christ's death and a mark that the believer would share in his resurrection: on this view, baptism itself was a real death to the old life. We find a similar idea in Acts 2:38, where Peter tells his hearers to be baptized, so that their sins can be forgiven and they can receive the Holy Spirit. Second, baptism was an initiation ceremony, symbolizing the fact that the person was joining the group of believers. Converts were baptized 'into' Christ and his church; to be baptized was to join a spiritual body. Matthew 28:19 testifies to the fact that they were baptized 'in the name of the Father and of the Son and of the Holy Spirit', presumably a formula that was spoken by the person doing the baptism.

However, we do not know precisely how baptism was performed. The measured formula of Matthew 28:19 was probably not used

Interior of the Baptistery of the Orthodox, Ravenna, Italy, featuring an early 5th-century baptismal font.

The baptism of Christ, from an 8th-century manuscript of a commentary on Revelation by the Spanish theologian Beatus of Liébana.

everywhere in the early stages. Different Christian groups also seem to have interpreted the ritual in different ways. In Acts 8:14–17, Peter and John lay their hands on recently baptized converts, who receive the Holy Spirit as a result. It seems, in this passage, that being baptized is *not* enough to get the Holy Spirit after all. Perhaps some Christians laid their hands on new converts as part of the baptism process, while others did not. In fact it is quite possible that some Christians did not baptize converts at all. There are large sections of Acts where we hear of missionaries converting many people, without any mention of baptism. For example, after the baptism of Cornelius in chapter 10, no one gets baptized again until chapter 16 – even though the intervening sections contain a description of the first leg of Paul's missionary journey. Acts 18:24–25 tells us of Apollos, a prominent Christian missionary, who 'knew only the baptism of John'; the same thing is said of a group of Christians in Ephesus in the next chapter, whom Paul meets, baptizes and then lays hands on, as a result of which they receive the Holy Spirit. However, people like this must have been in a minority. In Romans 6:3 Paul can assume that his readers have been baptized, even though he is writing to a Christian group he has never met. Evidently, baptism was the norm among most Christians, however it was performed and understood.

The Eucharist

Another distinctive feature of Christian liturgy was the Eucharist, which also came directly from Jesus. The word 'eucharist' comes from the Greek for 'giving thanks', and it was used to refer to this practice by the end of the first century AD. It was a ritual re-enactment of elements of the Last Supper, the final meal that Jesus shared with his disciples on the night before he was executed. The Gospels differ over the interpretation of this meal: in the Synoptics, it was a Passover meal; but according to John Passover was actually a day later and the Last Supper was simply an ordinary dinner. The earliest account we have of the event is from Paul:

> For I received from the Lord what I also handed on to you, that the Lord Jesus on the night when he was betrayed took a loaf of bread, and when he had given thanks, he broke it and said, 'This is my body that is for you. Do this in remembrance of me.' In the same way he took the cup also, after supper, saying, 'This cup is the new covenant in my blood. Do this, as often as you drink it, in remembrance of me.' For as often as you eat this bread and drink the cup, you proclaim the Lord's death until he comes.

1 Corinthians 11:23–26

The structure of the sentences in Greek suggest that this material had already been shaped by the oral tradition: this was a passage that people repeated in a liturgical context. Similar accounts are found in the Synoptic Gospels, although not in John. They indicate not only that Jesus treated the bread and wine at the Last Supper in a significant way, but that the Christians did the same thing when they shared the bread and wine together. However, we do not know precisely what form this ritual took. The Jewish Passover meal was – and still is – a proper dinner, which features ritual elements that bring to life the original Passover, eaten on the eve of the exodus. By recreating elements of that event, such as the use of unleavened bread, participants identify with their ancestors who took part in the original event. Was the Christian Eucharist something similar? If so, it would have been an actual meal which the believers shared together, in the course of which the words that Jesus had spoken at the Last Supper would, at one point, be repeated. The context of the passage from 1 Corinthians suggests this scenario, since Paul criticizes those who eat too much and allow others to go hungry, which implies that he is talking about a complete meal, eaten (in part) to satisfy hunger, and not simply a symbolic morsel of bread and sip of wine.

Acts mentions several times that the Christians would break bread together. Acts 2:42, 46, for example, tells us that they ate and

In Gleno, East Timor, Roman Catholic priest Domingos Soares distributes the bread during Mass.

prayed together. But all of these seem to be ordinary meals, without any mention of eucharistic elements. There is no reference to wine – which plays an important part in the Last Supper in both Paul and the Synoptics – or to any special words of Jesus or indeed any mention of Jesus at all. In Acts 27:35, while on a ship in a storm, Paul breaks bread, gives thanks to God, and shares it with everyone, including the sailors. This implies that the meals which Christians shared with each other – and sometimes with other people – were not the Eucharist.

Something similar seems to be suggested in a text known as *The Teaching of the Apostles*, normally called simply the *Didache* (the Greek word for 'teaching'). This short text, which was lost in antiquity and only discovered and published in the 1880s, is of enormous importance as a window into the early Christian church. It is usually thought to have been written in the late first or the early second century AD, although sometimes it has been regarded as a later composition which is 'looking back' to an earlier time. It contains a series of instructions about running the church. Among them are instructions for holding the Eucharist, which seem rather different from those in Paul. The *Didache* tells its readers to bless first the wine and then the bread. There is an eschatological angle: the bread was once different grains of corn, brought together into one loaf, and the Christians pray that the church may also be brought together into God's kingdom. But there is no mention at all of the Last Supper, or of the words Jesus spoke at it. The ceremony is explicitly Christian, invoking Jesus in the prayers, but there is no indication that it has anything to do with anything that Jesus himself actually did.

Some scholars, therefore, have suggested that the early church actually had two kinds of rituals that involved eating. The first was simply a normal meal, which might involve a semi-formal breaking of bread and prayer of thanks to God at the start. It might not involve wine at all. This is what the *Didache* describes and what Acts seems to presuppose. And the second was the Eucharist itself, a much more formal ritual with bread and wine – perhaps only small amounts of each – at which a fairly standard form of words, handed down from the Last Supper, was repeated. There must still have been variations in the words, however; it varies between the different Gospel accounts and Paul.

There was an important eschatological meaning to the Eucharist. The passage from Paul quoted above, for example, links it to the future return of Jesus: to perform the Eucharist is to proclaim him until his return. It is very likely that Jesus himself meant his actions at the Last Supper to be interpreted in something like this way. In Mark 14:25, immediately after his words over the bread and wine, he tells his followers that 'I will never again drink of the fruit of the wine until that day when I drink it new in the kingdom of God'.

In some texts, this eschatological dimension becomes an emphasis upon the future resurrection of those who participate in the Eucharist. In John 6:35–40, Jesus calls himself 'the bread of life', and states that those who come to him will be raised up on the last day. This passage may be a reflection upon the meaning of the Eucharist: by eating the bread, believers were actually eating Jesus himself, and looking forward to the time when God would raise them up.

Other texts, however, suggest an alternative meaning of the Eucharist. In another passage from 1 Corinthians, Paul writes:

> *The cup of blessing that we bless, is it not a sharing in the blood of Christ? The bread that we break, is it not a sharing in the body of Christ? Because there is one bread, we who are many are one body, for we all partake of the one bread.*

1 Corinthians 10:16–17

This late 13th-century Venetian mosaic depicts the traditional account of the attack on St Mark during the Mass in Alexandria.

On this view, to share in the Eucharist is to be united to Christ and to his whole church. For Paul, the Eucharist forms part of his theology of unity and identity, which we looked at in the previous chapter.

The breaking of bread is seen in this late 2nd-century fresco. It is found in the so-called Greek Chapel of the Catacomb of Priscilla, Rome, Italy.

Other services

We also hear of what seem to be other meetings of the Christians. Colossians 3:16 instructs its readers: 'With gratitude in your hearts sing psalms, hymns, and spiritual songs to God.' This was also something that expressed continuity with Jesus: according to Mark 14:26, Jesus ended the Last Supper by singing a hymn with his disciples. Colossians 4:16 also instructs its recipients to read the letter – that is, Colossians – itself, and for the letter to be read in the Laodicean church, and for another letter from Laodicea to be read too. We have already seen that many Christians were unlikely to be literate. In this context, it is very likely that Christian writings would be read out at meetings.

In 1 Corinthians, Paul describes what seems like quite an informal sort of gathering:

> *When you come together, each one has a hymn, a lesson, a revelation, a tongue, or an interpretation... If anyone speaks in a tongue, let there be only two or at most three, and each in turn; and let one interpret. But if there is no one to interpret, let them be silent in church and speak to themselves and to God. Let two or three prophets speak, and let the others weigh what is said. If a revelation is made to someone else sitting nearby, let the first person be silent. For you can all prophesy one by one, so that all may learn and all be encouraged.*

> **1 Corinthians 14:26–31**

Given that Paul felt the need to lay down these instructions, these meetings must have sometimes been rather chaotic affairs. Was anyone even in charge?

Leading the community

The 'pillars' of the church

In Paul's day there was, of course, a sort of *de facto* leadership of the church as a whole. These were the apostles, those who had actually known Jesus. In Galatians 2:9 Paul describes the most prominent of these as 'pillars' of the church. The 'pillars' he identifies are Peter, James (Jesus' brother, not mentioned in the Gospels), and John (who, together with his brother, another James, appears in the Synoptic Gospels). In Acts, too, there seems to be a general assumption that these people – including Paul himself – are senior to other Christians. We have already mentioned the story in Acts 8 of Peter and John travelling to Samaria to meet the new Christians there, and laying their hands on them to give them the Holy Spirit. Evidently it was thought that the new community in Samaria needed a boost from the 'pillars' of the faith. Paul himself

is another example of a 'pillar' of this kind, as we can see from all
of his letters, in which he instructs or even harangues the members
of the churches that he founded. Paul clearly regarded himself as
having authority over the churches he founded. We also hear of
other Christian preachers and leaders who moved around, such
as Apollos. People such as these must have led activities at the
churches that they visited, in virtue of their own spiritual standing
and personal charisma.

But these apostles and itinerant preachers were a small minority
within the church as a whole. What happened in a church when
no 'pillar' was around? It seems that in the 50s, at least, when
Paul was writing, each Christian community did not have its own
formally recognized leaders. Paul envisages different roles for
different Christians: in 1 Corinthians 12:28 we hear of apostles,
prophets, and teachers, as well as different abilities that different
people may have. But there is no indication of any kind of formal
ministry. These are functions that different Christians may perform,
not positions that they may occupy. When telling the Corinthians
that they should eat together in an orderly way, Paul tells them
simply to wait for each other to arrive, not that they should await
the instructions of the person in charge. And yet, in 1 Thessalonians
5:12–13, Paul asks his readers to respect those who are in charge
of them and teach them. These, presumably, were people who
performed these functions, but without any official title or office.
They had no formal authority, but it was believed that the Spirit had
given them the gift and task of looking after the community.

Prophets and apostles

This system of church leadership seems to have continued to exist,
at least in some churches, for some time. The book of Revelation,
probably written in the closing years of the first century AD by
one John of Patmos in the Asia Minor region, suggests this. John
regards himself as a prophet of some kind. That is evident not
merely from the visions which take up most of the book, but from
his reference to being 'in the spirit' (1:10) when they began, a
sort of prophetic trance. There were other prophets as well: John
denounces one in Thyatira, whom he accuses of misleading the
people (2:20–23). This prophet was a woman, whom John rather
misogynistically calls only 'Jezebel'. It seems that in the churches
of Asia Minor there was still a kind of 'prophetic' ministry: the
churches were led, in some way, by people who had a charismatic
ministry, who were believed to speak on behalf of God, but who
might not have held any 'formal' kind of office other than that
of prophet. Revelation 2:2 also mentions 'apostles', whom the
Christians in Ephesus judged and found to be false. The fact that
the Ephesians had their doubts about these apostles suggests that

they were not members of that church, but Christians who moved from place to place, exercising their ministry as they went. Clearly these were not 'apostles' in the sense of the leaders of the first generation of the church, but Christians who believed that they were continuing the same sort of ministry.

The *Didache* confirms this picture of a charismatic ministry in some churches at the end of the first century AD. The author has much to say about apostles and prophets and how to tell whether they are genuine or not. The picture this text paints is one where apostles and prophets are all itinerant, travelling from church to church. Exactly what apostles *do* in churches is not stated, but prophets speak 'in the spirit', just like John of Patmos. The author is quite strict about judging these people. Any prophet whose life does not reflect his or her prophecy is false and must be cast out, as must any who ask for money. Apostles are permitted to stay for only a day or two at most; any 'apostle' who hangs around expecting to be looked after is false and must be cast out. But prophets are allowed to stay for longer, and can even expect to be given gifts by the community.

The emergence of hierarchy

This informal, inspirational model of leadership was still operating at the end of the first century AD in Asia Minor, and may have continued to do so for some decades after, as we shall see in chapter 7 when discussing the Montanists. But a very different system had been developing in other churches. We can already see hints of it back in the 50s, in Paul's letters: in Philippians 1:1 he greets 'the bishops and deacons' in Philippi, titles that appear nowhere else in his undisputed letters. The Greek words are *episkopoi* and *diakonoi*, which mean something like 'overseers' and 'servants' or 'helpers'. We do not know at all who these people were or why Paul greets them in this letter and in no other; perhaps this reflects some special situation in the church at Philippi. It is worth mentioning that how we choose to translate terms such as these will affect how we interpret them. 'Bishop', for example, has overtones that the mere 'overseer' lacks. We should not imagine first-century 'bishops' as magnificent figures wearing special robes and hats. The more informal 'overseer' probably reflects their role more accurately. But was *episkopos* simply a description of what they did, or an actual title which was given to them? We cannot tell.

The 'bishops and deacons' appear much more clearly in later texts, however. They are especially prominent in the Pastoral Epistles – 1 Timothy, 2 Timothy, and Titus – which were probably written towards the end of the first century. In 1 Timothy 3:1–13, the author lays down stringent conditions for both bishops and deacons. The bishop is mentioned in the singular, implying that there is a single bishop in each church: he must be not only morally completely upright but also someone who has been a Christian for some time. Deacons – who appear in the plural – must also be morally upright, although the standards do not seem to be quite as high as for the bishop. The idea seems to be that the bishop is in charge of the church and the deacons are his assistants.

However, the situation implied by the Pastorals is complicated by the presence of another category of minister, the 'presbyters', a term which simply means 'old men'. Again, it is not always clear if this is a formal title or not. Are the presbyters identical with the bishop and deacons, or do they represent a quite different group, perhaps a different system of church leadership altogether? It is uncertain. 1 Timothy 5:17–19 speaks of presbyters who 'rule' the church. In Titus 1:5–9, meanwhile, the presbyters seem to be identified with bishops.

We find what seems to be a similar situation in Rome and Corinth in the 90s, as attested by *1 Clement*. This text is a letter written by the Roman Christians to the Corinthian ones, probably in AD 96; tradition tells us that its author was Clement, the bishop of Rome (Peter's third successor). The letter was written to plead for calm and unity in Corinth, where it seems that – for reasons we do not know – one faction in the church had expelled the church's leaders and installed their own instead. Clement calls these leaders 'presbyters'. He tells us that the first presbyters were commissioned by the apostles, and that their successors were similarly chosen with care to lead the church. He thinks it very wrong that presbyters who have served the church well should be dismissed for no good reason, and urges the Corinthian Christians to submit to their properly appointed presbyters. Here, then, we have what seems to be quite a formal arrangement of presbyters leading the church. 1 Peter 5:1–5 offers a similar picture. But Clement also talks about 'bishops' and 'deacons', at some points apparently taking 'bishop' to be synonymous with 'presbyter'.

But other groups seem to have developed rather different systems. We have already seen how Revelation and the *Didache* testify to a world of wandering prophets and apostles; but the *Didache* also talks about bishops and deacons, just like the Pastorals. Like their equivalents in the Pastorals, these bishops and deacons are chosen and appointed by the community (rather than simply turning up and exercising their charismatic powers), although we are not told exactly what they do. We *are* told that 'they are carrying out the ministry of the prophets and teachers for you,' which implies that the bishops and deacons are actually subordinate to the prophets. Perhaps we are to imagine the bishops and deacons as remaining in one place and running the local church, and then deferring to itinerant prophets when the latter arrive. What does seem clear is that the *Didache* implies a church in transition, where the older, Pauline, charismatic model of ministry was still operating, but a more formalized, official model of ministry was developing.

What can we conclude? There was certainly a tendency, throughout the first century, for Christian churches to become more formally organized, with a clearer distinction between those who were in charge and those who were not. To begin with, people simply took on a role in the church that seemed right for them, but by the end, those who were to lead had to meet many stringent criteria. We can say that a 'functional' model of church leadership gave way to an 'official' model. However, there was no single route that this development took. Different churches evolved different systems, and there may well have been different systems operating simultaneously in the same church. They also all developed at different rates. In fact, it is not really until the end of the *second* century AD that we can talk about a fairly uniform system of leadership throughout the Christian church.

Unity and division

As all of this suggests, the Christian movement in the first century AD was a mixture of uniformity and diversity. The existence of travelling preachers and other church leaders ensured that there was some uniformity to the movement, whose members all traced their spiritual heritage back to Jesus himself and the first disciples. But each community, in each city, was also self-governing, and different social structures evolved in different ones. Did the differences go deeper than that?

The question of the unity or diversity of the primitive church is one of the most vexed in New Testament scholarship. At one extreme is the traditional view, which is that the Christians were very unified. On this view, the different books of the New Testament certainly attest to different styles of leadership and different emphases in practice or doctrine, but there was no real disagreement between the churches. Some groups were aberrant in belief or behaviour, but they were rejected by the majority. Where there were distinctions between the mainstream churches – such as between the mission to the Jews, led by Peter and James, and the mission to the Gentiles, led by Paul – these were on the whole amicable. This picture derives, to a considerable extent, from the book of Acts. There, Luke generally strives to portray his characters as basically agreeing with one another, and disagreeing mainly over procedural matters rather than anything substantial. For example, in Acts 15:36–41, Luke tells us that Paul and Barnabas parted ways because of a disagreement over whether John Mark should accompany them in their travels, a rather trivial matter. But Paul himself, in Galatians 2:13, implies that he fell out with Barnabas over a much more serious issue, whether it was acceptable for Jewish Christians to eat with Gentile ones – a matter in which Paul tells us he disagreed with Peter himself, too.

German New Testament scholar, Ferdinand Baur (1792–1860).

On the basis of apparent discrepancies like these, some scholars have argued that the picture of Christian unanimity painted by Luke in Acts is a fiction. On this view, there were major and irreconcilable differences between different Christian communities, above all between those led by Peter and James and those led by Paul and his associates. Eventually, the Pauline faction 'won'. The later books of the New Testament, above all Acts, were written to demonstrate the superiority of the Pauline version of Christianity and to airbrush history to make it seem that no other version had ever existed. Only by reading between the lines, it is maintained, can we reconstruct the real story.

This account of early Christian history goes back to Ferdinand Baur, a major and very radical New Testament scholar of the early nineteenth century. Baur believed, furthermore, that the fundamental difference between the two major Christian factions was their attitude to Judaism. The churches of Peter and James were Jewish Christian churches, which sought to combine faith in Jesus as the Messiah with a basically Jewish lifestyle and theology. The Pauline churches, by contrast, were Gentile, and believed in Jesus as a personal saviour.

St Stephen Before the Judges, from the Altarpiece of St Stephen, c.1470, by Michael Pacher (1435–98).

How accurate is this interpretation? A few things, at least, are uncontroversially clear. The first is that there *were* disputes from a fairly early stage in the church. Acts 6:1 testifies to a disagreement among the Christians in Jerusalem between the 'Hellenists' and the 'Hebrews'. Although Luke tells us that the argument was over provision for widows, he does not tell us who these groups were. But one of the leaders of the 'Hellenists' is Stephen, who in the next chapter gives a speech to the Jewish council in which he attacks the system of Temple sacrifices and worship in very strong terms. As we saw in chapter 1, this view is hard to reconcile with the supposed habit of the early Christians of praying at the Temple. Was the disagreement between 'Hellenists' and 'Hebrews' over this matter? Unfortunately we can only speculate.

Probably in the late 40s, the church held what has become

known as the 'council of Jerusalem' to address matters of this kind. The event is described in Acts 15. According to this account, Peter, Paul, and James all agreed that Gentile converts to Christianity should not have to be circumcised. The church in Jerusalem wrote a circular letter stating that converts must not eat meat which had been sacrificed in pagan rituals, but this was the only condition placed upon them. According to Acts, this was the end of the matter. In Galatians 2:1–10, Paul describes what may have been the same event, but he says nothing about the circular letter. He also says nothing about that letter in 1 Corinthians 8, where he is discussing the problem of meat sacrificed to pagan idols, and where he states that it is permissible to eat such meat, although he advises against it. Also, in Galatians 2:11–14, Paul describes an incident at Antioch, after the council of Jerusalem, when – under the influence of messengers from James – Peter refused to eat with Gentile Christians, and Paul challenged him publicly about it. This disagreement reflects not only a personal argument between Paul on the one side and Peter and James on the other, but differences in practice between Christian communities. It seems that in Jerusalem Jewish and Gentile Christians did not mix, but in Antioch they did. All of this suggests that the disagreements between Paul and Antioch on the one hand and Peter, James, and Jerusalem on the other ran more deeply than Acts suggests.

But how one answers the question of divisions within the primitive church will depend, to some extent, upon the degree to which one is willing to take particular incidents or individuals as representative of groups. For example, when Paul stood up to Peter in Antioch and argued with him, was this simply a disagreement between two Christian leaders? Or did it reflect much deeper disagreements between two wings of the church? Scholars are often willing to assume that ideas expressed in New Testament texts reflect not simply the views of the author but of the whole 'community' which he represents ('community' is possibly a rather over-used word in New Testament scholarship). But this approach can sometimes be very tenuous.

The letter to the Galatians also indicates a subsequent controversy, in which a group of Christians arrived in Galatia – where Paul had founded a church – and told the converts there that it was necessary to be circumcised to inherit the promises made to Abraham, and that Paul had no real authority at all compared to those who had actually known Jesus in his lifetime. But who were these people? Were they the same as the 'Hebrews' of Acts 5, or were they agents of James like those who made Peter change his mind in Antioch? Were they Jews who had converted to Christianity but who retained a belief that Jewish practices were still essential, or were they actually Gentiles who converted to Christianity, investigated its roots, and became enthusiastic converts to the idea of following the Jewish law? Once again, we do not know.

If the diversity of scholarly opinions on these questions is anything to go by, we can conclude very little of any certainty. However, some things do seem fairly likely. One is that the intense arguments about circumcision, the role of the law, and so on had died down by the end of the first century AD. In the later documents of the New Testament, we do not find anything like the ferocity of Paul's letter to the Galatians.

It is also fairly safe to say that most scholars today would regard Baur's hypothesis of a complete split in the church as too extreme, but that they would also reject the traditional view of virtual unanimity as too simplistic. Undoubtedly, each community had its own distinctive approach to the shared faith, and undoubtedly, there were disagreements between both individuals and groups that were deeply felt on both sides. But at the same time, there is evidence of unity as well. Although Paul criticized Peter when they disagreed, his letters – even Galatians – do not indicate that he regarded Peter or James as fundamentally misguided or leaders of a faction that was wrong or unchristian. On the contrary, Paul was very concerned for church unity, and in his letters speaks frequently of a collection of money that Peter and James had commissioned him to make. This collection, which Paul made personally and took back to Jerusalem each time he visited there, was of great personal importance to the apostle, who regarded it not simply as a means of helping poor Christians in Jerusalem but as a sign of the unity between the churches he had founded and those of Peter and James.

If this is correct, then we should be wary of assuming the existence of various 'factions' within the first-century church. However, this does not answer the related question, which is: how 'Jewish' was the church? If we agree with Baur and think that the early church was highly divided, were those divisions ones between Jewish Christians on the one hand and Gentile Christians on the other? And if, on the other hand, we reject Baur's thesis and suppose that most of these groups mostly got on with one another, can we still distinguish between Jewish Christians and Gentile Christians during this period?

The question of the relations between Christianity and Judaism throughout this whole period is enormously complex and controversial. We shall look at just some of the issues involved in the next chapter.

Opposition and Persecution

The first thirty years of the church's existence were momentous. The church had begun as a group of fishermen, former disciples of Jesus, living in Jerusalem; it had become a movement with communities in cities all the way to Rome, all faithful to the Jesus they had never met and who they believed would return soon. The first great theologians had emerged and written the first great Christian texts.

But if the first thirty years were momentous, the next thirty were tumultuous. They saw the church come under fire from two directions at once – from the leaders of the Jewish religion, which was itself evolving at a frantic pace, and from the Roman authorities.

Detail of *The Taking of Jerusalem by Titus*, Flemish school. Titus was in charge of quelling the rebellion and of razing Jerusalem to the ground in AD 70.

Christianity and Judaism

We saw in the last chapter that there is considerable scholarly disagreement over how unified or divided the church was in the first century AD, and that this is closely connected to the question of how Jewish it was. One of the problems with discussing the Jewishness of the early church is that the very word 'Jewish' can mean so many things, which means that the question 'How Jewish was the early church?' can itself have many meanings. If we take 'Jewishness' to mean a racial category, then it is simply a question about ethnic origins. If we take 'Jewishness' to mean believing certain doctrines associated with the Jewish faith, then we are asking if the individual or community held these doctrines. If we take 'Jewishness' to mean belonging to a certain group within society, then we are asking whether Christians were members of that group or not. And finally, if we take 'Jewishness' to mean behaving in a certain way, then we are asking if the individual or community behaved in that way.

Some of these questions are fairly easy to answer. It is questionable whether 'Jewishness' is a racial category at all, but it certainly was not regarded as such in antiquity, when the modern biological notion of 'race' did not really exist. As for the doctrinal question, all Christians inherited some elements of Judaism, such as belief in one God who was the creator of the universe. To call Jesus the Christ or Messiah was to place oneself, to some degree, in a Jewish theological world, because 'Messiah' was a Jewish concept. We shall see in later chapters how some Christians did reject these Jewish elements of Christianity, but that they represented minority factions, firmly rejected by the majority.

What of the sociological and practical questions? These are much harder. They are also closely connected, since to practise a religion is, in part, to be a member of a group, and also, in part, to behave in a certain way. Group membership is often defined, in part, by how one behaves. So to ask whether Christians were 'Jewish' in the sense of belonging to a Jewish social group, and to ask whether they were 'Jewish' in the sense of behaving in ways characteristic of Jews, may be to ask much the same thing.

Another complicating factor is that Judaism itself was not a simple, monolithic religion. In fact, the first century was a time of huge change for Judaism. The emergence of Christianity was just one of a number of remarkable new developments that saw the religion change for ever.

Judaism in the first century AD

The decades after Jesus' death saw the political situation in Palestine continue to become even more complicated and strained. In the early 40s direct Roman rule was suspended and a Jewish

Peter Paul Rubens' portrait of Emperor Vespasian, who ruled from AD 69 to 79.

king, Agrippa I, ruled rather as Herod had. But after his death in AD 44 direct Roman rule returned, and a series of especially heavy-handed Roman officials led to rising tensions among the Palestinian Jews.

There had, perhaps, been revolutionary Jewish groups in Jesus' day; some modern commentators have even believed that Jesus was among them, or that Judas, the disciple who betrayed Jesus, was a revolutionary who was disappointed by Jesus' failure to overthrow the Romans. There is little evidence for such views. While there was no doubt plenty of anti-Roman sentiment in Palestine in Jesus' day, actual groups dedicated to the overthrow of Roman rule seem to have been very thin on the ground. But in the 40s more groups like this did emerge, who were opposed to Roman rule and who hoped to see it overthrown.

In AD 66, after a particularly dismal two years of rule by the procurator Gessius Florus, resistance groups broke out into open revolt against Rome. They ransacked the countryside, invaded Jerusalem, and defeated the small Roman garrison there. The legate of Syria invaded, but his men were routed at the battle of Beth Horon and an entire legion was destroyed. Jerusalem was firmly in the hands of the rebels, known as the Zealots. However, the Zealots seem to have been not a single group but a number of different organizations, who shared the goal of removing the Romans but could agree on little else. With the Romans ousted, the Zealots fell out with one another, and there was a protracted period of struggle for dominance among the Zealot groups and other Jewish groups in the city. Meanwhile, shocked by the loss of a legion and determined to crush the rebels with all the power the empire could muster, the emperor Nero was preparing a counter-attack. Under the leadership of the general Vespasian, Roman forces invaded Galilee and conquered it with ease. By AD 70 they had reached Jerusalem, and besieged it. At this point Vespasian became emperor of Rome, and his son, Titus, was put in charge of quelling the rebellion. Many scholars believe that the eschatological speech attributed to Jesus in Mark 13 was written during this time, since it reflects the situation in Palestine during the Jewish war:

> *But when you see the desolating sacrilege set up where it ought not to be (let the reader understand), then those in Judea must flee to the mountains; the one on the housetop must not go down or enter the house to take anything away; the one in the field must not turn back to get a coat. Woe to those who are pregnant and to those who are nursing infants in those days! Pray that it may not be in winter. For in those days there will be suffering, such as has not been from the beginning of the creation that God created until now, no, and never will be.*

Mark 13:14–19

The author was right to advise people to flee in the face of the 'desolating sacrilege' (often thought to be a reference to Titus entering the Temple). Thousands of people sought refuge in the precincts of the Temple as the legions entered Jerusalem, perhaps believing that God would never allow it to be destroyed. They were wrong: Titus had Jerusalem razed to the ground. The Temple itself was destroyed and its treasures plundered, to be exhibited in Titus' triumphal procession in Rome.

The destruction of Jerusalem, and above all of the great Temple, was a shattering blow to Judaism both in Palestine and beyond. After AD 70, many Jews referred to Rome as 'Babylon', because the Romans had destroyed Herod's Temple just as the Babylonians had destroyed Solomon's, six centuries earlier. Some Jewish groups seem to have completely ceased to exist. The Sicari, for example, had retreated to the great natural citadel of Masada, where in one of the most famous incidents of the war they were besieged by the Romans and defeated in AD 73; the historian Josephus tells us that they all committed suicide rather than submit, although modern historians are doubtful whether it really happened like this. The community at Qumran – apparently associated with the Essenes – was also destroyed. In fact the Essene movement disappeared from history

Above: Qumran, the home of an ascetic Jewish group that may have been connected to the Essenes, and who wrote the Dead Sea Scrolls.

Below: The ruins of Herod's Palace at Masada, the citadel where the Sicari were besieged by Romans in AD 73.

at a stroke after the war, as did the Sadducees. The priests also dwindled rapidly. With no Temple there was nothing for them to do.

One group that did not diminish, however, was the Pharisees. We saw in chapter 1 how they based their self-understanding around the law and its application in everyday life. Such an approach did not require the existence of the Temple or even of Jerusalem. The Pharisees seem to have grown in influence within Judaism in the years after AD 70. This was largely because of the work of Johanan ben Zakkai, a scholar who escaped the siege of Jerusalem (apparently being smuggled out in a coffin) and obtained Vespasian's permission to open a school in Jamnia, a small town in Palestine on the Mediterranean coast. The school became a major centre of scholarship, with Jewish scholars from across the empire coming to it. One of its features was the Great Bet Din, or 'house of judgment', which effectively functioned in some ways as a new Great Sanhedrin, or supreme religious court, in place of the old, priestly one which had met at the Temple and perished after Jerusalem's destruction. Although this is sometimes referred to as 'the council of Jamnia', as if it were a single brief event when the Jewish leaders got together and reinvented Judaism, it was really an ongoing process and one that took a long time. The scholars at Jamnia recognized that the Jewish religion needed to be rethought

An example of an illustrated Talmud is the abbreviated Talmud of Asher ben Jehiel, c. 1250–1328.

in the wake of the Temple's destruction; in particular, now that there was no central institution or priesthood, many matters which had previously been rather vague needed to be settled. They defined an official canon of Jewish Scripture, for example, distinguishing between old and useful but unscriptural books (such as 1 and 2 Maccabees) and truly canonical ones (such as the Pentateuch).

The Great Bet Din is normally considered the beginning of 'rabbinic' Judaism, so called because its scholars became known by the title 'rabbi' (a title that had not been used in the times of the Temple). Rabbinic Judaism, with its emphasis upon the study and practice of the Torah, and its learned scholars, did not instantly displace all other kinds of Judaism. After all, the Great Bet Din did not have any official authority, at least not in the time of ben Zakkai. Judaism remained diverse, but rabbinic Judaism gradually spread and became the dominant kind: indeed, it was, in effect, the ancestor of modern Judaism. The rabbis wrote down the oral traditions of the scholars and teachers who had preceded them, forming the Mishnah, the major source for our knowledge of Judaism in the first century AD and earlier. The Mishnah would later form part of the Talmud, together with commentaries upon it, known as the Gemarah. Yet the days of the Temple were not forgotten. Joshua ben Hanania, one of ben Zakkai's pupils, said:

> When a man plasters his house, let him leave a small portion unplastered as a remembrance of Jerusalem. Let a man prepare everything that is necessary for a meal, and then leave one small thing undone, as a remembrance of Jerusalem. Let a woman put on all her ornaments, and then leave aside one small thing, as a remembrance of Jerusalem. For it is said, 'If I forget thee, O Jerusalem, may my right hand forget its cunning.'[1]

The Jewishness of Christianity

Where does Christianity fit into this picture? Was it one of these internal developments of Judaism in the first century, a new movement which was nevertheless basically Jewish, like rabbinic Judaism, and only later became a distinct religion? Or was it distinct right from the start?

Some scholars have argued that Christianity was never very Jewish at all (in a sociological or practical sense) after its first couple of decades. On this view, some figures of the first generation, such as Peter and James, may well have continued to regard themselves as Jewish and to live a Jewish lifestyle, including following the law. They focused their missionary activities upon other Jews but met with limited success. Paul attests to this in Romans 9–11, where he grapples with the theological implications of the fact that most Jews weren't interested in the Christian message at all. So Paul preached to Gentiles instead, and enjoyed much greater success. The result was the existence within the church of two main groups, Jewish Christians and Gentile Christians. However, the success of the missions to the Gentiles and the relative failure of those to the Jews meant that Christianity became less and less Jewish in tone. In addition to these sociological factors, Paul's theological arguments led to a general acceptance that the law should not be binding. As a result, by the end of the first century AD, the original Jewish core of the church had largely died out or been marginalized, and Christianity had effectively become a Gentile religion, though with Jewish roots.

This has been the traditional understanding of the situation. But some scholars have taken this view to extremes, and suggested that even in the very first days of the church, the apostles and their

The Ebionites

One piece of evidence that Christianity ceased to be Jewish in any meaningful sense, at least by the second century AD, is the existence of a group known as the Ebionites. Their name seems to come from the Aramaic word for 'poor men', perhaps a reference to the 'poor in spirit' who would inherit the kingdom of heaven according to Matthew 5:3. The name is first used in the late second century AD by various writers, including Irenaeus and Tertullian, to refer to what seems to be a Christian group who were extremely Jewish: they continued to follow the law, denied the divinity of Christ, and argued that Paul was a heretic. The mainstream Christian writers regarded these people as heretics, and they seem to have dwindled over time, disappearing by perhaps the fifth century AD. Some scholars have argued that these Ebionites were actually spiritual descendants of the very first, Jewish Christians. On this view, the fact that the mainstream church in the second and third centuries AD rejected their highly Jewish theology indicates that that mainstream church itself had ceased to be Jewish in any meaningful sense a long time previously. To some modern critics of Christianity, the existence of the Ebionites shows just how much Christianity changed, and how far it became removed from

the original message of Jesus, to which the Ebionites remained faithful even though the mainstream church attacked them for it.

But however poignant such considerations may appear, we must be wary of romanticizing. The fact is that very little is known about the Ebionites, and nothing whatsoever of their history or origins. Moreover, the fact that other Christians rejected their insistence upon the law does not, in itself, prove that other Christians were any less Jewish. The difference between the two groups *may* simply have been that mainstream Christians mostly *were* Jewish, while the Ebionites believed that to be Christian, one *had* to be Jewish: specifically, one had to follow the law and be circumcised. It is also possible that the Ebionites were not 'remnants' of an early Christian group at all, but actually originated in the late second century. Perhaps they were a group of Christians – of Jewish or non-Jewish background – who decided, perhaps for some theological reason, that Paul had been wrong in his letter to the Galatians, and that in order to be a Christian, it was necessary to be circumcised and follow the Jewish law. One would not have to come from a Jewish background in order to develop such a view.

first converts always spent more time preaching to Gentiles than to Jews, and there was never a period when they or any major group within the church insisted upon conformity to the law.

Other scholars have argued for a quite different view of the Jewishness of the mainstream church. On this view, Christianity remained mostly Jewish for at least a generation or two after the time of the apostles. For example, Jean Daniélou, writing in the 1960s, argued that pretty much the whole church (Pauline and non-Pauline) was fundamentally Jewish for most of the first century AD, and only in the second century did Christianity largely abandon its Jewish outlook to move to a 'Hellenistic' one. The fact that the apostles regarded the mission to the Jews as largely 'failed' does not entail that most Christians were Gentiles – it only means that most Jews were not Christians. Indeed, it might be thought that an almost entirely Jewish church should be more intrinsically likely than a predominantly Gentile one. We have seen how small religions typically spread through existing social networks, and how Christianity seems to have conformed to this model. But the very first Christians were Jewish, and Jews typically associated mostly with one another, so we might expect Christianity to have spread almost exclusively among Jews.

Many Christian texts from the first century AD do suggest a Jewish background. Matthew's Gospel, which was probably written in the 80s, is a prime example. Traditionally, this Gospel is thought to have been written by a Jewish Christian, for an audience of Jewish Christians, since the author seems to be very familiar with Jewish ideas and practices. Moreover, it portrays Jesus as the fulfiller of the law: in Matthew 5:17–20, for example, Jesus states that the law will not pass away. The implication is that Matthew and his 'community' were Jews who probably continued to observe the law, but who believed that Jesus was the fulfilment of this law. Matthew even describes Jesus as stating that he has come only to the Jews; he tells his followers to preach only to Jews (10:5–6) and likens Gentiles to 'dogs' (15:26). This suggests that Matthew and his readers regarded themselves as Jews. We find something similar in the letter of James, which is highly Jewish; indeed, there is very little distinctively Christian in it, and were it not for a couple of passing references to Christ, it might have been classified as a piece of first-century Jewish wisdom literature. The letter is actually addressed to 'the twelve tribes in the Dispersion' (James 1:1), suggesting again a group of Christians who not only had much in common with non-Christian Jews, but who regarded themselves as Jewish.

Some scholars have argued that not only did Christianity remain largely Jewish throughout the first century AD, it continued to do so for the next two centuries, seeing a major influx of Gentiles only in the age of Constantine in the fourth century. On this view,

Christians may have agreed by the end of the first century AD that the law was not binding, but many of them probably continued to observe it anyway, and it remained the case for centuries that many – perhaps most – Christians were related to or friends with non-Christian Jews.

There are a few hints in later sources that support this view. For example, the Christians of Lyons who were martyred in AD 177 had been eating kosher meat, suggesting that they observed Jewish dietary regulations. There is also evidence that many Christian groups maintained Sabbath observances for centuries, perhaps even attending a synagogue on the Saturday as well as church on the Sunday.

Blandina was one of the Christian martyrs thrown to bulls in the amphitheatre in Lyons in AD 177.

A religious spectrum

As we have noted, Judaism itself was evolving rapidly and in different ways throughout this period, just as Christianity was. In fact there is good reason to suppose that the rabbis of the second and third centuries were influenced in a number of ways by Christian theologians. In place of the traditional model – Judaism came first and Christianity developed out of it – one might see both rabbinic Judaism and Christianity as developing in tandem out of the ashes of first-century Judaism and the rubble of the destroyed Temple. In fact, of these two, Christianity emerged first, so perhaps the real question is not how Jewish later Christianity was, but rather is how Christian later Judaism was. One Jewish text from third-century Palestine tells of the first-century Pharisee Rabbi Eliezer, who was mistaken for a Christian and arrested. He assured the judge of his loyalty to the emperor and was released. Afterwards, the rabbi recalled that he had been listening cheerfully to a Christian in the marketplace, and this must have been why he himself was mistaken for a Christian. Perhaps third-century Palestinian Jews often mixed with Christians in this way.

Some Christian sources hint at an even closer relationship between Judaism and Christianity. A particularly interesting one is the sixth-century Syriac life of Mar Abba, one of the leaders of the Persian church in that period. One passage recounts a meeting between Mar Abba (at that time a pagan) and a man who claimed to be both Jewish and Christian. Mar Abba asked him how this was possible, and the man replied:

> I am a Jew secretly; I pray to the living God, and I am faithful to his son Jesusmessiah and the Holy Spirit. And I run away from idol worship and all filth. I am a Christian truly, not like the Marcionites, who defraud and call themselves Christians. For Christian is a Greek word. And the interpretation of 'Christian' in Syriac is Marcionite. And [therefore] with respect to that which you have asked me: 'Do you worship the Messiah?,' I worship him truly.[2]

So even as late as the sixth century AD, in the border regions between the Roman and Persian empires, there were people who regarded Christianity and Judaism as basically the same religion; who worshipped Jesus but identified themselves as Jews because the very word 'Christian' was usually restricted to Marcionites (Christians who tried to purge the religion of all Jewish elements).

It may be best to think of these two religions as a spectrum. At one end were Jews who had nothing to do with Christianity, did not recognize Jesus, and perhaps even hated the Christians. At the other end were extreme Christians like the Marcionites, who believed that Christianity should be utterly non-Jewish. In between there were many shades of agreement, disagreement, contact, and distinction.

Justin Martyr, in his *Dialogue with Trypho*, seems to presuppose such a range of views. In the dialogue, the non-Christian Jew Trypho asks Justin whether there are Christians who follow the law. Justin replies that there are, and he comments that some other Christians – who do not follow it – think that they are not really Christians at all and refuse to have anything to do with them. He adds that he himself disagrees with that stance, and he has no problem with Christians who observe the law as long as they do not insist that other Christians do so. That, at least, suggests that in the middle of the second century AD there was a wide spectrum of practices and views among Christians on the issue of following the law.

The Christian apologist Justin Martyr (AD 100–165).

Church and synagogue: before AD 70

So the question of the relations between Christianity and Judaism at the theological, practical, and sociological levels is extremely complex. A simpler issue, however, is the *formal* status that Christians had within wider Judaism. What was the relation between the Christians and the leaders of the Jewish religion? Did they regard the Christians as part of their own religion or not?

In what follows I shall use the word 'Jewish' and its cognates to refer to people who practised the Jewish religion and who were not part of the Christian movement at all: they rejected the claim that Jesus was the Messiah or that he was going to return. By doing this I do not mean to imply that the Christians, or many of them, were not also Jewish in some important way or ways such as those discussed above, but they were distinct from other Jews in at least this way.

Because Judaism itself existed in such different circumstances before the destruction of Jerusalem and after it, it is reasonable to consider the two periods separately. The evidence of relations between Christians and Jews before AD 70 is not entirely consistent. On the one hand, we have some evidence of friendly relations between the two groups. Acts 5:34–39 represents Gamaliel, the leader of the Pharisees, as speaking in defence of the Christians. Indeed, if the very first Christians were in the habit of spending much of their time at the Temple – as Acts 2:46 suggests – then there cannot have been much tension between them and the Jews, since we hear of no disturbances there. On the other hand, however, there is evidence of persecution of Christians by the Jewish authorities. Acts 5:17–32 describes the Sadducees, in particular, as orchestrating a campaign against the Christians, in which the apostles are arrested. In Acts 7, Stephen becomes the first Christian to be killed for his faith, and in the following chapter Paul leads a campaign against the Christians in Jerusalem.

As usual, scholars disagree over the evidence. The traditional interpretation is that the Christians suffered a fairly systematic persecution at the hands of the Jewish authorities in Palestine in general and Jerusalem in particular, and that it was primarily theologically motivated. This is the impression that Acts gives: for example, it is after Stephen declares that he can see the Son of man standing at God's right hand that the Sanhedrin drag him outside and stone him to death. Evidently they interpret this as a blasphemous exaltation of Jesus on Stephen's part. Some, however, have argued that the systematic and theologically motivated persecutions depicted in Acts are anachronistic, and reflect the situation at the time when Luke was writing (the mid-80s?) more accurately than they do the situation in the first generation. On this view, the early persecutions were rather sporadic and were orchestrated by only some Jewish groups, such as the Sadducees; other groups, such as the Pharisees, were more inclined to tolerate the Christians. The persecutions were probably part of a political struggle on the part of these groups within Judaism, not inspired by a particular hatred of Christians or a belief that their views were blasphemous. Moreover, any such persecution would necessarily be restricted to Palestine and mainly Jerusalem, since that was the only place where there were Jewish 'authorities' in a position to do any persecuting.

Nevertheless, the early Christians were certainly encountering opposition from Jews even outside Palestine. In one passage, written in around AD 50, Paul complained:

> *The Jews ... killed both the Lord Jesus and the prophets, and drove us out; they displease God and oppose everyone by hindering us from speaking to the Gentiles so that they may be saved. Thus they have constantly been filling up the measure of their sins; but God's wrath has overtaken them at last.*

1 Thessalonians 2:14–16

There is nothing like this in Paul's other letters, so he cannot have been facing a constant Jewish blockade upon his missionary activities throughout his career, or we would hear more about it. But at some points, at least, he felt so hampered by them that he could denounce 'the Jews' in their entirety.

Although there was clearly at least some tension between some Christians and Jews outside Palestine, Jerusalem seems to have been the primary focus of conflict during this period. This was where James of Jerusalem, also known as James the Just, the brother of Jesus, and main 'pillar' of the church, was based. James seems not to have been a disciple of Jesus during the latter's lifetime, and does not appear in the Gospels; he should not be confused with James the Great (brother of John, a prominent figure in the Synoptic Gospels) or James the Less (a minor disciple also mentioned in the Gospels). Confusingly, there is another minor character in the Gospels, called James son of Alphaeus, who may be identical with James the Less or even (less probably) James the Just, or may simply be yet another James. James the Just and the other Christian leaders seem to have come into conflict with both political and religious leaders in Jerusalem. Acts 12:1–5 tells us of a persecution under Agrippa, confusingly named here as Herod. He imprisoned Peter and executed James the Great, the brother of John. This would have been in the early 40s. Assuming that this information is accurate, we still do not know why Agrippa would have sought to clamp down upon the

This painting by Altichiero da Zevio (1330–85) from the Basilica of Il Santo depicts the sentencing and beheading of James the Great.

Christians in this way, or whether the policy was continued by the Romans after his death in AD 44. The absence of evidence of any persecutions in Jerusalem on the part of the civil authorities for the next two decades suggests not.

Things seem to have flared up again in the 60s, when James the Just himself was killed. The sources do not agree about when and how this happened. Josephus tells us that he was stoned to death in AD 62, but Eusebius records another tradition according to which he was thrown off a tower of the Temple in AD 66 and then clubbed to death when the fall didn't kill him. Despite these contradictions, it is clear that James was not legally executed by the authorities as his brother had been, but lynched by a mob; moreover, this happened in the context of the rising tension and political splintering of the 60s, on the eve of the Jewish war against Rome. It may be, then, that we should interpret James's death as a sign not of particular hatred between Christians and Jews in Jerusalem but of the tension between many different groups at the time. Perhaps the leaders of certain factions within Jerusalem perceived James as the leader of yet another rival faction, and made a temporary alliance with one another to remove him from the scene. On this view, James was a victim of strife between different Jewish groups rather than of a systematic or ideological persecution of Christians by Jews.

But there are also good reasons to suppose that the 60s did see increasing violence by Jews against Christians in particular. This was the time when the Roman authorities were beginning the first persecutions against Christians, and it may be that Jewish leaders were keen to join in if only to demonstrate the clear difference between themselves and the Christians. It might have been wise to show that they were on the same 'side' as the authorities.

Church historian Eusebius of Caesarea (c. AD 263–339).

Church and synagogue: after AD 70

It is uncertain what happened to the Christian community in Jerusalem during the siege. The passage from Mark quoted earlier implies that the Christians fled Jerusalem when Vespasian's troops approached it, and Eusebius tells us the same thing. It may be that the Christians in Jerusalem, in fear for their lives after the death of James, fled from the Jews rather than from the Romans – to Pella, on the other side of the Jordan, according to Eusebius. Revelation 12:6, 14 may also mean that the Christians in Jerusalem fled at this time. In this case they seem to be fleeing persecution from the state authorities (as represented by a dragon). As we saw earlier, some scholars have argued that the later 'Ebionite' sect was actually descended from the original Christian church in Jerusalem. If that is so, then this flight to Pella might have marked the moment at which the Jerusalem Christian community ceased to play a central role in the Christian world, and began its journey to becoming what the mainstream church would regard as a heretical sect.

In this 15th-century illustration, Flavius Josephus is brought before Titus, at the siege of Jerusalem in AD 70.

In any case, the period after the destruction of the Temple certainly saw a worsening of relations between Christians and non-Christian Jews in many places. We can see this reflected in the Christian writings from this time. We have seen that Matthew's Gospel may well have been written by a Jewish Christian who continued to practise elements of the Jewish law. At the same time, however, there is a virulent anti-Jewish tone to much of the Gospel, shown above all in the portrayal of the Pharisees. In Mark's Gospel, the Pharisees and the scribes (many scribes were Pharisees) are portrayed sometimes positively and sometimes negatively. In Matthew, however, all of the positive elements have been removed and the negative ones exaggerated. Matthew's anti-Pharisee polemic is strongest in chapter 23, where Jesus delivers an extended attack on the Pharisees as 'hypocrites' and 'blind guides', who are so concerned to follow the law but have unclean souls. This, with other anti-Pharisaic material in the Gospel, indicates that Matthew was writing at a time of great tension. He regarded the Pharisees – or their equivalents in the 80s – as the church's greatest opponents. These, surely, were the leaders of rabbinic Judaism. Matthew's attacks upon Pharisaism indicate not only the hegemony of that tradition within Judaism during the 80s but also its particular antipathy towards Christianity. It can lead Matthew – apparently a Jewish Christian – to suggest that Jews were guilty of Jesus' murder, the notorious claim of Matthew 27:25, which appears in no other Gospel.

In around AD 90, perhaps a little earlier, the Great Bet Din at Jamnia addressed the rise of Christianity. It issued a new prayer which was to be read in all synagogues. One later report of this prayer suggests that it ran like this:

And for apostates let there be no hope; and may the insolent kingdom be quickly uprooted, in our days. And may the Nazarenes and the heretics perish quickly; and may they be erased from the Book of Life; and may they not be inscribed with the righteous.

In other words, the Christians – the 'Nazarenes', or followers of Jesus of Nazareth – were heretics, who deserved to be wiped out as quickly as possible. The issuing of this prayer is often taken to mark the official 'split' between church and synagogue. In reality, the situation must have been far more complex. The fact that a group of rabbis in Jamnia wanted all synagogue congregations to condemn Christianity does not mean that all the congregations did so; as we have seen, there is evidence, at the very least, of friendly relations between Jews and Christians for centuries after this point and that the boundary lines between the two religions were sometimes so unclear that they could hardly be called distinct religions at all.

Christian attitudes to Judaism

The notion which seems to have become standard among Christians by the end of the first century AD was that Christians were true Jews: they had inherited the promises God had made to Abraham and to Israel. This is what Paul had taught in Galatians 3:29. One important idea which developed to express this notion was that of 'typology'. A 'type' is an event or object of the past which somehow mirrors or foreshadows something in the future. Some Christians believed that much of the Jewish religion was a 'type' of Christ. The text which sets out this view most clearly is the letter to the Hebrews, an anonymous text of uncertain authorship and date. The author stresses that Jesus' death is enough to remove everyone's sin, and that it is only through Jesus' death that sin is removed. He does this by comparing the old covenant that God made with the Jews to the new one that he has made with the Christians. The old covenant was made through the mediation of angels and prophets, but the new one has been made through God's own Son. The old covenant involved a system of priests and sacrifices, but the new one has only one priest and one sacrifice – Christ himself. In fact, the old Jewish system of sacrifices was itself a 'type' of Christ and his sacrifice: the law was a 'sketch' of Christ's death, and the sanctuary of the Temple into which the high priest would enter a 'mere copy' of heaven, into which Christ entered. That means the law is good, and ordained by God, but its goodness is secondary, derived from the main event.

This qualifiedly positive assessment of Judaism as a 'type' of Christianity seems to have become less popular by the end of the first century AD and the breakdown in relations between Christians and Jewish leaders. Unsurprisingly, we find Christians in this period suggesting instead that Judaism is not so much a reflection of Christianity or a preparation for it as a rival

to it. So in Revelation 2:9, non-Christian Jews are called 'those who say that they are Jews and are not', implying that to be really Jewish is a good thing – but the Christians are the *real* Jews, and the non-Christian Jews are not Jews at all. This dual view – Christians are not Jews, and yet at the same time are more Jewish than the Jews – finds its most extreme expression in the letter of *Barnabas*. This text, which was probably written in the early second century AD, is anonymous – the attribution to Barnabas, Paul's companion, comes at the end and appears to have been added by a later editor. Most of the letter is an attempt to show that the Jewish Scriptures can be understood correctly only in the light of Christ. But where the writer to the Hebrews suggests that Judaism has become fulfilled in Christianity, *Barnabas* makes the more audacious claim that Judaism was *never* legitimate, and God's promises to the Jews were *always* applied to the Christians. He argues that the Jews abandoned the covenant that they had made with God at an early stage by worshipping idols; God therefore withdrew the covenant and applied it to Christians instead. So Christians, and not Jews, are the true heirs to the promises God made to the Jewish patriarchs.

Later Christians did not all share this negative attitude towards Judaism, but they did all seem to regard Judaism as, at the very least, a distinct religion. Later Christian authors never indicate that they regard themselves as a group within Judaism. Justin Martyr, writing in the middle of the second century AD, presents his *Dialogue with Trypho* as a debate between a Christian on the one hand and a Jew on the other. Tertullian, writing fifty years later, speaks of 'the Jews' and 'the Christians' as distinct groups.

Nevertheless, this was a significant moment and one which is also reflected in Christian writings of the time. John's Gospel is often considered to be one of them. In John 9:22 we are told that the Jews had decreed that anyone following Jesus would be cast out of the synagogue. But this is anachronistic; no such decree seems to have been issued in Jesus' lifetime at all. The verse is often taken as a reference to the decree of Jamnia, as are similar statements at 12:42 and 16:2. In fact, in John's Gospel we find that Jesus' opponents are no longer the scribes and the Pharisees but mostly simply 'the Jews', as if Jesus himself and his followers were not Jewish. It seems that when John was writing, he or his readers were at odds with Jews in general, not simply one party within Judaism. At the same time, much of John's language and themes are similar to those found in first-century Judaism, as the discovery of the Dead Sea Scrolls showed. Many scholars therefore believe that John and his readers were Jewish Christians who, like Matthew, were in conflict with Jews who rejected Christianity and who actively expelled the Christians from the synagogues.

Nero holds a golden lute while Rome burns in the background in this 1897 painting by Howard Pyle.

The imperial persecutions

Christians also faced a new threat in the form of persecution from the Roman empire itself. We know very little about this persecution, except that it occurred after the great fire of Rome in AD 64, on the orders of the emperor Nero. The Roman historian Tacitus tells us that many people thought that Nero himself had started the fire, and so to divert suspicion away from himself he blamed the Christians. Quite why he picked on them is a matter of speculation, but many were rounded up and executed in particularly horrific ways – including being set on fire to act as living torches for night-time revels. Tacitus tells us that although the Christians deserved to die because of their impiety and obstinacy, Nero was so cruel that many people felt sorry for them.

It is traditionally thought that both Peter and Paul were among those who died in this persecution, and this may well be the case. Certainly Paul's career probably ended at around this time in Rome. Peter is harder to place, especially given that his base of operations appears to have been Jerusalem. Tradition has it that he moved to Rome and led the Christian community there, which is why he is counted as the first bishop of Rome. Precisely what Peter's relation was to the Roman church is now impossible to assess, but there is no particular reason to doubt that he was in Rome acting as a Christian leader of some kind in the 60s or that he died at around this time. Both John's Gospel and *1 Clement* tell us that Peter died for his faith, although they do not give details.

Nero's purge of the Roman Christian community seems to have been a one-off event. We do not know if Christianity was made officially illegal or how Christians were treated in the years that followed. Nero himself was deposed and killed himself in AD 68, and was succeeded (after several very short-lived emperors) by Vespasian. There is no evidence that Vespasian or his successor, Titus, persecuted the Christians, but there is some that Domitian, who ruled between AD 81 and 96, did so. 1 Peter, possibly written during this time, contains several references to Christians suffering or being called to account by pagans. Revelation, also probably dating from this period, contains such references as well. But it seems likely that whatever persecution occurred was intermittent and unsystematic. It is not until the time of Trajan and Pliny the Younger that we learn anything of the official attitude towards the Christians, and we shall look at that in chapter 5.

Cornelius Tacitus, the Roman historian (AD 56–117).

Coin depicting Emperor Nero, who ruled the empire from AD 53 to AD 68.

Ignatius of Antioch

We know virtually nothing of Ignatius' life. He was the leader of the Christians in Antioch – or, at least, he regarded himself as their leader – when he was arrested, probably in AD 107. He was sentenced to death for his Christian faith and taken to Rome to face his punishment. As he travelled, he wrote seven letters to various churches in Asia Minor and in Rome. No doubt, as Ignatius wrote to the different Christian congregations while in chains, he was consciously taking Paul as his model. Just as the apostle had written to the Philippians of his determination while in prison awaiting judgment fifty years earlier, so too Ignatius wrote to the Roman Christians of his determination to face death boldly. In fact he insisted that he was looking forward to his own execution, since it would allow him to rise again with Jesus, and he begged them not to try to prevent it out of misguided concern for him.

Ignatius was also deeply influenced by Paul's emphasis upon the unity of all Christians with one another and with Christ. In Ignatius' case, however, this sense of unity came across in his emphasis upon obedience to the bishop in every church. We saw in chapter 2 how the model of church leadership evolved during the first century AD, with different texts suggesting different systems – some talking of 'deacons', some of 'presbyters', and so on. Ignatius presupposes a system not unlike that of the Pastoral Epistles, where each church has a single 'bishop' who is very much in charge. In fact, Ignatius instructs his readers to obey their bishop as if he were God himself. In Ignatius' system, the bishop is to the local congregation what Christ is to the church as a whole: just as Christ represents all Christians to God, and mediates God's saving grace to all Christians, so too the bishop represents his local congregation to God and mediates God's saving grace to them. Ignatius is

very clear that the bishop is the only person who can authorize liturgical activities. It is the bishop's job to celebrate the Eucharist: anyone who holds a Eucharist of their own without the bishop's blessing is a schismatic, someone who is breaking away from the church and setting up their own.

This very strong emphasis upon the authority of the bishop goes beyond anything in the New Testament. The fact that Ignatius stresses the point so strongly and so repeatedly is good evidence that not everyone agreed with him. Clearly there were Christians in these cities who were ignoring what the bishop told them to do, and who held services of their own without his authorization. In fact it may well be the case that the person Ignatius regarded as 'the bishop' was merely the leader of one faction among others within these churches. Ignatius also mentions deacons and presbyters, although he has far less to say about them than about the bishop; the implication generally seems to be that the deacons act as the bishop's assistants, while the presbyters' role is vaguer. Evidently different churches were still using different systems of government.

Nevertheless, Ignatius' ideas about the importance of the bishop would prove influential in later years. His letters testify to the emergence of what has been called the 'monarchical episcopate', where a single bishop rules a local congregation with the help of his deacons, rather as a king rules a nation with the help of the nobles. As for Ignatius himself, it is almost certain that he met his end in precisely the way that he anticipated and hoped for, as a martyr in Rome.

The book of Revelation

The bitter disputes with the synagogues and the persecutions at the hands of the Roman state did not simply change the exterior circumstances of the church. They also changed its internal characteristics: they influenced how Christians thought of themselves and of God's plan for the world. Christians, on this view, would have to suffer before they would see the glorious return of Jesus.

This view is found with unparalleled vividness in the book of Revelation, written by John of Patmos, probably around the end of the first century AD or perhaps the early second century. It seems to presuppose a geographical location of Asia Minor, and a background of Jewish Christianity.

John presents a starkly dualist picture of the world. In his view, the fact that the worldly powers persecute Christians shows that they are in league with Satan. He portrays Rome first as a cosmic dragon that tries to kill Jesus and his followers, and then as a 'beast' with ten horns and seven heads. The seven heads of the beast represent the seven hills of Rome, while the ten horns are the ten Roman emperors who had ruled at the time when John was writing. One of the horns is described as having suffered a mortal wound, but as having recovered, and this seems to be a reference to the popular belief at the time that the emperor Nero had not died in AD 68 after all but had in fact faked his own death and fled east, and would return at the head of a conquering Persian army to reclaim his throne. Nero, the first emperor to persecute Christians, is a particular object of fear and hatred: the 'number of the beast', 666 according to 13:18, may well be a numerological representation of the name 'Nero Caesar' in Hebrew characters.

A shepherd boy takes goats to graze on the hills below Chora on Patmos. It is from this region that the author of Revelation is thought to hail.

Taken from the demolished church of San Giovanni Evangelista on Torcello, the Great Whore (Revelation 17–18), is illustrated in the polyptych of the Apocalypse.

But John does not denounce Rome simply because Nero persecuted Christians. He portrays it as intrinsically corrupt and wicked, inspired by the devil and fundamentally idolatrous. The beast utters 'blasphemous' words, and is served by a second beast who performs miracles in its name and forces everyone to worship the first beast. This second beast may represent the imperial cult, whose priests portrayed the emperor as divine. Alternatively, it may be the Roman governor of Asia; the first beast comes from the sea (i.e., it is a foreign power, that of Rome) but the second comes from the land (i.e., it is home-grown). And later a new image is presented: a prostitute, identified with Babylon, seated upon the beast. As we saw earlier, many Jews used 'Babylon' as a code word for Rome. John uses the same terminology, but tells his readers that Babylon has made all the nations of the world drunk with the blood of Christians. This may be John's version of the famous 'Pax Romana', the peace of Rome, which brought prosperity to most of the known world. For John, the Pax Romana is a false peace, an intoxication with a harlot.

It is often suggested that John was writing, in part, to encourage the churches in this time of difficulty; that his predictions of the overthrow of the beast and the creation of a new heaven and a new earth in which the saints would live with God for ever were intended to comfort Christians. Undoubtedly that was part of his intention, but he also seeks to warn Christians not to compromise with Rome as well. The prophetess, 'Jezebel', in Thyatira, is portrayed as teaching Christians to fornicate and eat meat sacrificed to idols – typical 'pagan' behaviour in Jewish literature of the time. It seems that these Christians were combining Christianity with paganism in some way. And John also writes to Christians in Laodicea who were doing quite well in worldly terms, who were rich and prosperous. That would not have been possible without being closely involved in normal Roman society. To all of these, John issues stern warnings. In his eyes they were tainted by involvement with the beast, but Christians were called to something better.

Revelation, then, represents a new way of seeing the church's place in the world – one which by no means all Christians of the time shared, and one which John of Patmos was very keen to impress upon them. Paul had seen the church of his day as a sort of seed, which would grow and grow until everyone, first the Gentiles and then the Jews, would be part of it; eventually God would be 'all in all'. The Roman state had its part to play in this – its rulers and officials were appointed by God and should be obeyed. But for John, the church of his day was a remnant, those who remained faithful, who had stood alone against the beast, and who suffered for it. John writes not only to encourage them in their stand, but to warn them against compromise with the enemy.

Changing beliefs

Christians at the turn of the first and second centuries were living in a very different situation from their spiritual predecessors of the 50s and 60s, let alone that of the very first disciples in the 30s and 40s. Inevitably, the religion itself was developing in response to these changing times. One major development that we have looked at already was the changing relationship between Christians and non-Christian Jews, and another was the succession of controversies within Christianity over Jewish matters. But there were others as well.

The return of Christ

We have seen how early Christianity featured an important eschatological element. The first Christians believed that Jesus was going to return very soon, to such an extent that Paul had to tell his readers that it was still necessary to work. Even Paul did not anticipate, until his arrest, that he personally might die before Jesus returned. But it became increasingly apparent that Jesus was not returning as imminently as people had thought. It may well be that, after a time, many Christians came to believe that at least one of the original apostles would still be alive when Jesus returned. But then all the apostles died, and Jesus still had not returned. We can see traces of this in John's Gospel, which probably dates from the last decade of the first century AD. In 21:20–23, the author refers to a belief among the Christians that one disciple in particular, the 'beloved disciple', would not die before Jesus returned. He is at pains to point out that this rumour is false and that Jesus never made such a prediction. Evidently, this passage was written at a time when all of the apostles had died, and many people were losing heart because of the continued non-reappearance of Jesus. In John, the belief that Jesus will return remains, but there is no longer any sense that this return is imminent.

The problem is tackled even more explicitly in 2 Peter, often thought to be the latest book of the New Testament to be written. Chapter 3 tells us that people were laughing at the Christians for still believing that Jesus would return, pointing out that the apostles had long since died, and yet he hadn't come back. The author assures his readers that 'the day of the Lord' *will* come one day, but it could be a long way off. In this way, Christians retained the eschatology of Jesus' first disciples, but they removed its urgency.

Luke offered another approach to this problem. The authors of the other Gospels, including John, restricted their focus to the period of Jesus' ministry and the days following his resurrection. Luke, however, thought it worthwhile to write a sequel, namely Acts, in which he described what happened next. That very act implied a belief that what happened in the church after Jesus' departure was intrinsically significant. In fact, Luke presents the history of the church in the couple of decades after Jesus' resurrection as directly guided by God, through the Holy Spirit. The coming of the Holy Spirit at Pentecost, for Luke, ushers in a new age: the age of the church, during which new wonders are performed and new decisions taken, all under God's direct guidance. So where the first Christians believed that Jesus was the Messiah, that God had raised him, and that he would come again soon, Luke gives us a new worldview: one that agrees that Jesus was the Messiah and that God had raised him, of course, but which adds that God has now authorized Jesus' followers to found a new movement, one directed by the Holy Spirit. Luke is the only Gospel writer who tells us that Jesus not only rose from the dead but, some time later, ascended to heaven. The other Gospel writers imply no difference between the time of the very first disciples, who saw the risen Lord, and the time of their readers; but Luke implies that the time between Jesus' resurrection and his ascension was a special time, when the risen Lord might be seen, but now – after the ascension – Christians were living in a different time, the age of the church. God's plan had not come to an end with Jesus' resurrection; that was not the end of the story, with only the final 'day of the Lord' to come. On the contrary, it was the beginning of a whole new chapter – indeed, a whole new volume in Luke's work.

Giotto di Bondone's fresco, c. 1303, depicts *The Last Judgment*. Christ is seen here as having returned as king to judge the world.

The cosmic Christ

It has sometimes been argued that the late first century also saw developments in Christians' understanding of who Jesus was. In John's Gospel, for example, christology – the question of who Jesus is – is an overriding theme. The famous opening section tells us that Jesus already existed before he was born in Palestine – indeed, he existed 'in the beginning', and he existed in an extremely close relationship with God, so close that he could be called divine himself. The universe was created through him. This pre-existent divine being, the 'Word' (or

Logos in Greek), is the same entity who was born as Jesus and who was rejected by his people.

Such a christology is often classed as 'high', because it tends to stress how very exalted Jesus is and always was. We saw in chapter 1 how the primitive *kerygma* – the initial proclamation of the church – involved the claim that Jesus was the Messiah, that he had died to save people from their sins, and that God had raised and exalted him. A 'high' christology like John's portrays Jesus as *always* having been exalted and glorified, rather than as becoming exalted only at his resurrection. He was always Lord and full of the Holy Spirit even in his lifetime. So the Gospel describes a series of 'signs', or miracles, which revealed Jesus' glory during his lifetime, and even goes so far as to call his crucifixion his most glorious moment – something quite different from the primitive *kerygma*, in which it is the resurrection that is glorious.

Some readers have detected in John's Gospel a christology which is fundamentally opposed to that of the other writings of the New Testament. On this view, John regards Jesus as completely divine and not really human at all. This Jesus lacks the passion and human intensity of the Synoptics' Jesus. Instead of crying out in anguish on the cross, he calmly comments 'It is finished.' The Gospel teaches a form of 'docetism', the belief – later regarded as heretical – that Jesus only appeared to be human. However, other scholars have argued that the Gospel teaches no such thing. Compared to some docetic texts, such as those of the gnostics, John's Gospel is pretty mild stuff. This Jesus certainly eats, drinks, weeps, and dies.

In fact, 'high' christologies can be found in earlier Christian texts too. In Philippians 2:6–11, for example, Paul describes Christ as pre-existent, a divine figure who chose to become human, as much as John does. Yet not only was Paul writing in the 50s, but in this passage he seems to be quoting an earlier hymn. We find similar ideas about the pre-existence and cosmic significance of Jesus in Colossians 1:15–20, a passage possibly written by Paul or by a later writer strongly influenced by Paul. So this kind of view of Jesus must have existed from quite an early stage in the church's development, and did not first appear when John's Gospel was written, assuming that that Gospel was relatively late. Perhaps different Christians believed different things about Jesus right from the start. And perhaps they did not regard these as conflicting with one another. Paul was capable of quoting with approval both the view of Jesus associated with the primitive *kerygma* and the 'high' view of Jesus encapsulated in the hymn of Philippians 2:6–11. Christians had not yet reached the stage of setting out their views on such matters in a formal way – there was room for creativity and different approaches.

The Church in the Empire

The Roman empire covered an enormous expanse of land by the beginning of the 2nd century AD.

The most important Christian communities of the first couple of generations formed in cities such as Jerusalem, Rome, Antioch, Corinth, and Ephesus. These were the centres for expansion in the generations that followed. From Rome, Christianity spread quickly to the rest of Italy, and by the end of the second century AD it had spread over the whole of Gaul and apparently also parts of Germany and Iberia. A century later it had reached Britain, since there were

London

Colonia Agrippina

Danube

Bordeaux   Lugdunum

Tarraco   Rome   Byzantium

Cordoba   Thessalonica

Athens   Ephesus

Carthage   Antioch   Euphrates

Mediterranean Sea   Tyre   Damascus

Cyrene   Jerusalem

Alexandria

Nile

☐ area of Roman influence, 117 AD

0   600 km
0   400 miles

bishops from both London and York at the council of Arles in AD 314. Most of the strongholds of Christianity, however, were in the eastern, Greek-speaking half of the empire. Here, Antioch was the centre for rapid expansion, and major Christian populations could be found throughout Asia Minor. Cappadocia, the mountainous region in the centre of what is now Turkey, became another major centre of Christianity after the efforts of a missionary named Gregory the Wonder-Worker there in the middle of the third century.

To the south, vibrant Christian communities seem to have sprung up practically overnight in cities such as Carthage, the central hub of African Christianity. 'Africa' was the name given by the Romans not to a continent (no one knew how far south it extended) but to a province roughly corresponding to modern Tunisia and parts of Algeria and Libya. Carthage had been the ancient capital of the early Roman republic's most bitter enemy, the

Christian apologist Tertullian, c. AD160–220.

Carthaginian empire, but now it was the second city of the western empire, after Rome itself. It would produce two of the most famous names of the early church: Tertullian, who in the late second century was one of the first Christians to write in Latin and who pioneered much of what would become standard Latin theological language; and Cyprian, who was bishop there in the mid-third century and who was beheaded for his faith. By the end of the third century there were over a hundred Christian churches in Africa, compared to a hundred in France and Germany combined, nearly sixty in Spain, and five in Britain. Writing to Scapula, the proconsul of Africa, in around AD 212, Tertullian warned him that persecuting Christians was a bad idea, partly because there were so many in the province that killing them would have adverse economic consequences.

Map of the Christian diaspora in AD 200.

How many people were Christians in the Roman empire, and how large were the communities in each city? It is impossible to answer such questions with certainty. However, reasonable estimates are possible. One sociologist, Rodney Stark, has recently suggested a reconstruction based upon the evidence in Acts about church growth in the first generation and upon what is known of the proportion of Christians in later centuries. On this model, only 0.0126 per cent of the population of empire was Christian in AD 100 – a total of 7,530 people, a minute number out of the 60 million or so in the whole empire. A century later this had risen to 0.36 per cent, or 217,795 people. Only in AD 300 did Christians reach double figures as a population percentage – 10.5 per cent, or 6,299,832 people; fifty years later they represented just over half the population. If this model is roughly accurate, it means that Christians were a tiny minority throughout the empire until the third century, and they were still a small minority until the time of Constantine.

Alexandria

One city that would play a major role in the later history of Christianity was Alexandria, in Egypt, the greatest city of the eastern empire. It was built on the coast of the Mediterranean Sea, where it had two harbours and the famous Pharos lighthouse, considered one of the Seven Wonders of the World. To the south was Lake Mareotis, which was connected to the Nile by both natural channels and artificial canals. There was another harbour on this lake which was busier than the other two put together. Moreover, Alexandria controlled the grain exports from the enormously fertile Nile region. Rome alone received around 83,000 tons of grain from Alexandria every year, while in the fourth century AD the new capital of Constantinople would receive almost three times that amount. It has been calculated that, during the four-and-a-half-month period after the harvest when this trade was busiest, thirty-two fully loaded grain ships would have left Alexandria every week.

The magnificence of the city struck visitors with awe. Where the inhabitants of Rome lived in crowded flats on narrow, winding streets, the fortunate Alexandrians strolled along wide, paved streets, lit at night by lamps on tall stands. The main street was the Via Canopica, a thoroughfare over 30 metres wide which passed from the Sun Gate in the east to the Moon Gate in the west – the Champs-Élysées or Fifth Avenue of its day. Even more impressive was the famous temple of Serapis, the Serapeum, which was located in the southwestern corner of the city. The Serapeum was a great complex of buildings, housing libraries and research centres as well as more overtly religious structures. There were shrines to every god one could think of, but at its heart was the shrine of Serapis himself, the patron god of the city. Rufinus, a Christian theologian of the fourth century AD, described it like this:

The whole edifice is built of arches with enormous windows above each arch. The hidden inner chambers are separate from one another and provide for the enactment of various ritual acts and secret observances. Sitting courts and small chapels with images of the gods occupy the edge of the highest level. Lofty houses rise up there in which the priests... live. Behind these buildings, a freestanding portico raised on columns and facing inward runs around the periphery. In the middle stands the temple, built on a large and magnificent scale with an exterior of marble and precious columns. Inside there was a statue of Serapis so vast that the right hand touched one wall and the left the other.[1]

In addition to the libraries of the Serapeum there was the even more famous Great Library, part of the Mouseion (or Museum, that is, a centre of learning dedicated to the Muses), which was housed in a series of buildings throughout the city. Little wonder that Alexandrians were proud of their city to the point of arrogance; they often called it 'Alexandria next to Egypt', a title that defied geography but reflected the cultural divisions of the area. Alexandria was a Hellenistic city, where most people spoke Greek, but it was the one great metropolis in an otherwise rural area where most people spoke Coptic. It was quite possible for a Coptic-speaking villager in northern Egypt never to visit Alexandria at all.

It was here that the Jewish philosopher Philo developed the theory of allegorical interpretation of the Old Testament, and used it to create a religious philosophy that combined Judaism with Middle Platonism. Although a remarkable character, Philo seems to have been typical of the forward-thinking, intellectually engaged nature

Alexandria continued

of Judaism in Alexandria: it was here that, in the second century BC, a team of Jewish scholars made the Septuagint translation of the Old Testament into Greek. The same character seems to have marked Christianity when it arrived in the city. We do not know when this was, although given the cosmopolitan nature of this great sea port it seems intrinsically likely that it was at an early stage; tradition states that the apostle Mark brought the religion there. But we first hear of a Christian community there in the second century AD, and as we might expect from this setting, it seems to have been a philosophically inclined one right from the start. The first Alexandrian Christian of note was Basilides, a theologian closely associated with gnosticism, who lived there in the first half of the second century. Valentinus, one of the most influential gnostic theologians, came from the nearby countryside and spent many years in Alexandria. More mainstream Christianity, of an anti-gnostic character, emerged later on with the Christian scholar Pantaenus, who founded the Christian school in Alexandria in around AD 180. This school would presumably have been rather like the philosophical schools of the time: that is, not a public centre of education, but a group of friends and interested parties who met privately under the direction of a more experienced philosopher.

An illustration of a reconstruction of the Pharos lighthouse, one of the Seven Wonders of the World.

Christianity in the east

Christianity did not simply spread west from its early heartlands of Antioch and Asia Minor. It also spread east, beyond the Roman empire, to Edessa and Persia. However, we know much less about early Christianity in these areas than in the Roman empire. The sources are less numerous, and it seems that the Christians themselves were far less numerous than in the West. Not until the fourth century AD do we begin to encounter important literary remains from the Persian Christians themselves.

Edessa

Edessa – the modern town of Urfa – was located in a fairly fertile region near the River Euphrates. The Seleucid kings, the dynasty which inherited this region after the empire of Alexander the Great broke up in the fourth century BC, had founded it as a centre of Greek culture in the Middle East, and built walls and a fortress to defend it. The Parthians later conquered the city, but by the first century AD it had become self-governing and effectively independent. A series of kings, most of whom were called Abgar, ruled the city and the surrounding area, known as Osrhoene. This small country was increasingly friendly with Rome – which was keen to build allies in the region – and by the end of the second century AD, it was virtually a client state of Rome. In the early third century the monarchy was abolished and Osrhoene became a Roman province. During this period, Edessa was becoming increasingly important as a stopping point on the trade route to Persia and, ultimately, India and China.

At some point in all of this, Christianity came to Edessa, but we do not know how. It is highly likely that the merchants helped to spread it, but since we are uncertain when the trade routes began operating through Edessa, we cannot know how important a role they played in the early days. According to one document from around AD 400, known as the *Doctrine of Addai*, Christianity actually reached Osrhoene during Jesus' lifetime. The story goes that King Abgar V heard about Jesus and wrote to him, asking him to come to Edessa and heal him. Jesus wrote a reply, stating that he was unable to come, but he sent his disciple Addai to Edessa to preach to the king. This legend seems to have become widespread by the end of the fourth century AD; it formed part of Edessa's image as 'the blessed city', the first city to accept the Christian faith.

In fact we know nothing of when Christianity really came to Edessa, although it was certainly there by the end of the second century AD, when Abgar VIII 'the Great' ruled the city. In AD 201 there was a severe flood in Edessa, which, we are told, destroyed the Christian church as well as many other buildings. That makes this the earliest known Christian church building, although we know virtually nothing about what it was like except that it had a nave, which suffered the most damage.

It has sometimes been thought that Abgar VIII made Christianity the official religion of the kingdom – making Osrhoene the first officially Christian state – but it is uncertain if this ever actually happened. Nevertheless, it does seem clear that Christianity was at least tolerated during this period. One of the most prominent figures at the court of Abgar VIII was Bardaisan of Edessa, who was well known for his extravagant robes and jewellery, and was an expert in courtly pursuits such as archery. But he was also a Christian who wrote works of religious philosophy and hymns that remained popular for centuries. Bardaisan was a keen scholar, who knew Greek and sent his son to study in Athens (although he never travelled west of the Euphrates himself), and who was interested in Syriac and Indian philosophy of religion as well as astrology.

There were different factions of Christians in Edessa. Ephrem the Syrian, writing in the fourth century AD, attests to the numbers and varieties of those he regarded as heretics there – Arians, gnostics, Manichaeans, and more. One late second-century figure who led what would become the orthodox faction was called Palut, and so they were dubbed 'Palutians' by the other groups. Not until the fourth century do the Palutians seem to have become the majority

Dating from c. 50 BC and standing in a national park between Malatya and Urfa (previously known as Edessa), are the colossal heads at the Hierothesion of Antiochus I. The head of an eagle and that of a bearded man, toppled from gigantic stone statues, lie on the snow capped summit of Nemrut Dagi (Mount Nimrod), the site of a tumulus built for Antiochos I (69–34 BC), the first Commagene king. Several such statues of kings and gods once stood at this site in modern-day Turkey.

The Persian church

To the east lay Rome's great rival, the Parthian empire. The Parthians controlled what is now Iran and Iraq, with their capital at Seleucia-Ctesiphon on the Tigris, near ancient Babylon and modern Baghdad. In 20 BC Caesar Augustus agreed a peace with this powerful empire, setting the boundary between the two at the River Euphrates. But for centuries there were intermittent skirmishes and wars between them, broken by periods of uneasy peace. Although 'Persia' refers to just one province within the Parthian empire, the name is often used, rather inaccurately, as shorthand for the empire controlled by the Parthians and their later successors, and the 'Persian church' means the churches throughout this area.

According to the fourth-century Christian historian Eusebius of Caesarea, the apostle Thomas was the first person to bring Christianity to Persia. Although this is not intrinsically unlikely, historians are generally dubious about this claim, partly because there is no earlier evidence for it, and partly because other traditions claim that Thomas actually went to India – which is also possible, although there is no evidence for the existence of a Christian community there before the fourth century. Other legends tell of Mar Mari, whom Addai sent from Edessa into the Parthian empire; he travelled through Iraq, founding churches as he went.

It seems likely that in Persia as in Edessa, merchants played an important role in spreading Christianity. Moreover, it was probably closely associated with the Jewish Diaspora there. During this period, Jewish merchants controlled the silk trade with China; many of these merchants operated out of Edessa, across Persia, and on into Asia. Christianity would have been spread by these merchants from Edessa and taken root along the trade route. The central importance of Edessa for Persian Christianity is clear from the fact that the Persian Christians spoke Syriac, the form of Aramaic spoken in Edessa. And throughout the Syriac-speaking church, there seems to have been in general a much greater Jewish influence than there was in the Greek- and Latin-speaking churches. In Armenia, for example, Christians of the fourth century offered animal sacrifices at Easter. Many elements of Christian exegesis of the Old Testament during this period derived from older Jewish exegesis.

Little is known about the structure of the Persian church at this stage. It seems to have developed along the same lines as the Roman church, but more slowly. The first bishop from this church that we know of was Papa, bishop of Seleucia-Ctesiphon in the late third century AD. There seem to have been only about twenty Persian bishops at this time, indicating that the church there was much smaller than the Roman church at the same time.

Marble statue of Sanatrukes I, a Parthian king who ruled AD 167–190. It was discovered in Hatra, Temple X, Baghdad, Iraq.

Living as a Christian

Christianity dominated the lives of its adherents. Like everyone else, rich or poor, Christians got up at dawn and had a quick meal. They would wash their hands and pray. Christians who were shopkeepers or craftsmen would then get straight to work, since such people lived in their commercial premises. Those who were manual labourers would leave their homes and head out to work, or to find employment. On the way, however, they might manage to stop off at the house of the Christian instructor – someone like Pantaenus in Alexandria or Justin in Rome – and listen to a few words of Christian wisdom.

In the Roman empire, everyone – slave or free – worked hard all morning and stopped at noon for lunch. Again, the Christians were no different, although many would stop work briefly in the middle of the morning to pray, and they would pray again at lunchtime. In the afternoon, hardly anyone worked; it was customary to go to the public bath, and Christians might do this. Alternatively, they might stay at home and read, perhaps from the Bible or from some other Christian text. There would be more prayers before dinner and at bedtime, which was at dusk. Some Christians would also get up at midnight to pray again before going back to bed.

Regular prayer seems to have been a standard feature of the Christian lifestyle, although we cannot assume that all Christians followed precisely the same format. Some Christians seem to have prayed three times a day (as in Daniel 6:10), while others prayed seven times a day (as in Psalm 119:164). For some, prayer would have been a solitary business, perhaps following the guidelines that Tertullian offered in his book *On Prayer*: done kneeling down, and in silence. For others, prayer would have been a family affair; husbands and wives might pray together, or the *paterfamilias*, the head of the family, might pray on behalf of the whole household. Some Christians from different households would meet to pray together. When Pliny tortured Christian captives to force them to tell him what they got up to, he learned that they would meet each morning to sing a hymn to Christ, and again each evening to share a meal. It seems likely that this pattern of daily meetings was quite common, although some groups might have met less frequently, perhaps only once a week.

Pliny the Younger (AD 61–113). In a letter dated c. AD 111, he alludes to the spread of Christianity through the Roman empire.

Life and death

One of the most distinctive things about Christians was their opposition to killing. Violence was quite normalized in the Roman empire, where it was usual to watch people being tortured to death for entertainment, and where the empire was sustained by virtually incessant warfare and pillage. But the Christians rejected all of this. For example, they had at best an ambivalent attitude towards the military as a career option. Some Christians believed that it was

Christians and class

As we saw in chapter 2, the first-century church seems to have recruited mostly those from the lower classes of society: slaves, manual workers, and the morally suspect. This seems to have been at least the stereotype of Christians over the next couple of centuries too. In the middle of the second century AD, the anti-Christian writer Celsus attacked the Christians for the kind of people who joined them: the lower classes, idiots and illiterates, and criminals. But other sources suggest that Celsus was exaggerating. Certainly not all Christians were idiots or illiterates, as the existence of Christian philosophers from Bardaisan to Origen demonstrates. In the same period, Pliny reported that there were Christians of all social classes in Bithynia.

At the end of the second century, Tertullian tells us that there were Christians everywhere, even in the imperial palace. Perhaps some of these Christians were slaves or former slaves working there. The imperial civil service operated training schools throughout the empire where slaves could study and enter the service, with the plan of being freed and eventually retiring with their fortunes made. The sons and daughters of such people were born free and inherited their parents' hard-earned wealth; and *their* sons and daughters would generally have escaped the stigma of slavery and be wealthy, educated Roman citizens like anyone else in the upper echelons of society. It is easy to imagine a Christian slave working his way up in the civil service, resulting in a well-heeled, established

Christian family some decades down the line. There certainly were Christians in the civil service from an early stage: Clement of Rome, traditionally thought to have written *1 Clement*, was one, who not only worked in Rome itself but had a house in a prestigious location near the Forum.

In fact, by the end of the second century we find some positively aristocratic Christians. One of the most celebrated martyrs of this period – Vibia Perpetua – was the daughter of a Roman patrician from Carthage; she died together with her slave, Felicity, also a Christian. But Perpetua was a convert to Christianity, and did not inherit it from her family – her father tried to convince her to renounce her faith while she was in prison. In the mid-third century, Cyprian of Carthage testifies to specific penalties in the law for senators and knights who are found to be Christians. It seems that Christianity managed to widen its appeal as time went on, so that by the time of Cyprian it was plausible at least to expect to find Christians among the highest classes of society and even in the Senate. Even so, it seems never to have found much support there. Between AD 180 and 312, we hear of a total of ten people of senatorial rank or their families being Christians, out of what must have been several thousand people of that class over that period. It seems that although the religion largely shook off its associations with those considered the lowest in society, it was still not a religion of the elite.

acceptable for a Christian to be a soldier, provided he did not carry out executions, or act as a commanding officer, since such a role would involve giving orders to kill. Tertullian's book *On the Crown* describes an incident when a Christian soldier refused to wear the triumphant crown that was given to the troops, and ended up getting martyred. This man evidently did not see being a soldier as incompatible with being a Christian, but felt that some military practices were too pagan for him to perform.

But other Christians, such as Tertullian, believed that being in the army *at all* was fundamentally incompatible with Christianity. Soldiers who converted to Christianity should be careful never to do anything which contradicted their faith; better either to leave altogether or be martyred. And a Christian should never *join* the army. Tertullian wrote:

> Do we believe it lawful for a human oath to be added to a divine one, for a man to make a promise to another master after Christ...? Will it be held lawful to make a living by the sword, when the Lord proclaims that he who uses the sword will perish by the sword? And will the son of peace take part in the battle when it is not right for him even to sue somebody? And will he use the chain, and the prison, and the torture, and the punishment, when he is not even to avenge wrongs done against himself? Will he, indeed, either go on guard duty for others more than for Christ, or will he do it on the Lord's day, when he does not even do it for Christ himself? And will he keep guard before the temples which he has renounced? And will he take a meal where the apostle has forbidden him? And will he diligently protect by night those whom in the day-time he has put to flight by his exorcisms, all the time leaning and resting on the spear with which Christ's side was pierced? Will he carry a flag, too, hostile to Christ?[1]

These were practical issues of great importance to those who found their loyalties compromised. A document entitled *The Acts of Maximilian* describes the trial and death of a young man who was presented by his father to the proconsul, Dion, to join the army. But he refused to do so or to accept the military seal because, he insisted, he could serve only God:

> Dion said to Maximilian: 'Agree to serve and receive the military seal.'
>
> 'I will not accept the seal,' he replied. 'I already have the seal of Christ who is my God.'
>
> Dion said: 'I shall send you to your Christ directly.'
>
> 'I only wish you would,' he replied. 'This would be my glory.'
>
> Dion addressed his staff: 'Let him be given the seal.'
>
> Maximilian resisted and said: 'I will not accept the seal of this world; and, if you give it to me, I shall break it, for it is worthless. I am a Christian. I cannot wear a piece of lead around my neck after I have received the saving sign of Jesus Christ my Lord, the son of the living God. You do not know him; yet he suffered for our salvation; God delivered him up for our sins. He is the one whom all we Christians serve: we follow him as the prince of life and the author of salvation.[2]

Dion points out that there are Christians not only in the army but in the bodyguards of the emperors Diocletian and Maximian – a remarkable claim, given that these emperors persecuted the Christians. Maximilian replies that they must do what is best for them, but he cannot do the same.

The Christians' attitude towards life and death is also shown in their rejection of 'exposition', a traditional practice in which the parents of an unwanted baby would abandon it on a hillside, to be picked up and adopted by someone else or to die as fate decreed. This was done especially frequently with baby girls, since most people wanted sons, not daughters. In fact exposition of baby girls was so common that in the population at large there were many

In this 1446 fresco from the St Sebastian Chapel, Lanslevillard, France, the emperor Diocletian is shown with Sebastian, who, according to legend, entered the military and helped Christians who were suffering persecution.

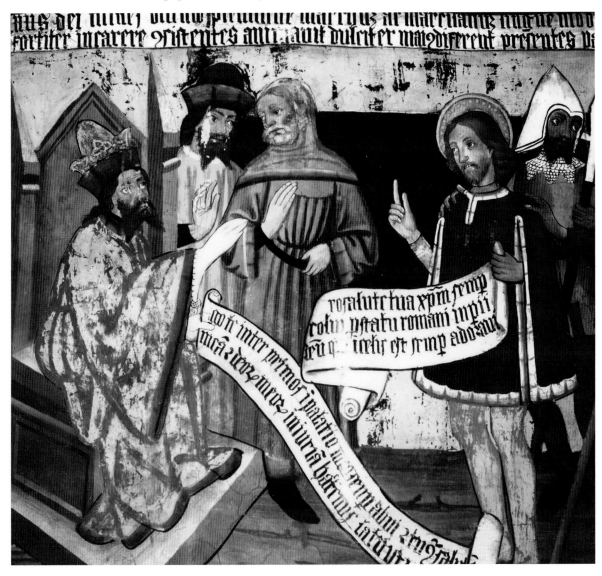

more men than women. It has been estimated that in ancient Rome there were roughly four men to every three women.

The Christians were equally uniformly opposed to abortion. The methods used to induce abortion in antiquity were crude and dangerous. Often, women would take small doses of poison, hoping to kill the foetus, but often killing themselves in the process. In other cases, the husband would attempt to induce a miscarriage by kicking his wife. If a doctor was involved, he might try to cut the foetus out by inserting blades and other contraptions into the mother. Many women died in the attempt – an attempt which had probably been ordered by their husbands, and over which they might have little or no say. The Christian condemnation of abortion thus seems to have been motivated by a concern for the safety of women just as much as for that of unborn children, although they will have believed both were important.

Women in the church

Most of the famous names of the early church were male names. Men appear in church histories as missionaries, bishops, priests, theologians, miracle-workers, and writers; women usually seem to be mentioned only when they are being martyred. Of all the Christian texts that have survived from this period, only one is known to have been written by a woman: Perpetua's journal account of her time in prison awaiting execution as a Christian – and that survives only because some man chose to incorporate it into his description of her death. This reflects the virtual invisibility of women in the ancient world in general. They generally did not receive any formal education and did not, as a rule, have careers (although there were exceptions, such as Lydia, the cloth-dealer of Acts 16:14). Their place in society was determined by their relationship to a man – their father, their husband, or their son. The only real exceptions were widows who had not remarried and had no sons, and in normal society at least, they were anomalies, expected to remarry if at all possible. We see this reflected in the roles of some of the most famous female Christians from antiquity, such as Monica, the mother of Augustine; Helena, the mother of Constantine; Macrina, the sister of Gregory of Nyssa; or the women with whom Jerome set up a monastery in Bethlehem. They all seem to play supporting roles to men.

And yet women also seem to have been more prominent in the church than they were in society at large, something that was partly caused by the Christians' attitude towards life and death. Because they were not forcing their wives to risk their lives by having abortions, or leaving their baby daughters to die, the Christian communities had a much larger proportion of female members than Roman society at large did. And pagan critics of Christianity, such as Celsus, noted the religion's special appeal to women. The

Christian women whom Pliny the Younger interrogated were titled 'deaconesses' in the church. So what sort of roles did women actually play in the church?

One of the most significant roles seems to have involved mission. Celsus sneered at the way in which Christian missionaries targeted 'gullible' women and children while the husbands were out at work. Later, Libanius of Antioch branded Christian women as a dangerous element of society, seducing their husbands away from proper respect for the pagan gods. It is worth remembering that until the fourth century, Christian activities, including prayer meetings, baptisms, and the celebration of the Eucharist, mostly took place in people's homes. It is easy to imagine a female Christian in a large household inviting other Christians to the house for some of these activities, something which might result in other members of the household becoming interested in the religion. She might also attract the interest of friends from outside the household. This would have made the proportion of women in the church even greater, since women would tend to socialize with – and therefore be more likely to convert – other women. As we have seen, conversion was normally a matter of friends joining their friends' religion. It is quite likely that a significant proportion of male Christians joined the religion primarily because their wives did, these wives having become enthusiastic about it through conversations with female friends who were already Christians. That would mean not only that there were more women – perhaps even outnumbering the men – but that the women would tend to be the most enthusiastic Christians.

The prominence of women within the church certainly did not mean that all Christian men were enlightened pro-feminists. Later, when Christianity became more established, we find male theologians denouncing women as spreaders of heresy, just as pagans had once denounced them as spreaders of Christianity itself. However, women do seem to have had, in general, higher social standing in the church than they did in wider society. For example, in Roman society, women were usually expected to remain faithful to their husbands, even while it was considered acceptable for their husbands to stray. But most Christians rejected these double standards and insisted upon fidelity from both sexes, meaning a greater equality between men and women. Moreover, Christian women seem, typically, to have had greater choice over their marriages in the first place. It was usual in antiquity for women to marry extremely young. Twelve was the official minimum age for a girl to marry, but there seem to have been no penalties for marrying someone even younger. Almost half of Roman girls could be expected to be married by the age of fifteen, invariably to a much older man. Christian women, however, typically married later. Only about one in five Christian girls was married by the age of fifteen, and almost half of them were over eighteen when they were married. All of this suggests that, in general, Christians regarded marriage as more of a partnership than was usual in society at the time. Moreover, Christian couples often practised sexual abstinence. This, once again, must have meant a better life for some of those Christian girls who did marry very young, in contrast to their pagan counterparts, who would often be having their first child at the age of thirteen. In short, young Christian girls were considerably less likely than their pagan peers to become what were effectively child concubines.

Women also enjoyed better social conditions at the end of their married lives. Pagan widows were generally expected to remarry as soon as possible, at which point anything they owned would become the property of their new husband. But Christian widows faced no such pressure; if anything, remarriage was discouraged. The church provided funds to support those who could not support themselves.

One other major role of women in the church during this period was as prophets. There was still a 'charismatic' sort of church leadership, based upon personal qualities and direct divine inspiration rather than formal hierarchy, and women were just as capable of exercising it as men were. We saw in chapter 2 that there is evidence of the existence of female Christian prophets in the first century, and they seem to have continued to exist for some time after. Perhaps Pliny's 'deaconesses' were spiritual leaders of this kind. The martyr Perpetua wrote of her visions while awaiting execution, and hints that she was already known in the church for such visions even before being arrested. The most famous female prophets of the period were Maximilla and Priscilla, the leaders of the Montanist movement, and there seem to have been other female Montanist prophets after them too. We shall see more of Montanism in chapter 7, but for now we can note that many of their orthodox critics condemned the fact that they had female leaders.

But some groups seem to have had women not only as prophets but as normal church leaders, especially in the east. A text known as the *Didascalia*, written in Syria in the early third century, recommends that both male and female deacons be appointed, to avoid potential scandals caused by men ministering to women.

Sexual morality and asceticism

Most Christian writers of the second and third centuries AD did not have a huge amount to say about sexual matters, and what they did say tended to reflect the views of pagan moralists of the time. The status of women in the ancient world meant that sex outside marriage was not a very large concern, since everyone was married. The only alternative to marital sex was adultery, which

Christians condemned just as Jews did. So when they discussed sexual matters, Christians of this period usually assumed that they were talking about sex between husbands and wives and did not generally offer different guidelines for different situations. One striking exception to this rule came in the prescription of Callistus, bishop of Rome in the early third century. It seems there was a problem of upper-class Christian women being unwilling to reduce their rank by marrying lower-class Christian men or compromise their faith by marrying pagan men of their own class. But at the same time they did not want to lead lives of chastity. No doubt this was a consequence of the fact that there were simply more Christian women than there were men. Callistus ruled that these women were allowed to sleep with whoever they liked, and they could be considered 'married' to their lovers in practice if not in law, thereby keeping their official social status intact. Callistus was known for his fairly liberal views on moral questions; he issued another ruling that Christians who had sinned and been expelled from the church could be allowed back in after a period of penance. His contemporaries Hippolytus and Tertullian bitterly attacked this ruling, in the first round of what would become a very long-running dispute within the church over how strictly its moral code should be enforced.

As a rule, the Christians had a fairly negative attitude towards sex. They generally regarded it as necessary, but to be done for the sake of having children rather than for any other reason. This went for sex in general, including that between husbands and wives. Many Christians seem to have practised complete abstinence; we hear of husbands and wives converting to Christianity and continuing to live together chastely. There seem to have been two main motivations for this sort of behaviour, although they were not clearly distinguished. The first was a belief that sex was, in itself, something to be avoided – not something bad, but at best a necessary evil. The *Acts of Thomas*, which was written in Syria in the early third century AD, describes the apostle Thomas as interrupting a newly married couple on their wedding night, and saying to them:

> *Know this, that if you abandon this filthy intercourse you become holy temples, pure and free from afflictions and pains both manifest and hidden, and you will not be girt about with cares for life and for children, the end of which is destruction. But if you get many children, then for their sakes you become robbers and avaricious, people who flay orphans and defraud widows, and by so doing you subject yourselves to the most grievous punishments. For the majority of children become unprofitable.*[3]

Rather improbably, according to the *Acts of Thomas*, the couple are convinced by the apostle's words. In the morning, the bride tells her parents:

I have set at naught this man, and this marriage which passes away from before my eyes, is because I am bound in another marriage. And that I have had no intercourse with a short-lived husband, the end of which is remorse and bitterness of soul, is because I am yoked with the true man.[4]

96

This is the second reason why sex was to be avoided. Christians were supposed to be focused not on the material world around them but on the spiritual world. Their primary allegiance was not to any family member or other human being, but to Christ alone. Abstinence from sex was a way of both showing this allegiance and strengthening it, and it formed part of a more generally ascetic lifestyle that many Christians followed. They might avoid eating meat and drinking alcohol, wear only simple clothes, and deprive themselves of sleep. We hear of the famous third-century Alexandrian theologian Origen, for example, sleeping on the floor. Many thought it a good idea to minimize contact of any kind between the sexes. Some Christian groups – known as the 'encratites' or 'abstainers' – took this further and dedicated themselves to complete abstinence. They rejected marriage altogether and lived extremely ascetic lifestyles. Such a lifestyle seems to have been especially common to the east, in the Syriac-speaking churches. It is possible that here, at least in some churches, a vow of celibacy was mandatory for all Christians. Some of these ascetic groups seem to have developed particular justifications for their behaviour. For some, eating and sex alike were closely associated with the sin of Adam and Eve in Genesis 3; they sinned when they ate the forbidden fruit, and upon being cast out of Eden, they slept together and had children. The encratites therefore avoided both eating and sex as far as they could. And some, at least, seem to have been associated with gnosticism. The gnostics believed that the physical world was fundamentally evil; it was therefore wise to live a life as free from matter as was humanly possible and force the body to submit to the soul. Other encratites were associated with Montanism, whose prophecies seem to have been concerned mostly with moral injunctions; they not only tried to live ascetic lifestyles but expelled those who failed to live up to their exacting standards.

Given their generally rather negative attitude towards sex, it is surprising to find that the Christians had more children than pagans usually did. Overall, and ignoring the influence of immigrants, the population of the Roman empire in the first couple of centuries AD decreased: people had too few children to keep the population level, despite various pieces of government legislation intended to encourage them to have more. The Christians, however, seem not to have suffered such a problem. The reasons for this are

A Christian moralist

One of the most interesting testimonies to the way some Christians tried to live is a book entitled *The Instructor*, written in the late second century by Clement of Alexandria. Clement – whom we shall meet more fully in chapter 6 – was probably born in Athens and worked in Alexandria, and he was one of the leading theologians of the day. In this book, he presents Jesus as 'the Instructor', who teaches Christians directly. The word translated as 'instructor' – *paedagogos* – meant a slave who lived with the family. His role was to teach, protect, and look after a child – a combination of nanny, personal tutor, and servant. In Philippians 2:7, Paul had stated that Christ took on the form of a slave; why not, then, portray him as the universal *paedagogos*, who looks after, trains, protects, and teaches his people?

Most of the book consists of advice about how Christians are to behave in everyday life. We are told, for example, that Christians should eat a moderate and healthy diet and avoid too much luxurious sauce; they can make jokes and laugh at genuine wit, but not get carried away and fool around (and 'filthy speaking' is entirely unacceptable). Women should have only a couple of pairs of shoes – tough shoes for travelling, and a plain white pair the rest of the time – while men ought to go barefoot or in slippers except when in the army. Men shouldn't shave and certainly shouldn't wear jewellery. The public bath should be indulged in only infrequently, and one should never get other

Icon depicting Clement of Alexandria
(c. AD 150–215).

people to pour water over one, because in the bath everyone is equal. Clement even offers advice for the bedroom: the bed should be comfortable but not too soft, since that is unhealthy, and Christians are called to be wakeful and alert. Sex should be confined to married couples and should be engaged in only in the evening, never in the morning.

Clement bolsters his advice with passages from the Bible as well as arguments drawn from natural science (for example, too-soft mattresses hinder digestion), but his version of the correct lifestyle really seems to owe more to upper-class Roman ideals than to anything distinctly Christian. Indeed, some passages – including those on sexual matters – are lifted straight from Roman moralists such as the first-century Stoic Musonius Rufus. Moderation in all things is Clement's guiding principle, a principle which had been taught by pagan philosophers for centuries. Indeed, Clement praises the virtue of 'passionlessness', a sort of calm serenity where a person never becomes flustered or too emotional. This ideal was central to Stoicism, and Clement suggests that it is an essential prerequisite to the spiritual life. Only someone who has become passionless stands a chance of becoming closer to God – and, conversely, the closer we become to God, the more passionless we become. This idea would have a long future in Christian ethics and spirituality.

not entirely clear, although the fact that there were proportionally more women in the church than in society as a whole must have played a major role.

Liturgy

In the second and third centuries, becoming a Christian was a much more protracted and serious affair than it had been in New Testament times, when the apostles were apparently happy to baptize people they had only just met. By at least the middle of the second century AD, converts to Christianity were expected to meet certain standards of behaviour and belief before they could be baptized. By the end of the century, there was a formal period of instruction, the 'catechumenate' (from the Greek for 'oral teaching') before baptism. A document known as the *Apostolic Tradition*, probably written in around AD 215 and usually ascribed to Hippolytus of Rome, testifies to the practices in that city at that time. According to this document, even becoming a catechumen was a difficult business: candidates would be grilled, and their friends and employers interviewed, to ensure that they were of good standing and worthy to be baptized. Many professions were excluded, such as actors, athletes, governors, magicians, prostitutes – anyone the Christians considered to be immoral or enmeshed in pagan practices. Artists were acceptable provided they swore never to paint idols, and soldiers were acceptable provided they swore never to execute anyone or swear a military oath. Once accepted, the catechumenate lasted for three years. During that time, the catechumens would remain in a separate area within the church. When the time for baptism drew near, the lifestyles of the catechumens would be checked, to ensure that they were living properly; the bishop would lay hands on them daily to exorcise them. A final exorcism would be performed on the day before the baptism, after a period of fasting, and they would then spend all night in vigil. The ceremony itself took place at dawn, at a flowing spring. The catechumens would remove their clothes – men, women, and children together – and the women would let their hair down. The bishop would then anoint them with 'oil of exorcism' as they swore to renounce Satan. Then they would enter the water itself, where a deacon would wash them three times – once in the name of the Father, once in the name of the Son, and once in the name of the Holy Spirit. Finally, they would be anointed with 'oil of thanksgiving', and dress themselves again before returning to the church.

Hippolytus mentions that children would be baptized before adults, and this is one of the earliest witnesses to the practice of baptizing children. Origen tells us that this practice went back to the apostles. Cyprian defended it, arguing that the grace of God should not be restricted from anyone, least of all newborn babies, who have never sinned, and who need all the help they can get. But others regarded it as a dangerous innovation. Tertullian thought it wrong, largely on the grounds that it exposed the baptized children to a greater risk of condemnation. Because post-baptismal sin was such a serious matter, Tertullian advised that baptism should be delayed whenever possible; and single people should wait until they are married, because then there is less danger of sin. Furthermore, if a child is baptized, his sponsors risk damnation when they make promises on his behalf. Tertullian pointed out that the unbaptized would still be saved if their faith were sound, so people should not rush to be baptized out of a fear of damnation – baptism was a serious commitment that should be undertaken seriously.

We have little information on other Christian liturgies and communal practices in the second and third centuries, but they seem to have been much the same as in the first. Hippolytus' description of baptism indicates that they could be quite elaborate, similar in form – in some respects – to pagan mystery-cult practices of the time. There were differences, though. For one thing, the Christians seem not have used incense in their ceremonies. Tertullian wrote of it as something used in pagan ceremonies, but admitted that he was willing to burn it himself to get rid of a bad smell; the notion of incorporating this pagan religious element into Christian ceremonies seems not to have occurred to him.

Christians would hold their meetings and ceremonies in their own homes. This would not have been a matter of simply going to one another's houses and praying in the living room; rooms would have been set aside specially for the purpose, probably in the home of whoever in the group had the largest house. This practice parallels that of the mystery religions, where adherents would also set aside chapels within their homes for use by everyone in the group – although a key difference is that the Christians seem to have met much more frequently than members of most mystery religions or other pagan cults did. If the Christian group became really big, they would convert an entire house for religious use. The earliest known Christian church, in Dura-Europos on the Roman–Persian border, was of this type. The house was converted to Christian use in AD 232 and follows the normal Roman plan of a large family home, a square with a courtyard in the middle. Most of one side of this square has been converted into a large meeting hall, and other rooms in the complex serve as vestibules. One is a baptistery, where initiates were baptized into the religion.

The congregation of such a church could not have been very large. Each church would have been largely autonomous, but they maintained links with one another of varying closeness. A Christian travelling away from home could meet up with Christians wherever he or she was, and find not only a warm welcome but material help if required. This was also a difference from pagan cults. For example, there were worshippers of Dionysus all over the Roman empire, but different groups had very little to do with one another. The second-century AD satire *The Golden Ass* by Apuleius describes the main character joining the cult of Isis, but when he travels to different places, he has to be reinitiated each time. This would never have happened among Christians, for whom baptism was a once-for-all affair. In fact, the Christian church – considered as an empire-spanning entity – was an organization like no other in antiquity. This was increasingly the case as its organizational structure became

Depicting scenes from the Old Testament, these frescos decorate the walls of a synagogue (built c. 200 BC) in Dura-Europos, Damascus.

more clearly defined, and the 'monarchical episcopate' system – with a single bishop in charge of the community, assisted by a number of presbyters or priests – was becoming standard.

The church at Rome seems to have developed the monarchical system a little later than some other churches, which means that although tradition lists the names of 'bishops of Rome' going right back to Peter himself, we cannot be certain at which stage these people really began to exercise episcopal authority over the whole Christian community there. They were certainly doing so – or attempting to – by the end of the second century AD. The first known ruling by a Roman bishop took place in AD 190, when Victor of Rome decreed that all Christians in that city, including the immigrants from Asia Minor, should follow the Roman dating of Easter and not the Asian one. The decree seems to have been extremely controversial, and Victor had to excommunicate those who disagreed, even Polycrates, bishop of Ephesus. This ruling was therefore intended to apply not only to the Christians in Rome but to those beyond as well. This was the first time that the bishop of Rome had acted in a way that implied that he had authority over other churches.

Orpheus was venerated by some adherents to the Dionysian mysteries. He is seen here with Eurydice in Peter Vischer the Younger's bronze relief, c. 1516.

The mystery religions

How distinctive was the religion of the Christians, as described above? Was this a quite distinctive religion, with original ideas and practices? Or was much of it copied from other cults of the time? Many people have claimed that Christianity had very few distinctive elements. On this view, Christians took many of their beliefs and practices from various contemporary cults, above all the mystery religions.

These cults were usually not distinct religions, but revolved around elements of the standard public Roman religion: for example, they might involve the special worship of one of the Roman gods. Members of these cults might thus regard themselves as going beyond everyday piety; their cults were advanced forms of Roman religion rather than rivals to it. To become a member of one of these cults, you generally had to go through an initiation process. The uninitiated were not allowed at their rituals, which often took place at night. Typically, the rituals involved the re-enactment, to some degree, of the central myths of the cult. It was believed that by doing this, the eternal truths embodied in the myths could be manifested in the lives of the individual members. These myths often revolved around life, death, and fertility, as represented in the colourful activities of the gods. For example, some versions of the Dionysian mysteries involved the veneration of Orpheus, the legendary lyre-player and lover of Eurydice. These Orphic mysteries had a myth according to which the Titans ripped Dionysus to pieces and ate him. In his fury, Zeus not only remade Dionysus but destroyed the Titans with a lightning bolt. From the ashes, human beings were created. The Orphic mysteries thus had a myth of sin, death, and rebirth which was linked to their devotees' hope for a life after death, a hope which seems to have been important to all forms of the Dionysian mysteries.

In the nineteenth century, a school of thought arose in Germany which has since been given the rather uninformative name of the 'history of religions' school. The historians and theologians associated with it believed that the study of any particular religion should focus upon its cultural context and its relations to other religions of that time. They argued that one should examine, in particular, the ways in which a given religion takes ideas from its predecessors. In this light they examined Christianity in the context of imperial Roman religion and concluded that pretty much everything in Christianity came from pagan religions such as the mystery cults. Like those cults, Christianity had a myth which involved life, death, and resurrection. Like them, its members re-enacted key elements of that myth in their meetings, with food and drink playing an important role. Like them, its rituals were open only to members, and one became a member through a long period of initiation involving more secret ceremonies. So Christianity was itself simply another mystery religion, one that by a sort of accident of history survived and prospered while the others died out.

Since then, however, scholarship has changed. The 'history of religions' scholars were, perhaps, overreacting somewhat to the tradition of scholarship which preceded them, which was overtly Christian and either ignored the pagan context of the early church or acknowledged it only as something fundamentally different from the true faith which would displace it. The scholars of the nineteenth century were the first to deal with Christianity and pagan religions on the same terms and as different examples of the same sort of phenomenon, and, as in the case of many rebels, their enthusiasm for a new way of looking at things may have clouded their judgment in some matters. Today, scholars are more aware of how fragmentary our knowledge of the mystery religions is. There is certainly no reason to believe, for example, that they all featured myths of gods dying and being resurrected, let alone that these myths were the source for Christian beliefs about Jesus. Even the Egyptian myth of Isis and Osiris, where Osiris dies but is somehow reborn in his son Horus, is not definite enough to form the basis of such a claim.

Moreover, it is true that any given religion must be understood in its context, and that ideas or practices from one religion may percolate into another – but one should still not ignore what makes different religions unique. For example, Christianity may have possessed a myth similar in some respects to those of the mystery religions, but in other respects it was very different. It was the only one whose spiritual narrative revolved around an identifiable individual from recent history, and the only one to have books that preserved historical information about him. The rites of baptism and the Eucharist are similar in some ways to the rites of the mystery religions, but they developed out of the rather different context of Jewish ritual washings and meals and the particular actions of Jesus himself.

One sometimes encounters (especially on the internet) lists of Christian doctrines or practices, with parallel doctrines or practices from the mystery religions and other contemporary cults, the implication being that the former were just copies of the latter. In light of what we have seen, it should be clear that such an approach can prove little, given how little we really know about these other religions. But more fundamentally, such an approach misunderstands the nature of these religions. In them, as in all religions, doctrine, spiritual experience, and practice formed a closely woven fabric which cannot be unpicked without doing

A relief from the 2nd century AD shows a mystic banquet of the Mithraic faithful.

Mithraism

One of the most dramatic examples of how commentators can get somewhat carried away when comparing Christianity to other religions of the time is the case of another mystery religion, Mithraism. In many popular books, television shows, and (above all) internet sites one can find a series of startling claims about Mithraism and its close parallels to Christianity. Mithraist priests, we are told, called themselves 'bishops' and wore mitres, and had rings that believers would kiss; the head priest was called 'pope'. They believed that Mithras – the central deity of the religion – was killed and rose again, and that he saved believers from their sins. The implication is that the Christians simply borrowed all these ideas and others for their own religion, which is little more than Mithraism under a new name, and that the Jesus worshipped by Christians is just a reworking of old myths about Mithras.

However, there is no evidence for most of these claims. There is no evidence that Mithraists believed that Mithras was killed at all, let alone that he rose again. In fact we know very little about Mithraism, which is known primarily from archaeological evidence rather than written texts. We possess many Mithraist sculptures and other artefacts, but in the absence of written explanations, it can be very hard to explain them. The key Mithraist image, which is found in every mithraeum (or Mithraist temple), is the 'tauroctony', an image of Mithras killing a bull. But precisely what this central element of the religion meant is uncertain. There is also doubt over the origins of Mithraism. Mithras, its central deity, was a god from the Middle East, who had been worshipped for well over a thousand years before the birth of Jesus. But it is uncertain whether Roman Mithraism was a continuation of this cult or a new religion inspired by the old one. Certainly the Roman cult seems to have emerged towards the end of the first century AD, *after* the appearance of Christianity.

There were clearly some similarities between Christianity and Mithraism, especially in the celebration of a ritual meal. Christian authors such as Justin Martyr and Tertullian believed that the Mithraist version was a demonic mockery of their own Eucharist. In fact, such meals were common to many religions of the time, and most of the similarities between these two religions can be explained more easily as common features of the time rather than as the result of 'borrowing' one way or the other. It should be remembered, moreover, that any 'borrowing' that did occur could just as easily have been Mithraists borrowing from Christianity rather than vice versa. And there were significant differences between Mithraism and Christianity. Like most of the deities of the mystery religions, Mithras seems to have been conceived not as a historical figure but as a cosmic god, whose deeds were performed in some mythic time before creation or eternally in the cycle of the seasons. Jesus was quite different in that his worshippers knew that he was a historical figure of recent times. And Mithraism was an elitist cult. It was very male-dominated (it was unusual among mystery religions in apparently featuring no female deities), and is usually thought to have excluded women altogether. It was particularly popular among civil servants and the military, although not politicians; most of its members seem to have been drawn from the equivalent of the middle classes rather than the political elite. Most of the known mithraea outside Rome itself are on the empire's borders, where soldiers were garrisoned. We might imagine Mithraists as a small, select group, membership of which was seen as something rather special. Christianity, by contrast, was open to all, especially those most despised in society, and women were among its most important members. It was most popular in the big cities of the empire and its heartlands, not the frontiers. Christianity and Mithraism thus addressed almost completely different sectors of society.

violence to it. The beliefs and practices of these people were not arid doctrines or meaningless motions, but arose out of spiritual experiences, those of individuals and also of cohesive societies too. This means that the meaning of these elements must be understood in the context of the religions of which they form a part. An apparently similar idea may appear in two religions, but it may mean completely different things in those two religions.

A good example of this is the Christian understanding of Jesus, which developed throughout the period we are looking at, until in the fifth century the church declared that he was one person with two natures, fully human and fully divine. There are, perhaps, parallels to some ancient pagan beliefs, such as the divinity of emperors and pharaohs. But the doctrine developed within Christianity mainly as a result of factors that were internal to the religion. One of the main reasons Christians became convinced that Jesus must have been fully human and fully divine was that they believed that salvation comes through Jesus. And they believed that salvation is a matter of humanity being divinized, which could occur only if divinity and humanity had literally been joined in a single person. So the notion of Jesus' two natures – fully divine and fully human – developed as a way of defending and explaining this fundamentally soteriological (or salvation-related) aspect of Christianity. There was an internal logic to the doctrine, which developed as a part of the spiritual tradition in which it was rooted. It was not simply cobbled together from elements of other religions.

That is not to say that there is no cross-fertilization between religions. There were many elements in Christianity which may have come from the mystery religions, and perhaps other traditions too. The point I wish to make here is that even if that is the case, it does not mean that Christianity was just the same thing as these religions, with the names changed – a charge which some nineteenth-century scholars made, and which is still repeated at the popular level today. The role that these common elements played within the religion, and the way in which the adherents of the religion understood them, make all the difference.

However, the mystery religions do help us to understand what people looked for in religion at this period. The mystery religions must have given people a sense of belonging to a special group, one with its own traditions and rituals, as well as a myth or set of myths that meant something profound and important to its members. The mystery religions were about fertility, life and death, the purpose and destiny of human beings, and similar matters. Christianity must have offered believers similar rewards. Those who were baptized as Christians must have felt much the same way as those who were initiated into the mysteries of Isis or Attis, that they were being reborn into a new society that offered not only hope for a life beyond the grave but a sense of belonging and community in this life too.

Christian art

Christian art was, at this time, an extremely modest affair. In fact, Christian texts from the second and third centuries AD often criticize pagan religion for its reliance upon images and objects, implying that the Christians themselves did not use or make any. Some scholars have even concluded that, during this period, Christians – like Jews – regarded religious images as fundamentally idolatrous, banned by the second of the Ten Commandments.

However, some Christian images do survive from this time, in a number of contexts. There is some evidence that Christian house churches were decorated with murals. A few such murals have been discovered, although it is impossible to tell how common the practice was. Moreover, the council of Elvira, held in Spain in the early fourth century AD, condemned this practice.

Archaeologists have had more success discovering murals and other artworks from a funerary context. These have been found mainly in the catacombs, above all near Rome, although a few are known in other locations as well; the oldest are in the Catacomb of Callistus, from the early third century AD. Many of the images found here are taken from pagan art – for example, a woman praying with outstretched hands represents piety, a common pagan motif. Others are based on pagan images, but Christianized. The most common of these represents Jesus as the Good Shepherd, carrying a sheep over his shoulders – an adaptation of the pagan image of Hermes and of philanthropy. However, images of Jesus or of the apostles are rare during this period; when Jesus does appear he is usually performing a miracle (often healing someone by touching them with a stick, as the Roman god Asclepius was also represented). There are no images of his death or resurrection. Jesus always looks like a beardless young Roman, who does not particularly stand out from the people with him. There are also images of various animals with symbolic meaning: the phoenix, for example, which represented the resurrection, or the dove, which represented the Holy Spirit. Fish also appear. The Greek word for 'fish', *icthos*, was used as an acrostic: its letters stood for the Greek for 'Jesus Christ, Son of God, Saviour'. This again may have been an adaptation of pagan imagery, since the fish was already a traditional religious symbol. Boats were a particularly common Christian symbol, possibly representing the church. Finally, the *chi-rho* symbol was also important: this consisted of the first two

The *chi-rho* symbol illustrates this 3rd-century AD fresco from the Roman villa at Lullingstone, Kent, in the UK. The additional letters "A" and "W" represent *alpha* and *omega* – the beginning and the end.

The fish had a symbolic meaning within Christian circles. Above is a piece of funerary graffito from Rome, dating from the 2nd–3rd century AD.

letters of the name *Christos* in Greek, X (ch) and P (r), superimposed upon each other.

We also find representations of biblical scenes, mostly from the Old Testament, which has led some scholars to believe that early Christian art was based, to a large extent, upon Jewish art. Particularly popular scenes include Daniel in the lions' den, Abraham about to sacrifice Isaac, or Moses miraculously creating water in the desert. Jonah and the whale are also popular, with the whole story sometimes being told in several panels. Christians regarded all of these Old Testament stories as prefiguring Christ. The three youths in the fiery furnace, from the book of Daniel, was also a popular subject, apparently as a reference to the sufferings of the Christian martyrs. As these examples indicate, Christian art was about conveying a message, often one that a casual viewer would not understand. Much of this early art is of relatively poor quality too, with rather slapdash painting and uninspired composition compared to the usually superior pagan equivalents of the time. Although this may have been partly because the Christians were often too poor to afford good painters, it may also have been because the actual execution of the art was not considered important. What mattered was the religious message that it conveyed. The notion that contemplating a beautiful image might help bring the soul to the contemplation of the divine beauty itself – which was so important in later Orthodox Christianity – had not yet developed.

In addition to these funerary images, which would not have played a very significant role in the lives of most Christians, archaeologists have also found a large number of everyday objects featuring Christian motifs. These include goblets, signet rings, glasses, lamps, and the like. They might be carved not with scenes from the Bible but with simple motifs with Christian significance, such as fish, doves, ships, or anchors (representing the steadfastness of faith). Such items might serve to help Christians recognize one another, but are more likely to have been simple reminders of the owner's faith as he or she went about daily life.

The catacombs from Maresha, an ancient city in Judah. It is in catacombs like these that many examples of Christian art have been found.

Christians in a Hostile World

The Christians seem to have been model citizens. They worked diligently, spent their spare time attending services or praying at home, and held themselves to very high moral ideals. And yet the authorities brutally persecuted them. Why were Christians so hated? And what effect did these persecutions have on the Christians themselves?

Roman religion

One of the main virtues that the Romans prized was *pietas*, or 'piety'. Originally, this word meant showing proper respect to one's parents and relations, and to society as a whole. Later, it came to mean having a proper and loyal attitude to Roman society and the Roman state, a sort of deferent patriotism. And finally it acquired religious overtones, so that a 'pious' person was one who showed respect for the traditional gods and rituals. But the word still kept the overtones of its earlier meanings. So in Roman society, to adhere to the traditional religion was closely bound up with acting in a socially responsible way and patriotism.

A 1st-century Roman mosaic from the House of Neptune in Herculaneum, Italy, depicts Neptune and Amphitrite.

Indeed, the emperor himself was a religious figure. In Greece and Asia, powerful rulers such as Alexander the Great had been regarded as gods for many years, and this practice seems to have spread to Rome in the first century BC, when Rome acquired a powerful dictator of its own for the first time in the person of Julius Caesar. A number of inscriptions in the east, dating from late in his lifetime, hail him as a living god. Caesar himself clearly approved of the development, since he had a month named after himself, built a temple to himself, and appointed his friend Mark Antony as his own chief priest.

Caesar's nephew, Augustus, the first true Roman emperor, developed some aspects of this idea and abandoned others. He did not have temples and priests dedicated to himself, but since he was Caesar's adopted son, he was known as 'the divine son'. He avoided actually calling himself a god, but he did not stop other people from doing so – especially in the provinces and the eastern part of the empire. He revived the old position of *pontifex maximus* or chief priest in the city of Rome, but he took over the position himself. All of Augustus' successors adopted the same title until AD 382. And after Augustus' death, he was officially deified. This became standard procedure for every emperor, except for the particularly unpopular ones; a witness would swear to the Senate that he had seen the dead emperor's soul ascend to heaven from his funeral pyre, and the Senate would agree that he was now a god. Even in their lifetimes, the emperors were held to be inspired by a divine spirit, 'Caesar's genius', and people were expected to worship this spirit. The words 'the piety of the emperor' often appeared on coins; the supreme example of the virtue of *pietas* was thus the emperor himself. Augustus also revitalized the Roman elements of the old religion by building new temples, hiring many new priests, and encouraging writers such as Ovid and Horace to praise the traditional Roman religion. This helped to strengthen the connection of religion to traditional Roman virtues and culture.

So Roman religion was quite pragmatic; to worship the gods in the proper way was part of what it was to be a good member of society. Indeed it was essential to the running of society at all. Public events such as games or theatrical performances would have prayers and offerings to the gods, just as sporting events in some countries today feature the playing of the national anthem. Public prayers and sacrifices were offered on certain days of the year or before important events, and observance of the rituals was generally considered to be essential to being a good Roman. Even events such as private parties had religious overtones: people would send out invitations to their friends in the name of the god who was to 'host'

A triumphal chariot is pulled by elephants on this sestertius coin dating from the reign of Augustus (27 BC–AD 14). The inscription reads: 'To the divine Augustus, SPQR' [the Roman senate and people].

The emperor Augustus, depicted here in a contemporary cameo, was deified after his death in AD 14.

the party. And people's private homes contained shrines of various kinds. Some were niches in the walls, which might contain statues of the gods; others were rather like bookcases or cupboards attached to the walls, just like shrines in modern Chinese homes. There were also small free-standing altars like tables, as well as small models of temples kept on plinths, and sacred paintings. The father of the household – the *paterfamilias* – acted as chief priest for his family and their slaves – indeed, he had a 'genius' just like the emperor did.

The Romans believed that their *pietas* was something that set them apart from other peoples. Cicero – the great politician and philosopher of the first century BC – declared:

If we care to compare our national characteristics with those of foreign peoples, we shall find that, while in all other respects we are only the equals or even the inferiors of others, yet in the sense of religion, that is in worship for the gods, we are far superior.[1]

Attitudes to the Christians

Popular attitudes

Imagine someone living in present-day Australia who hates sport so much that he or she refuses ever to come into contact with it or hear about it at all. Such a person would be unable to go to the pub, where sport would probably be playing on TV; or read a newspaper, which would probably have a story about sport on the front page; or watch television at all, in case a commercial referring to sport came on. He or she would be unable to talk much to people at work, in case they start discussing sport – indeed, such a person would probably be unable to do much socially at all. He or she would have to find refuge with other extreme sport-phobes and make friends with them instead. And such a person would probably be regarded as very peculiar by others.

That is what it must have been like for the Christians in the second or third centuries AD, when a religion they believed to be fundamentally wicked pervaded all aspects of life. They couldn't go to sporting events or the theatre; they couldn't attend parties or eat at the homes of non-Christians; they couldn't make the customary gestures of respect and deference to the political authorities. Little wonder that Celsus, a second-century philosopher who wrote a book attacking Christianity, denounced 'the cult of Christ' as 'a secret society whose members huddle together in corners'[2].

The attitudes of many ordinary people to the Christians are reflected in a short dialogue entitled the *Octavius*, written at the end of the second century AD by a Christian named Marcus Minucius Felix. In the dialogue, the character Caecilius Natalis launches a tremendous attack upon the Christians from the viewpoint of educated Roman paganism. The Christians, we are told, are simply rude:

> They despise our temples as being no more than sepulchres, they spit after our gods, they sneer at our rites, and, fantastic though it is, our priests they pity – pitiable themselves; they scorn the purple robes of public office, though they go about in rags themselves. How amazingly stupid, unbelievably insolent they are.[3]

Their secretive nature makes them obviously suspicious:

> One is always happy for honorable actions to be made public; crimes are kept secret. Why do they have no altars, no temples, no publicly-known images? Why do they never speak in the open, why do they always assemble in stealth? It must be that whatever it is they worship – and suppress – is deserving either of punishment or of shame.[4]

Despite their secrecy, Caecilius seems to know precisely what happens at the Christians' ceremonies. He describes the orgies that Christians hold: a dog is tied to the lampstand, and encouraged to run away, knocking it over and plunging the room into darkness; this is the cue for everyone to have sex with each other at random, even close family members. Even worse, they disguise a baby by covering it with flour and trick initiates into stabbing it to death, before dismembering the corpse and eating it. After this speech, the character Octavius – a Christian – points out the absurdity of these tales, asking where the grieving parents are whose babies have been murdered by the Christians. He retorts that in fact it is the pagans who are sexually immoral and given to bloodlust. Caecilius is convinced by his arguments and the dialogue ends with everyone cheerfully congratulating one another. In real life, things did not generally end so happily. The bizarre stories were well known, and for many people, to call oneself a Christian was effectively to admit to murder and incest. Indeed, Minucius Felix tells us that the accusations made by his character Caecilius are based upon real-life ones by Marcus Cornelius Fronto, who had been the tutor of the emperor Marcus Aurelius. In his *Apology*, written at around the same time as Minucius Felix's *Octavius*, Tertullian railed ineffectively against the injustice and incoherence of the system: the authorities never investigated any rumours of murder or the like against Christians, they simply executed them on the basis of the name 'Christian' alone.

The philosophers and the Christians

At the same time, educated people mocked Christian doctrines as credible only to those with weak minds. It seems to have been a commonplace among intellectuals that Christianity was a religion for stupid people. The second-century AD physician Galen, for example, made it clear that he thought Christians not enormously intelligent; in one passage he gives advice 'in order that one should not at the very beginning, as if one had come into the school of Moses and Christ, hear talk of undemonstrated laws'[5]. But he did admire the Christians for their lifestyle, which he thought just as good as that of 'real' philosophers.

Others were less prepared to see any good in Christianity. In his long attack upon the religion, Celsus ignored scurrilous rumours like those mentioned above and focused on the intellectual shortcomings of his targets. He noted that Christians spent their time trying to convert children, idiots, and women, since even they could see that intelligent people would never be convinced by their ideas. He attacked the Christian belief in a God who rewards and punishes people as fundamentally immoral, and the Christian belief that God made the world for human beings as arrogant and anthropocentric. For Celsus, whatever is good in Christian doctrine was simply a garbled version of something that philosophers had already said, and said better. In particular, the Christian God was no real God at all:

> They say that God has form, namely the form of the Logos, who became flesh in Jesus Christ. But we know that God is without shape, without color ... Their absurd doctrines even contain reference to God walking about in the garden he created for man; and they speak of him being angry, jealous, moved to repentance, sorry, sleepy – in short, as being in every respect more a man than a God. They have not read Plato, who teaches us in the Republic that God (the Good) does not even participate in being.[6]

Celsus' attack on Christianity goes beyond the mere charge that it was a false religion. It represents a fundamentally conservative viewpoint, according to which the established mores of religion and philosophy are necessarily more reliable, and more central to society, than the new-fangled foreign nonsense being peddled by this secretive sect. Jesus, on his view, was a con-man who fooled the gullible; the real mystery was that people were still being taken in.

A somewhat different view can be seen in the work of Porphyry, a philosopher of the late third century AD who wrote at least one major book attacking Christianity, although little of it has been preserved. Porphyry was a disciple of the great philosopher Plotinus. He also attended lectures by the Christian theologian Origen, but he was not impressed by his attempt to combine Greek philosophy with Christianity. Unlike Celsus, Porphyry seems to have made a serious study of the Christian Scriptures and based much of his criticism of Christianity upon a demolition of the Christian interpretation of these books. For example, he argued at length that the book of Daniel was not really a prophecy of the future written in the sixth century BC (as Jews and Christians believed), but was actually written in the second century BC (a conclusion with which most modern scholars agree) and described what were to the author contemporary events *as if* they had been prophesied four centuries earlier. In this way, Porphyry argued that the Old Testament could not be taken seriously as containing useful prophecies about the Messiah or anything else. He seems also to have argued that the four Gospels could not be taken as reliable historical records about Jesus, because they were written to glorify him, and actually contradict one another at various places.

However, Porphyry did not denigrate Jesus himself as a trickster, as Celsus had done. In his book *Philosophy from Oracles*, intended to show the agreement of pagan oracles and philosophy, Porphyry

Averroes (Ibn Rushd), who lived 1126–98, is seen here in an imaginary conversation with Porphyry (c. AD 232–305).

presented Jesus as a great teacher who, after his death, had been wrongly proclaimed a god by his followers. On this view, Jesus was a pious pagan who worshipped the true God of the philosophers and the oracles, and the Christians had misunderstood his message and foolishly worshipped him instead of God. Little wonder that Porphyry's work caused such consternation among Christians; this was the first attempt to co-opt Jesus into paganism, showing respect for his teachings while attacking Christianity.

To philosophers and ordinary people alike, Christianity was not simply antisocial, ludicrous, immoral, and unpatriotic; it threatened the very stability of the world. The Roman gods, it was believed, protected the empire, and divine providence kept things running smoothly provided it was given the respect it was due. Christianity was a form of 'atheism' in that it disrupted this arrangement. According to the Christian historian Eusebius of Caesarea, one pagan critic of Christianity – probably Porphyry – wrote:

How can men not be in every way impious and atheistic who have apostasized from the customs of our fathers, through which every nation and city is sustained? What good can reasonably be hoped for from those who stand as enemies and warriors against their benefactors? What else are they than fighters against God? What types of pardon will they be worthy of who have turned away from those recognized as gods from the earliest times among all Greek and barbarians, both in cities and in the country, with all types of sacrifices, and mysteries and initiations by all, kings and lawgivers and philosophers, and have rather chosen what is impious and atheistic among men?[7]

Many of these anti-Christian attitudes were simply new versions of old pagan attacks upon Judaism. Jews were also commonly regarded as 'atheists' because they worshipped only a single god and refused to acknowledge those of Rome. They were also often thought to be annoyingly arrogant, looking down upon pagans and sneering at the Hellenistic culture in which most of them lived. These criticisms and others like them may have contained a grain of truth – many Jewish writings *did* contain trenchant criticisms of pagan morality and religion – but they also partly derived from common fears of immigrants that can be found in any society. The large Jewish Diaspora throughout the Roman and Persian empires had been in existence for at least a couple of centuries before Jesus, but the distinctive behaviour and appearance of many Jews meant that they remained 'outsiders' in other people's eyes nevertheless. Some of the anti-Christian sentiment seems to have derived from the same source:

Column with a bust of Trajan, who reigned from AD 98 to 117.
The columns were part of a Roman monument of the 2nd century.

some Christian communities found themselves scapegoated because they behaved differently from other people or their members were immigrants. It must also have been easy for people to transfer the traditional complaints against Jews to the Christians – especially if those scholars are right who argue that most Christians *were* Jews during this period in at least some important senses. If that is so, then to many pagan critics, one Jewish sect was doubtless much the same as another.

The persecutions

Nevertheless, the authorities tolerated the Jewish religion. This was not the case for the Christians, who had no official protection against the slanders that were directed against them, and who were subject to arrest and execution by the authorities for their faith. The persecutions were, for the most part, intermittent – in fact, in most places, most of the time, no persecutions of Christians were going on. Although Christianity was illegal, and theoretically punishable by death, in practice most emperors largely ignored it and allowed local governors to deal with it as they saw fit. As we saw in chapter 3, the first persecution was conducted by Nero in AD 64, but we do not know exactly how or why it was carried out, and we know virtually nothing of what sort of persecutions happened during the following half-century.

The first we hear of anti-Christian activity from those actually conducting it is in AD 112, when Pliny the Younger, governor of Bithynia, wrote a famous letter to the emperor Trajan asking him for advice about Christianity. Apparently many people had been accused of Christianity, but when Pliny interrogated them, he found that they seemed to be innocent of the crimes of which they were usually accused. He executed them anyway because he thought that their 'obstinacy and unbending perversity' should be punished, but he was unsure whether it was a crime simply to be a Christian, or whether the criminality lay in the things that Christians were said to do. Trajan replied (rather briefly, suggesting that this matter was low on his list of priorities) that Pliny was acting quite correctly. Any Christians that turned up should be executed if they refused to sacrifice to the gods, or freed if they did sacrifice, but it was not worth making a special effort to find and arrest them. In around AD 125, the emperor Hadrian told the proconsul of Asia that Christians needed to be shown to have done something illegal before being punished, and that people making groundless accusations should themselves be punished severely. Most governors during the second and early third centuries seem to have taken this approach, and many Christian communities seem to have been quite open about their faith. When one governor in Asia Minor began to persecute Christians, the whole Christian community demonstrated outside his house in protest. Evidently they regarded his actions as not just unreasonable but remarkable. Some governors were even sympathetic to Christianity to some degree. Origen of Alexandria was on one occasion summoned by the governor of Syria, not to answer charges of treason but for a theological chat. Even the imperial household was capable of showing interest in Christianity. Victor, bishop of Rome in the 190s, was able to ask Marcia, the mistress of the emperor Commodus, to release Christians who had been sent to the Sardinian mines, and his request was successful – one of the released slaves was Callistus, who would later become bishop of Rome himself. Later, Origen was summoned to meet the powerful mother of the emperor Severus Alexander, Julia Mammea. In fact, another Christian intellectual, Julius Africanus, seems to have acted as Julia Mammea's spiritual adviser. Severus Alexander himself had a chapel containing statues of the gods worshipped throughout the empire, among which was one of Jesus.

And even when Christians were arrested, governors might try to resolve the problem peacefully. In many accounts of martyrs' trials, the governors are portrayed as doing their best to be merciful; they try to encourage the Christians to sacrifice to the gods so they can be released. Perhaps such behaviour was sometimes a sham – a sort of 'soft cop' act intended to win the trust of the accused and get them to hand over information about their friends – or perhaps sometimes it is exaggerated by later writers, hoping to emphasize the parallels to the Gospel accounts of Jesus' trial before a largely sympathetic Pilate. But (unlike the real Pilate) most Roman governors were not monstrous tyrants, and it is quite reasonable to suppose that many of them really were perplexed by the Christians brought before them and genuinely wanted to avoid needlessly executing apparently decent citizens, no matter how odd their religious beliefs. Tertullian tells us of one governor who instead of ordering Christians to sacrifice to the pagan gods ordered them to recite a pagan formula of faith, and released them if they agreed – but he had carefully worded the formula so vaguely that it would be acceptable to Christians as well as to pagans. Unfortunately, Tertullian doesn't tell us what this ecumenically minded formula was.

This 15th-century painting, by Pedro Garcia de Benabarre, shows Sebastian and Polycarp destroying idols. Sebastian was martyred in AD 288, having been killed during Diocletian's persecutions. Polycarp died a martyr in c. AD 155.

Christians on trial

One Christian document, *The Acts of the Scillitan Martyrs*, offers a terse account of a trial that indicates how a hearing before a judge inclined to be merciful might progress:

> The proconsul Saturninus said: 'If you return to your senses, you can obtain the pardon of our lord the emperor.'
>
> Speratus said: 'We have never done wrong; we have never lent ourselves to wickedness. Never have we uttered a curse; but when abused, we have given thanks, for we hold our own emperor in honour.'
>
> Saturninus the proconsul said: 'We too are a religious people, and our religion is a simple one: we swear by the genius of our lord the emperor and we offer prayers for his health – as you also ought to do.'
>
> Speratus said: 'If you will give me a calm hearing, I shall tell you the mystery of simplicity.'
>
> 'If you begin to malign our sacred rites,' said Saturninus, 'I shall not listen to you. But swear rather by the genius of our lord the emperor.'
>
> Speratus said: 'I do not recognize the empire of this world. Rather, I serve that God whom no man has seen, nor can see, with these eyes. I have not stolen; and on my purchase I pay the tax, for I acknowledge my lord who is the emperor of kings and of all nations...'
>
> The proconsul Saturninus said to Speratus: 'Do you persist in remaining a Christian?'
>
> Speratus said: 'I am a Christian.' And all agreed with him.
>
> Saturninus the proconsul said: 'You wish no time for consideration?'
>
> Speratus said: 'In so just a matter there is no need for consideration.'
>
> The proconsul Saturninus said: 'What have you in your case?'
>
> Speratus said: 'Books and letters of a just man named Paul.'
>
> The proconsul Saturninus said: 'You are granted a reprieve of thirty days: think it over.'
>
> Once again Speratus said, 'I am a Christian!' And with him all the others agreed.
>
> Saturninus the proconsul read his decision from a tablet: 'Whereas Speratus, Nartzalus, Cittinus, Donata, Vestia, Secunda, and the others have confessed that they have been living in accordance with the rites of the Christians, and whereas though given the opportunity to return to the usage of the Romans they have persevered in their obstinacy, they are hereby condemned to be executed by the sword.'
>
> Speratus said: 'We thank God!'
>
> Nartzalus said: 'Today we are martyrs in heaven. Thanks be to God!'[1]

As this suggests, the authorities and the Christians might be almost unable to understand one another even where a peaceful solution was sought. For the governor in this case, being merciful meant offering the accused the opportunity to sacrifice to the gods. But not only would the Christians never do this, they actually welcomed the chance to die for their faith.

But while we should be aware that arrests and executions were usually rare during this period, we should also bear in mind that they were always a possibility. Even when the Christians enjoyed peace and prosperity, this was entirely at the discretion of the local governor; and one never knew when a governor might change his policy, or be replaced by a new and less sympathetic one. And in the second half of the second century, it seems that both provincial governors and the populace in general were becoming less and less sympathetic to the growing (although still tiny) Christian community in their midst. Tertullian complained that governors were quite happy to execute people simply for calling themselves 'Christians', without investigating what they actually did, contrary to Hadrian's instructions. There are plenty of stories of Christians' trials where the judges are not accommodating at all.

The church and the mob

Even when Christians were being left in peace, they were not particularly popular in society at large, and they were a ready-made scapegoat whenever anything did go wrong. It was not only the authorities that they had to fear. The rulings of Trajan and Hadrian that unsubstantiated accusations of being a Christian were not to be taken seriously indicate that such accusations did happen; people were quite willing to denounce those they disliked to the authorities as 'Christians', even, perhaps, if there was no basis to the accusation at all. In his *Second Apology*, Justin Martyr tells the story of a woman who converted to Christianity and tried to divorce her pagan husband; he responded by denouncing her to the emperor himself. And individual accusations like this were not the only danger faced by Christians. They were vulnerable to violence from the mob too; in AD 222, Callistus, the bishop of Rome, seems to have been killed by being thrown down a well by such a mob. In AD 248 there was a series of mob attacks on the Christians in Alexandria, in which pagans killed some and dragged others into temples to force them to sacrifice to the gods. These mobs seem often to have included Jews, many of whom were perhaps quite happy to see a new group emerge as the scapegoats of society, and who might also have wished to demonstrate their antipathy towards Christians for the benefit of pagans who might have been hazy about the distinction between the two groups. Thus we hear of Jews helping with the execution of Polycarp, for example, and of Jewish mobs alongside the pagan mobs in Alexandria.

Even if some governors were inclined to be sympathetic towards Christians, they seem often to have withheld mercy for fear of angry mobs. This was apparently the case in one of the best-known persecutions of the period, which occurred at Lyons. The surviving Christians later sent a letter describing this persecution to the Asian churches. Most of the Christians at Lyons (including the most famous one, Irenaeus, who survived this episode) were immigrants from Asia Minor; it is very likely that the hostility against them was partly inspired by anti-immigrant feeling on the part of the locals. In AD 177 this hostility boiled over into a full-scale riot, as the Christians were dragged from their homes:

> They heroically endured all that the people en masse heaped on them: abuse, blows, dragging, despoiling, stoning, imprisonment, and all that an enraged mob is likely to inflict on their most hated enemies. They were dragged into the forum and interrogated before the entire populace by the tribune and the city authorities. When they confessed, they were locked up in prison to await the arrival of the governor.[8]

The aged bishop, Pothonius – over ninety years old – was a particular target:

> He was brought to the tribunal by the soldiers, accompanied by some of the civil magistrates and the entire mob, who raised all kinds of shouts at him as though he were Christ himself. He gave a noble witness. And when asked by the governor who the god of the Christians was, he replied: 'If you are worthy, you will know.'
> At this they dragged him heartlessly along giving him all kinds of blows: the bystanders attacked him in every way with their feet or their fists, without any respect for his old age; and those who were far away tried to hit him with whatever they had at hand, and everybody acted as though it were a serious fault and impiety to fall short in their viciousness towards him, for they thought that in this way they could avenge their gods. And so, scarcely breathing, he was thrown into gaol, and two days later he died.[9]

The city authorities gave the violence a patina of legality. The governor, however, was more of a stickler for the rules, and when he found that there were Roman citizens among the Christians he wrote to the emperor Marcus Aurelius for advice. The emperor – who had, in his youth, been tutored by the anti-Christian writer Marcus Cornelius Fronto – replied with the now standard line that those who refused to sacrifice to the gods should be executed while the rest should be freed. The governor took his advice; few of the Christians were prepared to sacrifice; and forty-seven of them were killed in the amphitheatre before a baying crowd.

Co-ordinated persecutions

Things remained much the same in the early third century, although this period saw a new development, the co-ordinated persecution, taking place in more than one place at once. This happened between AD 202 and 206, when some kind of clampdown against Christianity took place in Rome, Carthage, Corinth, and Alexandria, all at the same time. The authorities seem to have arrested only new converts, presumably in an attempt to discourage people from joining the religion. It was in this persecution that Perpetua – a convert from a prominent Carthaginian family – and her slave Felicity were killed. Things then went generally quiet again, especially under the emperor Severus Alexander, who ruled from AD 222 to 235 and did not persecute the Christians. His successor, Maximin, ordered a persecution in AD 236. Maximin was emperor for only a couple of years, after which the church enjoyed peace once more – culminating in the rule of Philip (AD 244–9), who was so sympathetic to the Christians that later Christian writers believed he had actually been one himself. However, Philip was succeeded in AD 249 by Decius, who had quite a different attitude. Faced with a crisis on the Danube border, where the Gothic tribes were invading, Decius ordered everyone to sacrifice to the gods. These sacrifices were to be done in front of local officials, and certificates were handed out to those who had done it. Evidently Decius hoped not only to secure the favour of the gods in his battles with the Goths but also to keep his empire united by appealing to traditional, patriotic values; and he seems to have succeeded, as the vast majority of people offered their support to him and the gods.

Most Christians did the same thing. In Smyrna, almost the entire church – including its bishop, Euctemon – sacrificed to the gods. Perhaps these were the kinds of cleric whom Tertullian had lambasted fifty years earlier as 'lions in peace, deer in the fight' (*On the Crown* 1); or perhaps they simply wanted to avoid giving the authorities an excuse to kill their congregations. In Carthage, the bishop, Cyprian, described how so many Christians were going to the temple to sacrifice that the priests had to turn them away. Perhaps many of these Christians believed that making the sacrifice was their patriotic duty and did not regard it as a betrayal of their faith. Some Christians did see the sacrifice as a betrayal, but were unwilling to face death for refusing to perform it. They managed to obtain certificates stating that they had performed the sacrifice without actually doing it. Some Christians simply fled; Cyprian was one of these. Just a few stood up for their faith. In Smyrna, a priest named Pionius and a small group of followers refused to do as their bishop had done, and they were executed. The account of their trial indicates that the rather bemused attempts by officials to treat Christians as well as possible had become a thing of the past. Pionius was jeered at, dragged bodily to the temple, and told to sacrifice:

> Lepidus said: 'Pionius, why do you and your people not sacrifice?'
>
> The group around Pionius said, 'Because we are Christians.'
>
> 'Which god do you worship?' asked Lepidus.
>
> Pionius answered, 'The God who made heaven and earth and the sea and all that is in them.'

Lepidus said: 'You mean, then, the one who was crucified?'

'Yes,' said Pionius, 'him whom God sent for the redemption of the world.'

At this the officials gave a loud guffaw and Lepidus cursed Christ.[10]

The bishops of Rome and Antioch – Fabian and Babylas – were also killed. But this was not a systematic persecution; the sacrifices had not been ordered in a deliberate attempt to catch Christians out. And after the day of sacrifice had passed there was little attempt by the authorities to search out those who had been disobedient.

In AD 257, however, the emperor Valerian began a new persecution that was deliberately aimed at the Christians. This seems, in part, to have been inspired by the series of crises then gripping the empire. The third century as a whole was a dire period for Rome, and the empire itself was almost unequal to the challenge. In the east, a renewed Persian empire was conquering considerable territories. In the north, the Germanic peoples who lived beyond the borders of the empire were beginning a series of migrations which saw them move across the border, triggering a series of invasions and border skirmishes. Reforms to the Roman military had reduced the flexibility of the legion system, and the army could not respond to these threats effectively. And all this coincided with a terrible economic crisis. The currency had become appallingly debased as successive emperors tried to cut costs by lowering the silver content of the denarius. The central authorities in Rome had even lost control of the minting process, with independent coiners setting up business throughout the empire and debasing the currency still further. The result was inflation so extreme that the denarius became effectively worthless, and people throughout the empire simply stopped using it and reverted to a barter economy. This in turn meant that economies became localized; people no longer travelled about to sell or buy goods but traded only with their neighbours. The great Roman roads fell silent, trade dried up, merchants went out of business, and the economy withered.

In these difficult times Valerian decreed that it was necessary for everyone to worship the traditional Roman gods, protectors of the empire, as diligently as possible, and for the Christians in particular to be dispersed. Their leaders were summoned to the authorities and sent into exile. Cyprian of Carthage and Dionysius, bishop of Alexandria, were among them. But a year later, a harsher edict was passed. Property was to be seized from the Christians; any Christian civil servants were to be reduced to the status of slaves; and their leaders were to be executed. Cyprian was beheaded, while the bishop of Rome, Xystus II, was killed as soon as he was discovered in a catacomb. Many others, including Origen of Alexandria, lost

Executing the Christians

Criminal executions of this kind took place in the middle of the day, sandwiched between animal hunts in the morning and gladiator fights in the afternoon. The gladiators were supposed to be brave, voluntarily risking death for the entertainment of the crowd; they symbolized the courage and power of Rome in the face of danger. The criminals were supposed to be pathetic wretches, justly killed for transgressing the sacred norms of society. The sight of Christian criminals subverting this expectation by facing their deaths bravely – even joyfully – must have astonished the crowds. Many were furious, seeing the bravery of the martyrs as yet more defiant of society. We hear of mocking taunts shouted at the victims, such as 'Well washed!' – a traditional greeting to someone coming out of the baths – aimed at a Christian covered in blood. Some spectators, however, were impressed by the bravery of the martyrs. We hear of a soldier named

Basilides, who had to accompany a Christian called Potamianena to her execution. He was so impressed by her bravery as she had boiling pitch poured over her that he converted to Christianity himself and ended up being beheaded.

In theory, Roman citizens were executed by beheading, while anyone else could be killed more painfully. In practice, Christians tended to suffer protracted deaths irrespective of their nationality. Many were burned at the stake or roasted alive on iron griddles; many more were killed by wild animals such as lions or leopards. Possibly the worst death was being killed by bulls, which was slow and inefficient; the victims were often tied up in nets to make the process easier. Sometimes the animals failed to kill the victims, in which case guards might be sent out to dispatch them more quickly, or the victims might simply be taken back to prison and executed on another occasion.

Gladiators are shown fighting wild beasts in this 4th-century Roman mosaic from Terranova, Italy.

their lives, until Valerian was captured by the Persians and the persecution ended. Decades of almost complete peace followed.

The Great Persecution

By far the worst persecution of the period came at the end of the third century, under Diocletian, one of the greatest emperors of the period. When he became emperor in AD 284, the empire was still in a sorry state. Not only had it lost land to the east but the financial crisis was continuing and infrastructure was crumbling. In fact the situation had become so bad that parts of the empire actually broke away and declared independence. In AD 260 much of the western part of the empire, including what are now France, Spain, and Britain, broke away as the 'Gallic empire' and began issuing their own coins. The Gallic empire was reabsorbed back into the main empire through political means in AD 274, but that was not an end to the problem. In AD 286 a Roman naval commander in the English Channel, Carausius, declared himself emperor of Britain and set up a breakaway state there, apparently with the support of British merchants. The weak and overstretched state of the Roman military is amply demonstrated by the fact that this independent British empire lasted for a decade, seems to have enjoyed prosperity at home, and even controlled parts of what is now the French coast, including Rouen and Boulogne.

Diocletian's priorities involved reinventing the economy by effectively scrapping the old coins and issuing brand new, good-quality ones, and also reforming the political system of the empire itself so that the military could be controlled more effectively. He recognized that the empire was simply too vast for one man to keep on top of everything. So he divided the empire, retaining control of the east but putting the western half in the charge of Maximian, who ruled as co-emperor. In AD 293 he reintroduced the old system of the emperor appointing someone – his 'caesar' – as his heir and co-ruler. Both Diocletian and Maximian did this, so there were

Valerian, the Roman emperor who ruled AD 253–260, is shown after being captured and mistreated by the Persians. Here, King Shapur I uses Valerian to mount his horse.

Palace of Diocletian at Split on the Bay of Aspalathos. Diocletian spent the last years of his life here, having abdicated in AD 305.

two emperors and two caesars: the 'tetrarchy' or 'rule of four'. This system was extremely effective at sorting out the military threats to the empire. Maximian's caesar, Constantius Chlorus, successfully invaded Britain in around AD 296, killed Carausius' successor Allectus, and reintegrated the island into the Roman empire.

Diocletian seems, at least at first, not to have been bothered about Christianity. His court contained Christians and he could even see the Christian church in Nicomedia from the windows of his palace there. He was an instinctive conservative in cultural matters, though, and seems to have become angry with the Christians when they interfered with traditional religion. A series of divinations held by his court in AD 299 failed to make the expected predictions, and this was blamed upon the presence of Christians making the sign of the cross to ward off demons. Diocletian ordered all members of the imperial household to sacrifice to the gods, and then extended the order to the whole army. In AD 302 a Christian deacon named Romanus broke into a session of the imperial court while the emperor was in Antioch, shouting during the sacrifice with which the session began. An angry Diocletian had Romanus' tongue cut out and he was thrown into prison, to be executed a year later.

But the prime instigator of the persecutions seems to have been Diocletian's caesar, Galerius, a passionate pagan who hated the Christians. In AD 297 Galerius' stock with Diocletian rose after he won an important victory against the Persians. Perhaps flushed with confidence from the more secure political position this afforded him, he began rooting out Christians from his army. By early AD 303, both Diocletian and Maximian had been persuaded to roll out the persecutions empire-wide.

Like the persecution of Valerian, this one involved the confiscation of property (including all Bibles) and the closing of churches. At first Diocletian forbade the killing of Christians, for fear of creating more martyrs. But the following year he became ill and Galerius ruled in his stead; both he and Maximian ordered a general sacrifice by all Christians. Much the same thing happened as before: some Christians sacrificed and some didn't, and some governors tried to persuade them to sacrifice, usually without success. In Sicily, we are told of one Christian named Euplus who marched up to the governor's office and shouted that he was a Christian and was ready to die; the surprised governor found that he had little option but to grant the request. In Iberia, we hear of a twelve-year-old girl named Eulalia whose family retreated to their family estate to avoid the trials going on in town; she ran away at night, made her way to the town, marched up to the governor and told him she was a Christian. When he told her to think of her parents and go home, she spat in his face and kicked over the pagan altar; she was eventually condemned to death.

Far more Christians died in this persecution than in any other before, and for the first time, it seems that the carnage went beyond what the mob was happy with. We hear, for example, of pagans hiding Christians from the authorities in order to protect them. The sympathy that Christians began to attract from many quarters may have been a factor in the gradual easing of the persecution. In AD 305, both Diocletian and Maximian abdicated and retired. In the west, Maximian was succeeded by his caesar, Constantius Chlorus, who was quite tolerant of Christians. He had never permitted any Christians to be executed in the territories that he had controlled as caesar (although he had destroyed churches), and he ended the persecutions. In the east, Galerius became emperor, and continued the persecutions. His caesar, Maximinus Daia, paid a backhanded compliment to the Christians by reorganizing the pagan priesthood in imitation of the Christian one. He also had literature disseminated that sought to undermine Christianity, such as an account of Jesus' trial which was supposedly written by Pontius Pilate, and which was posted publicly everywhere and even taught in schools. In AD 311, however, Galerius fell ill, probably with bowel cancer. Terrified of death, he issued a new edict reversing his previous ones against the Christians, and ordered them to pray for his recovery. Five days later, he died. Maximinus Daia, who now ruled Asia Minor and Egypt, at first respected the new edict, but after a few months he overruled it and ordered fresh persecutions in his territories. It was to prove the last persecution Christians were to suffer at the hands of a pagan Roman state.

A theology of martyrdom

It is not known how many Christians were killed in the Roman persecutions; estimates range from hundreds to thousands. For a community that represented a small minority of society at large, these deaths – even coming only occasionally – were of major significance to the whole group. Not enough Christians were killed for the survival of the religion to be in serious doubt, but still these persecutions must have stunted church growth, especially given the fact that they were followed by periods of soul-searching and bitter recriminations among the Christians, because some of them had given in, sacrificed to the gods, and must now be cast out of the church. Such problems effectively prolonged the misery caused by the persecutions themselves and must have hampered the attempts of Christians to spread their faith. In fact, there is considerable doubt whether the church expanded at all during the second and the third centuries. We hear virtually nothing of any Christian missionaries anywhere during this period, with only occasional exceptions such as Gregory the Wonder-Worker, who helped spread Christianity in Cappadocia in the third century. Although there are a few reports of pagans converting to Christianity after witnessing the bravery of the martyrs, there is no real evidence that this was a common occurrence.

A Byzantine manuscript in the Biblioteca Nazionale, Turin, Italy, depicts Christian martyrs.

A more important consequence of the persecutions was their effect upon how Christians saw themselves. One consequence was the rise of 'acts of the martyrs' as a genre of literature, describing the trial of the accused before the authorities, stressing their refusal to renounce their faith, and their deaths. The parallels to the account of Jesus' trial before Pilate and his death in the Gospels would have been obvious to their first readers. Jesus' conduct before his enemies and bravery in facing death were the model which later martyrs tried to follow, and which their chroniclers represented them as achieving. After all, Jesus himself had told his followers: 'The cup that I drink you will drink; and with the baptism with which I am baptized, you will be baptized' (Mark 10:39); and 'If any want to become my followers, let them deny themselves and take up their cross and follow me. For those who want to save their life will lose it, and those who lose their life for my sake, and for the sake of the gospel, will save it.' (Mark 8:34–35).

For the early Christians, martyrdom was not simply a danger that anyone joining the church faced; it was not even merely an opportunity to prove how devoted they were to Christ. It was a way to emulate Christ, to become perfect in one's union with him. It was, in fact, the pinnacle of the Christian calling. Generations of Christians read the following famous passage from the letter of Ignatius of Antioch to the Roman church, written in AD 107 as he was being taken to Rome for execution. In that letter, he warned the Roman Christians not to try to save him from death:

> I am writing to all the churches and assuring them that I am truly in earnest about dying for God – if only you yourselves put no obstacles in the way. I must implore you to do me no such untimely kindness; pray leave me to be a meal for the beasts, for it is they who can provide my way to God. I am His wheat, ground fine by the lions' teeth to be made purest bread for Christ. Better still, incite the creatures to become a sepulchre for me; let them not leave the smallest scrap of my flesh, so that I need not be a burden to anyone after I fall asleep. When there is no trace of my body left for the world to see, then I shall truly be Jesus Christ's disciple ... How I look forward to the real lions that have been got ready for me! All I pray is that I may find them swift. I am going to make overtures to them, so that, unlike some other wretches whom they have been too spiritless to touch, they may devour me with all speed. And if they are still reluctant, I shall use force to them. You must forgive me, but I do know what is best for myself. This is the first stage of my discipleship; and no power, visible or invisible, must begrudge me my coming to Jesus Christ. Fire, cross, beast-fighting, hacking and quartering, splintering of bone and mangling of limb, even the pulverizing of my entire body – let every horrid and diabolical torment come upon me, provided only that I can win my way to Jesus Christ![11]

For Ignatius, being alive was a sort of death; by dying for Christ he anticipated that he would live. Dying for Christ was thus the supreme prize, the greatest step on the spiritual journey; it allowed one literally to share in Christ's own death and see God. Martyrdom was often called a 'crown', or a 'birth' into new life – martyrs would be remembered on the anniversaries of their deaths, but these were called their 'birthdays'. (There is some evidence that Christians did celebrate their literal birthdays, but some, including Origen and Tertullian, denounced this as a pagan practice.) This emphasis upon Christ as the ultimate model for martyrdom meant that, although Christians greatly venerated the martyrs, this veneration was secondary to their worship of Christ himself. The account of the martyrdom of Polycarp, bishop of Smyrna in the second century, mentions the fears of the authorities and the Jews that the Christians might start to worship Polycarp after his death. But the author comments:

> Little did they know that we could never abandon Christ, for it was he who suffered for the redemption of those who are saved in the entire world, the innocent one dying on behalf of sinners. Nor could we worship anyone else. For him we reverence as the Son of God, whereas we love the martyrs as the disciples and imitators of the Lord, and rightly so because of their unsurpassed loyalty towards their king and master. May we too share with them as fellow disciples![12]

Many Christians actively hoped for martyrdom, and the 'acts' often portray the martyrs as thanking God when sentence is passed on them. Indeed, they often use the very phrase 'Thanks be to God' that appears in early liturgies. Their greatest fear was not the physical suffering, but the possibility that one might not prove steadfast. Indeed, some Christians regarded the persecutions themselves as heaven-sent tests, designed to show who in the church was a true Christian and who only appeared to be. On this mindset, persecution was actually something to be thankful for.

Often, Christians were arrested but not actually executed, partly because the authorities were aware of the danger of creating martyrs. These Christians were known as 'confessors', because they had bravely confessed their faith in Christ and been willing to die if necessary; they were regarded as just one step below martyrs. These confessors enjoyed enormous respect from other Christians.

The relics

Christian veneration of the martyrs also reflected an attitude to the body that was quite at variance with the norm in antiquity. Then as now, death was something of a taboo; dead bodies were to be avoided. Most philosophers taught that the soul, the true self, was immortal and distinct from the body; a dead body was simply an empty vessel, worth nothing. But the Christians believed that the body would be raised again at the end of time. The martyrs – it was believed – had a holy power in their bodies. Some of the accounts of the martyrs drew attention to their physical power. Pionius, for example, is described as appearing handsome and youthful, like an athlete, even after being burned to death. Sanctus, one of the Lyons martyrs, was disfigured by the tortures one day until his entire body was one bruise – and the next day the same tortures healed him and he was restored to his original appearance. Stories such as these not only reflect a belief that miracles were possible where the martyrs were concerned, but indicate that the Christians believed the power of God was at work in the martyrs' very bodies.

This belief led the Christians to venerate the physical remains of the martyrs themselves. They would hang around at the place of execution – or return later – and take away whatever was left of the body. Sometimes, churches would pay the executioner to turn a blind eye to this. When the body itself was not available, any physical memento would do. When Cyprian of Carthage was beheaded in AD 258, the last thing he saw as the blindfold was tied over his eyes was the handkerchiefs laid out by other Christians on the ground in front of him. They were put there to soak up the blood, so that they could later be venerated as holy relics. The story of Saturus, a Christian mauled by beasts in the amphitheatre of Carthage together with Perpetua and Felicity, is especially remarkable. Saturus asked a nearby soldier for his ring, dipped it in his own blood, and handed it back so that the guard would have a relic of his own. Sometimes the authorities acted deliberately to prevent this sort of thing: the bodies of the Lyons martyrs were dismembered and guarded, before being burned and the ash thrown into the river, to prevent other Christians from rescuing the relics.

Some Christians seem to have owned relics and carried them around like lucky charms. We hear of one wealthy Christian in Carthage named Lucilla who owned the bone of a martyr, which she took to church and kissed before taking the Eucharist. More often, however, the relics were shared by the community. They might be kept in shrines in the church, or buried in chambers where Christians could go and venerate them. By far the most famous of these chambers were the catacombs under Rome. These systems of tunnels and caves were traditional burying places, especially for the poor, who could not afford proper plots in cemeteries. At first the Christians did the same, digging simple tunnels and putting the dead into unadorned stone niches, wrapped in white cloth, as Jesus had been when he was buried. By the third century AD, however, the Christian catacombs had become separate from the common ones, and far more extensive and elaborate. Most began with a stairway descending 40 feet (12 m) into the ground, leading to narrow, high tunnels lined with several layers of niches for the dead. These galleries might open on to more, sometimes going down several storeys; they contained literally millions of bodies and altogether extended for hundreds of miles, a remarkable achievement given that they were dug by the Christians themselves, by lamplight, carrying the soil to the surface in bags. The old romantic stories of Christians literally hiding out here, in fear of persecution, or conducting most of their services here, are probably not true. But the catacombs did feature special caves devoted to the martyrs who were buried there, and services of some kind were probably held there in memory of them.

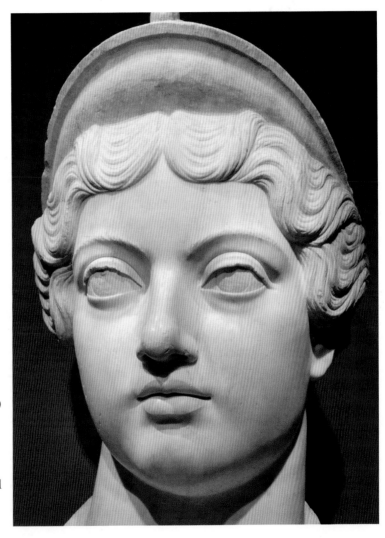

2nd-century AD marble bust of Lucilla, found in Carthage in 1845.

Boethius (c. AD 480–524) is seen to be visited by Philosophy in prison in this 11th-century illustration.

Christian Philosophy

As we saw in the last chapter, many intellectuals in the second and third centuries thought that Christianity was a stupid religion for the simple-minded. But a new breed of thinker was emerging who sought to answer this criticism – indeed, whose very existence was itself an eloquent answer. These were Christian philosophers, who believed that their religion offered answers to intellectual and spiritual problems that were every bit as sophisticated as pagan philosophy. Their efforts would result in the emergence of Christian philosophical theology, which would rapidly become as technical as the pagan philosophical schools it sought to rival.

The first Christians who tried to use contemporary philosophy creatively in a Christian context were those who wanted to present Christianity as an attractive option to pagans. These writers – of the second and early third centuries AD – are often called the 'apologists', from the old meaning of the word 'apology' as a defence or argument. In chapter 5 we saw the kinds of criticism that pagans brought against Christianity: that it was immoral, that Christians were unpatriotic, dangerous, and so on. The apologists tried to answer these criticisms.

The earliest apologists that we know of were Quadratus and Aristides of Athens, who in around AD 125 presented the emperor Hadrian with books they had written defending Christianity. Quadratus' book is lost. At least parts of Aristides' survive, incorporated into an early medieval story known as *Barlaam and Joasaph*. He seems to have devoted most of his energies to denouncing the errors of paganism and describing the virtuous lives lived by Christians.

However, new apologists soon appeared who took the argument further. These writers also tried to answer the charge that Christianity was a stupid religion, that it was a sort of debased version of philosophy. Indeed, they took the attack to their opponents. They argued that Christianity was actually the truest kind of philosophy. What the philosophers had perceived dimly, the Christians had had revealed to them by God himself. In their eyes, Christianity addressed precisely the same concerns as pagan philosophy and pagan religion, but it did so more successfully.

Justin Martyr

The first, and most important, of these apologists was Justin Martyr, who was born in Palestine in around AD 100 and grew up as a pagan. He became a Platonist philosopher and moved to Rome. According to his own testimony, however, he was inspired to read the Old Testament prophets after an encounter on the beach with a mysterious old man who insisted that they had taught the truth about God. Justin converted to Christianity, but he remained a philosopher – he always wore the distinctive cloak sported by professional philosophers – and regarded Christianity as another school of philosophy, the one that happened to be true.

In AD 155, Justin wrote his *First Apology*, addressed to the emperor Antoninus. In this he covered the same ground as Aristides, arguing that Christians were innocent of the charges laid against them. But Justin also offered arguments for the reasonableness and truth of Christianity. He pointed out that there were parallels between Christian doctrines and pagan ones. For example, Jesus was said to have done miracles, but so were many characters from traditional mythology. Christians believed in a judgment after death, but so did Plato. He concluded that it was unfair of pagan intellectuals to brand Christian doctrines as absurd when they believed similar things themselves.

Indeed, Justin believed that the pagans had got many things right. As a Platonist philosopher he venerated Plato above all, but he also believed that the truth could be found in other philosophers such as Socrates or Heraclitus, as well as in the poets such as Homer and Hesiod. He had two main explanations for this. The first was historical: the Old Testament was older than Plato and Homer, and they had read it and taken many of its ideas. This argument reflects the common belief in late antiquity that the older an idea is, the better. People liked to trace their beliefs as far back as possible, often identifying some shadowy figure of the past as a great sage who had been privy to special information.

Despite the common belief that Romans and Greeks were the only truly civilized people, and that everyone else were 'barbarians', these ancient sages were usually foreign – mysterious figures from the exotic east or south, such as Zoroaster or Hermes Trismegistus. In late antiquity, the orient – meaning the Middle East, Persia, and India – was often regarded as the home of the most profound religious and philosophical teachings.

In fact, many philosophers took it almost for granted that the great wisdom of the Greek philosophers and poets was itself ultimately derived from oriental peoples such as the Egyptians, the Indians, the Persians, and the Babylonians. Those who sought the truth often travelled to the East to find it. Both Clement of Alexandria and Plotinus are said to have done this – although perhaps this reflects the belief of later writers that great philosophers *should* have done so, rather than any journeys they may really have made.

In this context, it was perhaps only natural for Christians and Jews to identify characters from the Old Testament (all suitably ancient and exotically barbarian) as ancient sages. In Philo's works, Abraham and Moses both play this role; we are told that Plato based his account of the creation of the world in the *Timaeus* upon the biblical version in Genesis. The Christians agreed with this assessment and usually identified Moses (universally accepted as the author of the Pentateuch, including Genesis) as their great ancient sage. Justin, for one, insisted that Moses was older than Plato. As we saw in chapter 5, some pagans argued that Christian doctrines were a garbled version of pagan ones; that Jesus had simply repeated what Plato had already said better. Justin turned the argument on its head by making Plato simply the interpreter of Moses, which meant that he could accept Plato as a teacher of the truth, but a lesser one than Moses. Strikingly, some pagans seem to have accepted this argument. One philosopher named Numenius of Apamaea said that Plato was nothing but 'Moses speaking Greek' – a remarkable statement given that Numenius was a pagan, not a Christian or a Jew. Others, however, were unconvinced. For example, the second-century physician Galen compared Genesis to Plato and concluded that Plato was preferable, because he gave reasons for why things are the way they are, while Moses simply appeals to the will of God.

Justin's second explanation for the agreement of the pagans and the Christians was based upon the basic philosophical belief that the world is fundamentally rational. Many Platonists in Justin's day believed that below the highest God there was a lesser God, the world-soul, which actually ran the universe. The Stoics believed that the universe is run by the divine Reason – Logos – which is immanent throughout the world like fire. Justin approved of these ideas. He too spoke of a second God below the highest God, and he called it the Logos, the Reason of God. But, following the opening chapter of John's Gospel, he identified this Logos with Christ. Christ is thus the divine Reason, intimately associated with the supreme God and yet also distinct from him, and he is the explanation for the rationality of the world. It is through Christ that God created and maintains the universe, and it is through Christ that human beings are rational. The Stoics believed that the rational ability of each individual person is a fragment of the universal Reason of God, and Justin agreed with this. He spoke of the 'seed of the Logos' existing in all people. Whenever anyone acts or thinks rationally, he or she is actually following Christ, even without knowing it. This was how both the pagan philosophers and the Jewish prophets could speak truth about God despite not knowing Christ: they did know Christ, but were unaware of it. As Justin put it:

> I confess that I both boast and with all my strength strive to be found a Christian; not because the teachings of Plato are different from those of Christ, but because they are not in all respects similar. And neither are those of the others, Stoics, and poets, and historians. For each man spoke well in proportion to the share he had of the seed of the Logos, seeing what was related to it.[1]

Still, the seed of the Logos is not as impressive as the full Logos. As Justin sees it, Christians have received the full revelation of which that seen by the philosophers and poets is only a part. So there is fundamental agreement between paganism and Christianity, but Christianity is the real thing, the original truth, and paganism is a sort of blurry reflection of it.

Justin's *First Apology* seems to have made little impression upon the Roman authorities. He followed it up with a *Second Apology*, which restated the same ideas, and also a *Dialogue with Trypho*, an apologetic work aimed at Jews rather than pagans. Justin apparently wrote many other books intended for a Christian readership, but these have been lost. This is unfortunate, as it is difficult to reconstruct his theology properly from just these apologetic works alone. For example, his theology of the Logos appears only in passing; Justin makes occasional references to it but never gives a proper systematic treatment. We know that he thinks that Christ is the Logos, which he explains like this:

> We call him the Logos, because he carries tidings from the Father to men: but maintain that this power is indivisible and inseparable from the Father. It is just as we say that the light of the sun on earth is indivisible and inseparable from the sun in the heavens. When it sinks, the light sinks along with it. In the same way, we say, the Father, when he chooses, causes his power to spring forth, and when he chooses, he makes it return to himself.[2]

Later apologists

In AD 165, Justin was arrested – together with some companions – and tried for his Christian faith. He was beheaded, which is why he has always been known as 'Martyr' almost as a kind of surname. However, his ideas remained very much alive. A host of apologists appeared, all attempting to present Christianity as a school of philosophy, and all using the same basic idea of Christ as the divine and universal Logos. One was Tatian the Syrian, a former student of Justin's, whose *Oration to the Greeks* took a much more critical stance towards pagan philosophers than Justin had. For Tatian, the philosophers had failed to embody in their lives the moral ideals that Christians achieved every day. Another was Athenagoras of Athens, who was apparently a pagan philosopher who studied Christianity in order to attack it, like Celsus, but ended up converting to the religion instead. Finally, we must mention Theophilus, bishop of Antioch. His *To Autolycus* is written to a pagan friend, attempting to convince him of the truth of Christianity, much like Justin. But unlike Justin, Theophilus has a strong sense of both the Logos *and* the Holy Spirit as divine agents. Indeed, he is the first Christian writer to use the word 'Trinity' to refer to all three of them. This was an important step from the Logos theology of the second century towards the Trinitarianism of the third and fourth.

The work of the apologists often seems rather strange to readers familiar with later Christian literature. In it, Christianity comes across as little more than a combination of monotheism and the doctrine of the future resurrection of all humanity. Those, at least, are the main doctrines these writers focus on. Christians themselves are presented as incredibly virtuous monotheists, living up to pagan ideals even better than the pagans. There is surprisingly little attempt to deal with distinctively Christian doctrines other than the resurrection, or with any distinctively

Christian understanding of how to live a moral life. Jesus, in particular, is conspicuous by his absence. We hear a lot about the Logos, and its role in mediating between God and the world, but very little about the incarnation. It is as if the Logos is *already* a mediator, even before it becomes a human being. Both Tatian and Athenagoras are capable of writing entire defences of Christianity without once mentioning the names 'Jesus' or 'Christ'. To some degree, this must be explained by the fact that they were writing for non-Christian audiences and trying to find common ground with their readers. Tatian certainly knew all about Jesus: he wrote a book called the *Diatessaron*, a harmony of all four canonical Gospel accounts into a single story of Jesus' life. This proved so popular in the Syriac-speaking churches that it displaced the canonical Gospels there for some centuries. Stranger, however, is the case of Marcus Minucius Felix, one of the first Christians to write in Latin, who wrote an apology called the *Octavius* at the end of the second century. In one passage, he denies that Christians worship a crucified criminal at all – a passage that has puzzled readers ever since.

A 19th-century reconstruction of Alexandria, showing
Cleopatra's Needle.

But scholars disagree over how to interpret such passages. Is Justin taking this idea from Greek philosophy? Or is he taking it from the Wisdom literature of the Bible, where the divine Wisdom is also presented as a semi-independent entity? Had Justin read Philo? Scholars are uncertain.

Clement of Alexandria

We know little of Clement's life. He was apparently born to a pagan family in the middle of the second century AD, perhaps in Athens, but later converted to Christianity, travelled around the empire studying various philosophies, and eventually settled in Alexandria, where he became a student of Pantaenus, the first non-gnostic Christian philosopher in the city. In around AD 200, he took over the leadership of Pantaenus' school, but not long afterwards he fled from persecution there. He had apparently died by AD 215, but we do not know how or where.

Like Justin, Clement regarded himself as a philosopher all his life: he was simply a philosopher who taught the Christian philosophy. In fact, more than any other Christian figure of this period, Clement was extremely enthusiastic about philosophy in general. He believed that the pagan philosophers had come close to the truth – Plato being the best of them all – and he criticized other Christians who thought philosophy to be the work of the devil. Clement believed that God had inspired the pagan philosophers just as he had inspired the Jewish prophets, and for the same reason – to prepare the ground for the coming of Christianity. Like Justin, he believed that the philosophers got their best ideas from reading the Old Testament. Clement's works are packed full of quotations not only from philosophers but from all kinds of pagan sources, such as Homer and other poets; it is as if he were desperate to refute the popular image of Christians as uneducated idiots. His interests were not confined to the classical tradition, either; he is the first western author to mention the Buddha, although he says disappointingly little about him.

Again like Justin, Clement identifies Christ with God's Logos or Reason. It is through this Logos that God creates and runs the world. Clement also reproduces the Platonist idea that God transcends human understanding, so that he can be known only as what he is not rather than what he is. He argues that we know God by the method of abstraction, a method which is also found in pagan philosophers of the period, such as Alcinous or Maximus of Tyre. Think of an ordinary physical object, and then mentally remove (or 'abstract') from it all the qualities that make it physical, and you end up with the notion of pure existence. That is what God is – he is quite unlike anything physical. But unlike the pagan philosophers, Clement believes that one can know this only through Christ, the Logos. There is a personal, experiential element to knowing God; Clement is the first Christian to speak of 'the vision of God', a notion that would become central to later mysticism.

Clement calls the enlightened Christian a 'gnostic'. But unlike those we call gnostics (whom we shall look at in chapter 7), Clement does not believe in any kind of esoteric knowledge which is passed down secretly and made available to only a few. Rather, it is publicly available in the teachings of the church and, above all, in the Bible. Yet not everyone can understand the Bible properly. Most Christians just read it and absorb the obvious sense of the words. But there is a deeper, spiritual sense, which must be gleaned from it by the use of allegory. In theory anyone can do this, but in practice only a few do. These are the 'gnostics' in Clement's sense of the word, and they are at the second stage of a three-stage spiritual journey. This journey begins with faith, progresses to 'gnosis', and finally reaches love – but all three stages are characterized as knowledge of some kind. 'Faith' is when you know the basic teachings of Christianity. 'Knowledge' is real understanding of those teachings. And 'love' is direct, personal knowledge of God.

Clement tried to reflect this spiritual journey in his own writing. He wrote three major works: the *Exhortation to the Greeks*, *The Instructor*, and the *Stromateis*. The *Exhortation* is an apology similar to those of Justin Martyr and his imitators, so it is a call to faith. *The Instructor* sets out Clement's vision of the ideal Christian lifestyle, as a prerequisite for the spiritual journey. The *Stromateis* – literally 'patchwork' or 'miscellanies' – tackles a vast range of subjects in no apparent order. It is here that we find Clement's most important ideas, but he does not make things easy for the reader: it is up to us to use our powers of spiritual discernment to read between the lines. The advanced Christian philosophy is there, but we must work hard to get at it – just as we must when reading the Bible itself. So Clement's work is designed not simply as instructions for the 'gnostic' but as training: by reading it we learn how to think spiritually for ourselves.

Christian scholar, Origen (c. AD 185–254).

Origen

In the last chapter we met Celsus, the second-century pagan philosopher who wrote a book attacking the Christians as feeble-minded fools who mangled philosophical doctrines to suit themselves and preyed upon the vulnerable. It is possible that he wrote partly as a response to Justin Martyr. He had probably died before he had a chance to read anything by Clement of Alexandria, even assuming that he would have wanted to. But a century after he wrote his book, it was finally answered by a man whose entire life and career was itself a sort of response to Celsus. That man was Origen 'Adamantios', the most brilliant and influential Christian writer of the pre-Constantinian era.

Origen's life

Despite his pagan name (it means 'born of Horus'), Origen was born to Christian parents in Alexandria in around AD 185. He studied under a number of teachers in Alexandria, probably including Clement and also Ammonias Sacchas, a mysterious philosopher who also taught Plotinus.

However, when Origen was a teenager, his father was executed for his faith and Origen had to support the family by teaching. But before the age of twenty he replaced Clement as head of the Christian school in Alexandria, and promptly renounced all studies of pagan philosophy and literature. He sold his books and took up an extremely ascetic lifestyle, sleeping on the floor; it was for this reason that he acquired the nickname Adamantios – 'unbreakable' – a word which also gives us the English words 'adamant' and 'diamond'. It is during this stage of his life that he is supposed to have read Matthew 19:12 – where Jesus talks about 'eunuchs who have made themselves eunuchs for the sake of the kingdom of heaven' – and unwisely interpreted this as a direct command. In fact the evidence is rather conflicting. Self-castration as an ascetic act was uncommon, but by no means unknown among more fervent Christians at this time; it was frowned upon by the church, though, and eunuchs were not allowed to become priests. The only hint in Origen's surviving writings comes in his commentary on Matthew. When he deals with the fateful verse, he tells his readers that some people take the verse literally, but this is a very bad idea. This is sometimes taken as evidence that Origen himself had never taken it literally – although one might equally think it evidence that he *had*!

Despite giving up his secular studies, Origen continued his theological ones and soon became one of the most prominent Christian scholars in the world. He attended a lecture given by Hippolytus of Rome – at that time a far more famous figure – and the great man not only recognized him in the audience but pointed him out and applauded him.

A turning point in Origen's career came when he converted a wealthy man named Ambrosius from gnosticism to mainstream Christianity, and Ambrosius showed his gratitude by funding Origen's work. He paid for seven secretaries to write down in shorthand everything Origen said; another seven to write out the notes longhand so that Origen could check them over (something he loathed doing); and another seven to copy out the final versions in calligraphy. As a result, Origen became enormously prolific. A century later Epiphanius of Salamis would estimate his output at 6,000 volumes; Jerome reckoned it at the more modest but still incredible 2,000. Eight hundred actual titles are known to us now. These works included immense commentaries on books of the Bible, devotional treatises, dogmatic works, and letters. Many were left incomplete; Origen seems to have been one of those people who begin a new and very ambitious project with great enthusiasm but later get tired of it. His commentary on John's Gospel, for example, runs into at least thirty-two volumes but only covers two-thirds of the Gospel. He also had to deal with requests from fans and supporters, especially Ambrosius; it was Ambrosius who came across Celsus' *True Doctrine* and commissioned Origen to write an eight-volume refutation of it.

Like Philo and Clement before him, Origen believed firmly that the truth was to be found in the letter of Scripture, and he recognized that if this was so then it was essential to establish what that letter was. Origen collected several different Greek translations of the Old Testament and copied them out next to the original Hebrew. Like all Christians of this period, Origen believed that the inspired text was not the original Hebrew but the Septuagint Greek translation, and his aim in comparing these various versions was to establish the true text of the Septuagint. He saw, however, that study of the Hebrew original might help with this, and to this end he learned the Hebrew language and consulted Jewish rabbis. The result was the *Hexapla*, so called because it combined six versions of the Old Testament in parallel columns (more, for some books); a study Bible so immense that in those days of papyrus scrolls it occupied a whole room.

The *Hexapla* was housed in Caesarea in Palestine, where Origen relocated in the 230s after falling out with the bishop of Alexandria, Demetrius. One of Origen's books, *On First Principles*, had been leaked to the public – something that annoyed Origen since it had been written only for private circulation. This book was the first attempt at systematic Christian theology ever written. In it, Origen sought to provide a philosophically rigorous overview of the Christian faith, taking in the nature of God, the Trinity, the person and work of Christ, the role of the church and the function of Scripture. Some passages, however, caused outrage, especially one where Origen apparently argued that the devil might ultimately be saved. Unable to satisfy the concerns of either Demetrius or his successor at Alexandria, Heraclas (a former student of Origen's who seems to have had no love for his former master), Origen remained in Caesarea. He also seems to have worked as a sort of spiritual troubleshooter, being called in to help deal with doctrinal disputes – even though he was only a priest, not a bishop. The record of one such dispute exists – the *Dialogue with Heraclides*, a transcript of a meeting at which Origen discusses the nature of the soul with a bishop suspected of heresy before taking questions on related matters from the other bishops present. The questions he is asked are quite revealing of the sorts of problems that worried intelligent, but not philosophically trained, Christians of the time. They include: 'If the body dies and is placed in a tomb, how will the spirit find it again and how will the dead be raised?' 'Is the soul the blood?' 'Is the soul immortal?'

In AD 250, the Decian persecution broke out, and Origen was arrested and tortured for several days. The 'unbreakable' ascetic held out until finally they released him rather than make him a martyr. But that was the end of Origen's career; he seems to have never recovered his health or his spirit. He wrote nothing more, and he died in obscurity in Tyre in AD 254. Perhaps it was being released, rather than the torture itself, that crushed the old man's spirit: he had always shared the common Christian veneration of martyrdom and perhaps hoped to emulate his father's death.

Origen's philosophy

Perhaps the central notion in Origen's thought, and the one which shows most clearly his Platonist heritage, is the distinction between the physical and the spiritual. Origen agrees with pagan Platonists that there exists a spiritual realm above and beyond the physical one, and that this spiritual realm is fundamentally intellectual and comprehensible – indeed, the physical world is itself rational because it is a reflection of that spiritual realm. He agrees that there is a God who is a supreme mind, and that the human mind is basically the same sort of thing as this God. In fact, Origen extends the physical/spiritual distinction to every aspect of the human person. It is not simply that we have physical bodies and spiritual minds – there is a spiritual body too, a whole spiritual person, corresponding to the physical one, with spiritual arms and legs and spiritual senses. It is because we have these spiritual senses that we can come to know God. The Bible, too, is both physical and spiritual. There is an 'obvious' meaning to every text (usually, although not always, a literal meaning); but there is also a 'spiritual' meaning, which must be extracted through the use of allegory. In *On First Principles*, Origen famously argues that Scripture has a body, a soul, and a spirit, just as human beings do, and he suggests that each text has three meanings to correspond to them. But in practice, like most exegetes of the period such as Clement, he offers only two interpretations of most texts – an 'obvious' one and an 'allegorical' one.

Despite this, Origen does not praise pagan philosophy as Clement did. Clement was keen to find common ground with pagan philosophers; Origen prefers to find differences. This was a man who, at an impressionable age, had seen his father killed by a pagan state for his Christian faith, and who sometimes wished to see the persecutions return so that younger, more carefree Christians could be tested as his father had been. He agrees with Clement and Justin that philosophers such as Plato had grasped some parts of the truth, but not that this makes them Christians before the fact. On the contrary, it just makes them more blameworthy for not realizing the rest of the truth.

Origen's theology is at once less rationalist, and more so, than that of the pagan philosophers he criticized. He stresses that knowledge of God can come only through acquaintance with Christ, not through the exercising of human rational powers. It must be given by grace. But like Justin and Clement, he characterizes Christ as God's Logos, his Reason. It was common among philosophers of this time to emphasize the unknowability of God, a tendency we see reflected in Clement. Origen largely rejects this view. For him, God is intrinsically quite knowable. He states that in practice we generally cannot know him, but this is simply because God is so great and our minds so small; it is like being dazzled by a bright light, so that we effectively cannot see it. There is too much information, not too little.

Origen believes that, originally, all created souls had perfect knowledge of God. They were united to God perfectly and understood him perfectly. But for some reason, the souls fell away; Origen is prepared to entertain the supposition that perhaps they actually got bored with God! The story of the fall of Adam and Eve in Genesis is an allegory of this great event. The souls fell to varying degrees, and God created the physical world for them to become incarnate in. Those that fell far became demons, those that fell only a bit became angels, and those in between became human beings. For Origen, the physical world is a sort of arena created by God to allow these souls to struggle and overcome problems, to grow morally, and gradually to come closer to God. This may take many lifetimes. The Stoics believed that when the world ends, another world will begin, which will be identical to the old world, and we will all live our lives again in exactly the same way. In fact there is an infinite succession of these identical worlds. Origen also believes that there will be a new world after this one, and that we will live in it once again, but that it will be different: each individual's place in life will be determined by how well they did the last time. This will continue for a vast number of worlds, but eventually everyone will find their way back to God: evil and sin are inherently limited and unsatisfying. In Origen's eyes, punishment – both in the physical world and after death – is inflicted only as a sort of extreme cure, like an unpleasant medicine or surgery. It can only be temporary. It is uncertain whether Origen really taught explicitly that all souls – even those of demons – would eventually find their way back to God, but the logic of his theology certainly seems to suggest it. Origen takes it as a fundamental axiom that the end must be like the beginning. The universe began with all created souls existing in perfect union with God; it must therefore end like that too.

This 17th-century painting by an unknown artist shows Teresa of Avila (1515–82), a Carmelite nun and mystic, sheltering a community of Carmelite nuns under her cloak.

The spiritual life

The process of coming closer to God is one of learning. The mind is the part of us most like God; it is therefore through the use of the mind that we come close to him, above all by studying the Bible and seeking to understand it. Origen argues that spiritual progression comes in three stages, which reflect the three books of the Old Testament attributed to Solomon. The book of Proverbs shows us how to lead a good life. When we have mastered that, the book of Ecclesiastes shows us how to study the world around us, both the seen and the unseen objects of science and philosophy. And finally, the book called the Song of Songs describes how we learn of God himself. Origen's commentary on Song of Songs is one of his most famous and remarkable works, the first real Christian mystical treatise. He takes the Song of Songs to be an allegory of two things: Christ's relationship with the church, and his relationship with the soul of the individual Christian. On the latter (and dominant) interpretation, the character of the Bridegroom in the book represents Christ, and the Bride is the soul. Origen explains that the erotic imagery in this poem should not be taken literally (God is not really male, and the soul is not really female), but it is still appropriate because erotic love in the physical person is the closest analogy there is to the love of God in the spiritual person. Just as, in physical love, we greet a lover with a kiss, so too Christ greets the soul with a kiss when he grants it knowledge of God.

In two famous passages, Origen expands upon the experience of God. In the first, he offers his thoughts on the passage of Song of Songs that speaks of a wound of love:

> *If there is anyone anywhere who has at some time burned with this faithful love of the Word of God; if there is anyone who has received the sweet wound of him who is the chosen dart, as the prophet says; if there is anyone who has been pierced with the loveworthy spear of his knowledge, so that he yearns and longs for him by day and night, can speak of nought but him, would hear of nought but him, can think of nothing else, and is disposed to no desire nor longing nor yet hope, except for him alone – if such there be, that soul then says in truth: 'I have been wounded by love.'*[3]

This erotically charged language would be enormously influential on later Christian mystics, such as the sixteenth-century Teresa of Avila. Yet Origen also speaks of what happens when the soul cannot find Christ:

> *The Bride then beholds the Bridegroom; and he, as soon as she has seen him, goes away. He does this frequently throughout the Song; and that is something nobody can understand who has not suffered it himself. God is my witness that I have often perceived the Bridegroom drawing near me and being most intently present with me; then suddenly he has withdrawn and I could not find him, though I sought to do so. I long, therefore, for him to come again, and sometimes he does so. Then, when he has appeared and I lay hold of him, he slips away once more; and, when he has so slipped away, my search for him begins anew.*[4]

Origen's work was a watershed in intellectual history. It was the first real attempt to use ideas and categories drawn from contemporary philosophy to set out a systematic Christian theology. It puzzled pagan philosophers; the fifth-century Neoplatonist Proclus commented on how strange it was that a man as brilliant as Origen should have got mixed up with Christian nonsense. And it inspired later generations of Christians to continue the attempt. But Origen had tried to pull the rug from under the feet of philosophy; he had tried to use the philosophers' own tricks against them. He agreed that Plato said many profound things – but that just showed how guilty Plato was in God's eyes, because he saw the truth yet remained a pagan. He agreed that there was a spiritual realm of beauty and intellect – but insisted that it could be found only through study of the Bible, granted by the direct inspiration of Christ. Later Christian philosophers would not, as a rule, share his antagonism to pagan philosophy. Raised in a Christian empire, never knowing the fear of persecution, they would treat classical philosophy and the Christian religion as parts of an organic and mutually supporting whole.

Heresy and Orthodoxy

In the third century AD, a Christian could travel from Syria to Britain and find communities recognizably the same as his own all the way, performing the same rites with much the same words. But he could also find plenty of people who would disagree with him on fundamental matters, even while professing the same religion. Different groups and individuals had different understandings of the Christian message. But how much disagreement was acceptable? This period saw the rise of the notion of orthodoxy and heresy, as Christians tried to answer that question and come to some kind of agreement about what they believed. 'Orthodoxy' means the set of beliefs which came to be standard – those that the church agreed were true. 'Heresy' means beliefs which disagreed with orthodoxy in some way. And the emergence of the notions of 'orthodoxy' and of 'heresy' also involved the emergence of theories about these beliefs and their origins.

In this mosaic on a triumphal arch dated c. AD 579–90, Christ sits on a globe between the apostles Peter and Paul. Lawrence and Pope Pelagius are on the left, and Stephanus and Hippolytus are on the right.

The emergence of orthodoxy

There are two points to make at the outset here. The first is that Christians had been disagreeing with one another since New Testament times; the new element here was the emergence of explicit criteria for telling which doctrines were true and which were not. Paul attacked his opponents by insisting that they *were* wrong; theologians such as Tertullian thought they could show *why* their opponents *must*, in principle, be wrong. They were not simply identifying what was orthodoxy and what was heresy – they were explaining the difference.

The second point is that orthodoxy and heresy were usually defined against each other. In fact, events normally followed a fairly standard pattern. First, there would be no consensus about a particular subject, often because no one had thought about it much. Then someone would come up with a definite view on the matter. Others would disagree with him, and a dispute would begin. The dispute would end with one party victorious, as everyone came to agree that their opponents were wrong – although this might be quite an informal and lengthy process, since no formal mechanisms for deciding such disputes yet existed. The victorious party would declare their view to be orthodoxy, and their opponents' view to be heresy. Those opponents would generally be given a label, often derived from the person identified as the 'originator' of the heresy; thus we hear of 'Valentinians' from Valentinus, 'Arians' from Arius, and so on. Such labels helped to demarcate, in the minds of the 'orthodox' and their readers or listeners, between themselves and the 'heretics'. They made the 'heretics' into outsiders, the followers of some new-fangled nonsense that had recently been invented by a false prophet. But they usually oversimplify the situation dangerously. For one thing, they often ignore the fact that the 'heretics' lumped together in this way might be quite varied among themselves. And for another, it ignores (indeed, deliberately obscures) the fact that the supposed founder of the heresy – the 'heresiarch' – was not necessarily inventing some new perversion of the true faith, but simply articulating something that many people had already believed for a long time. And before that point there might have been no consensus on the matter at all.

All of this means that it is often anachronistic to refer to 'the orthodox party', or 'the orthodox doctrine', during the period when the doctrine in question had not yet been settled. We can, perhaps, apply the term to those who held what would later become recognized as the orthodox doctrine. And sometimes we can talk of a 'mainstream' view, which most people believed but which had not yet been formally defined as orthodox. For example, most major theologians of the third century held that Christ was divine, but it was not until the fourth century that this was officially defined and explained. On other occasions, however, what would become the orthodox view was actually held by only a minority to begin with. An example of this is the doctrine of Christ's human soul. Until the fourth century, most theologians did not teach that Christ had a human soul, and at least some thought that he had none at all; only Origen was clear that he did. But in the fourth and fifth centuries it became a matter of dispute after one theologian, Apollonarius of Laodicea, argued that Christ definitely had no human soul, and the church eventually decided that he had been wrong and Christ definitely had had one. The minority view had become orthodoxy.

Variant Christianities

To categorize certain groups simply as 'heretics' or their views as 'heresies' is usually a simplification, and often an anachronism, for the reasons discussed above, not to mention unobjectively pejorative. 'Variant' is perhaps a more neutral term, although again that might suggest that these groups consciously deviated from a pre-existent standard, which was usually not the case.

Modalism

The second and third centuries saw a huge variety in opinions among Christians about what would eventually be known as the doctrine of the Trinity. We saw in the previous chapter how the second-century apologists identified Jesus with the Logos or divine Reason, by which God created and runs the universe. This way of speaking became quite common among subsequent Christian theologians, including Hippolytus of Rome, one of the leading Christians in that city at the beginning of the third century AD. For these theologians, to call Jesus the Logos was to say something about the role he plays in the relationship between God and the created universe. Increasingly, however, the term came to have connotations of the relation between Jesus and the Father. Theologians were less interested in the relationship between God and the world and more interested in the relationship between the Father and the Son, or the Logos. What did it mean to say that Jesus was God's Reason? We can see this process beginning in Hippolytus, who stressed the distinctness of the Father on the one hand and the Logos on the other to such an extent that the bishop of Rome, Callistus, accused him of ditheism, that is, belief in two different gods.

Hippolytus, for his part, reacted by accusing Callistus of the opposite error, modalism. Theologically, this word normally means the claim that the Father and the Son (and the Holy Spirit) are identical with one another in every way. They are actually the same person, operating under different names, just as Clark Kent is the same person as Superman. The first person to have explicitly stated and defended modalism seems to have been Noetus, who came from

Smyrna and was active in Rome in around AD 200. He was brought before a tribunal of some kind in the Roman church, presided over by the presbyters. He asked them, rather innocently, 'What harm am I doing by glorifying Christ?', but the presbyters were unconvinced and expelled him from the church. He founded a church of his own but died soon after. His cause was taken up a decade or two later by Sabellius, about whom we know even less, except that he was the most prominent and famous modalist of the period. In fact, despite our almost complete ignorance of who Sabellius was and what he said, modalism is often known as 'Sabellianism' after him.

The fact that the Roman church could be divided to such a degree, with opinions varying from those of Hippolytus on the one hand to Noetus on the other, with Callistus perhaps somewhere in the middle, shows how little consensus there was at this time over questions such as these. Christians had not yet agreed on what kind of language was appropriate for talking about what would later be known as the Trinity. Indeed, the term 'Trinity' itself was only now beginning to be used (the Greek word was first used by Theophilus of Antioch, and the Latin by Tertullian). By the middle of the third century, however, most Christians seem to have agreed at least that modalism was unacceptable.

Marcionism

Modalism was a *belief*, or set of beliefs, rather than an organization. We do not hear of a Sabellian church structure set up as an alternative to the mainstream church. In traditional terminology, this means that modalism was a heresy but not a schism. Other groups during this period, however, did set up rival organizations. One of the most prominent of these was the Marcionite church.

Marcion of Sinope was one of the major figures of second-century Christianity. He was born in Pontus on the Black Sea coast and moved to Rome in around AD 140, where he taught his distinctive doctrines. According to Marcion, the God of the Old Testament was evil, and a different entity from the God of the New Testament. He believed that salvation involved turning away from the creator God and embracing instead the God of love preached by Jesus. This doctrine was very similar to that of many of the gnostics. But scholars are uncertain whether Marcion should be considered a gnostic or not. He seems not to have taught that the physical world is intrinsically evil, for example, or that he possessed any special 'secret teaching' unavailable to the majority of Christians. Instead, his belief in two Gods seems to have come from his study of the Bible: in the Old Testament, God is portrayed as doing things which seem immoral, such as ordering the deaths of many people. Marcion concluded that this must be a different entity from the loving God of Jesus.

Marcion therefore sought to remove all Jewish elements from

Christianity altogether. He argued that Christians should have nothing to do with the Old Testament. As for the New Testament, the church had not yet settled on which books should be considered canonical, and different groups used somewhat different collections; but Marcion's canon was considerably more spartan than most. He rejected all of the Gospels except for a version of Luke's, which he edited to remove the pro-Jewish elements; and he rejected all of the letters apart from Paul's, which he also edited in the same way.

After only a few years at Rome, Marcion was expelled by the Christian community there and returned to Asia Minor. But he was no isolated figure of scorn. On the contrary, he had many followers; perhaps many were attracted by his reputation as a holy man, since he was renowned for living an ascetic lifestyle. Marcion was also independently wealthy, and he seems to have used his own resources to set up churches throughout Asia Minor as rivals to the mainstream churches. In fact, the Marcionite churches were quite widespread, and they continued to exist for a long time after his death despite the condemnation of his ideas in Rome. We still hear of them in the fourth century, and it is quite possible that they lingered for longer and helped to influence later movements.

Montanism

Another splinter group within the wider Christian movement, which proved just as resilient as Marcionism, was Montanism. Like many of these names, 'Montanism' was only used by its opponents, and then only in the fourth century and afterwards. But the name 'Montanism' has stuck, even when referring to its early stages.

Montanus, the man after whom the movement's opponents named it, began preaching in Phrygia, in what is now Turkey, in the middle of the second century AD. Nothing is known of his background. His preaching was remarkable and striking: he spoke as one possessed, with odd ecstatic exclamations, and he drew great crowds. Precisely *what* he taught is uncertain, and it may be that Montanus' teaching did not contain any doctrinal elements that most Christians would have objected to. But what alarmed many at the time was his style of teaching, and also his organizational ability, as he gathered a large group of followers. Foremost among these followers were two women named Priscilla and Maximilla, who also spoke in a frenzied, ecstatic way, issuing what their followers believed to be divine prophecies. Montanus, Priscilla, and Maximilla were collectively known as the Prophets, or the Three, and the movement called itself the Prophecy or the New Prophecy. Montanus died before the others, although we do not know exactly when, and Priscilla and Maximilla continued as the 'main' prophets of the movement.

We saw in chapter 3 that 'prophets', both male and female, were a major feature of some churches in the first century, and that evidence from the book of Revelation indicates that this may have been especially true of the churches in Asia Minor at the end of the first century. It is perhaps unsurprising to find a dynamic Christian movement centred on particularly charismatic prophets emerging a few decades later in nearby Phrygia. But the prophetic ministry in general seems to have been dwindling during this period, to the extent that the New Prophecy could seem remarkable to contemporaries. According to John's Gospel, Jesus had promised his followers that they would be sent the Paraclete – the Holy Spirit – and the followers of the New Prophecy revered the Three as the spokespeople of the Paraclete, giving new revelation to his people. Two particular areas that the teaching of the Three is often thought to have focused on are ethics and eschatology. The New Prophecy taught quite a strict system of morality, even by normal Christian standards of the day, with particular emphasis on fasting and sexual abstinence. And it is quite likely that the Three had much to say about the return of Christ, perhaps telling their hearers that this event was coming soon.

The followers of the New Prophecy congregated in the towns of Pepuza and Tymion, which they called 'Jerusalem'. They had many enthusiastic missionaries, and despite condemnation by Apollinarius, bishop of nearby Hieropolis, the movement spread first throughout Asia Minor and then throughout much of the rest of the empire, especially Rome, Gaul, and Africa.

The Three were not the only Montanist prophets, and new ones emerged after their deaths to continue their teachings. There continued to be many women among these prophets. A subgroup of the Montanists, known as the Quintillianists, were named after one of them. They are said to have ordained women as priests and bishops, perhaps basing their practices on the claim in Galatians 3:28 that in Christ there is no male or female. But there is evidence that other Montanist groups did the same thing. One leading prophet – possibly Quintilla or Priscilla – had a famous vision of Christ in female form, and this may well have been a partial inspiration for the practice of female ordination. However, despite the fact that women were especially prominent in Montanism, there is no evidence that they were *more* important than men or that most of their leaders were female. It should also be remembered that at least some non-Montanist churches had female deacons. We should therefore avoid the temptation, to which some commentators have succumbed, to contrast the patriarchal orthodox churches with the feminist Montanist ones. The reality was much more complex.

But they came under increasing attack from other Christians. The main charge directed against the Montanists was that of false prophecy: the prophecies of the Three, and of their later heirs, were not true prophecies, because they were delivered in an unchristian fashion. The dramatic, ecstatic preaching of the prophets was felt to have more in common with pagan prophecy than with anything in the Bible. And the reverence which the movement's members felt for these prophecies – which included writing them down and compiling them into books – was considered excessive. Christians were at this time developing the notion that the beliefs of the church were handed down in a 'rule of faith' that went back to Christ and the apostles, and which was contained in the public preaching of the churches and, in written form, in the writings that would become the New Testament. The Montanists' use of new texts, containing new teachings, violated this principle.

By the fourth century, Montanism seems to have been waning. Like other variant forms of Christianity, its terminal decline coincided with the Christianizing of the Roman empire and the attempts by successive emperors to impose uniformity of practice and belief upon all Christians. By the middle of the fifth century it had largely disappeared.

Gnosticism

Probably the most famous and widespread 'variant' form of Christianity during the second and third centuries AD was gnosticism. Until the twentieth century, our knowledge of the gnostics – like our knowledge of most of the heretical groups mentioned above – depended entirely upon hostile reports by orthodox authors. That changed when a number of texts by the gnostics themselves were discovered, above all the famous Nag Hammadi codices in 1945. Nevertheless, our knowledge is still very patchy. Scholars disagree over who wrote many of these texts and when. One thing is certain: gnosticism was not a single, easily identified movement like the Marcionite church or the Montanists. It was a rather vague movement, or tendency, that took many forms. It is often unclear if a particular text or individual should be considered 'gnostic' at all. In the end, such words are just labels. It is more important to focus on what that text or individual actually taught, and why, rather than whether one label for that teaching is better than another.

It is perhaps surprising to learn that neither the gnostic texts themselves nor their orthodox opponents ever talk about 'gnosticism'; that word was coined in the seventeenth century. They do, however, talk about *gnosis* ('knowledge'), something to be acquired, and *gnostikoi*, ('gnostics', or 'knowers'), people who have

The Nag Hammadi Codices, discovered in Egypt in 1945.

acquired it or are in the process of doing so. Some people called themselves 'gnostics'. But the term seems to have meant different things to different people. For example, Clement of Alexandria – who was not a 'gnostic' in the usual sense of the word, and who attacked the gnostics in his works – talked frequently of 'gnosis' and described the ideal of the 'Christian gnostic'. For him, to be a 'gnostic' simply meant to be enlightened in some important way, and it was something highly desirable. We could perhaps draw a comparison with the word 'democrat' in the United States. Most Americans would regard themselves as 'democrats' in the sense of supporting democracy, and believe such a stance to be a good one; but only some would regard themselves as 'Democrats' in the sense of supporting the Democratic Party. Similarly, for an Alexandrian Christian such as Clement, to be a 'gnostic' (in one sense) might be an almost unquestionably desirable ideal, shared by most people, even while the same term was used by others in a more restricted, technical sense. Little wonder that Clement so hated these 'so-called gnostics' (as Irenaeus called them), who had effectively appropriated the term for their own warped use.

The twentieth-century philosopher Hans Jonas, who sought to address gnosticism as a living religious tendency, believed that the whole movement revolved around the single notion of 'alienation': the feeling that one is somehow at odds with both society and with the visible world, that one belongs in – but has been abandoned by – a higher, spiritual realm. This seems to be a common idea throughout the texts that we can (perhaps tentatively) identify as 'gnostic'. Gnostics typically regarded the world around them as evil or wrong in some way. Many believed that physical matter itself was intrinsically evil. On this view, the physical world is a sort of prison. The spirit is completely unlike the body, and the spirit yearns to escape from its bodily prison. The focus of the gnostic was therefore upon the spiritual realm, the gnostic's true home. Some gnostics believed that only a few human beings even had a spiritual element to them at all. Other people, they thought, might have souls, but they conceived of these souls as basically akin to the physical stuff in which they were embodied. There is a real 'them and us' feel to the texts that teach ideas such as these. These people considered themselves outsiders, different from the rest of society, different even from the natural world around them.

There were two particularly important features associated with this worldview. The first was mythology. If the world is basically bad or wrong, but the spirit (or at least, for a gnostic, his or her spirit) is good, how did this situation come about? Many gnostics developed elaborate mythological explanations for this. Some groups, notably the Sethians and Valentinians, believed that the divine realm contained many different divine beings, known as Aeons ('eternals'), arranged in a sort of hierarchy from the unknowable

Gnostic movements

The origins of gnosticism are uncertain and much debated. Suffice to say that scholars remain unable to agree whether it had its roots in Judaism, in Greek philosophy, in Eastern religions such as Zoroastrianism, or in all or none of these. In the nineteenth century, some scholars believed that gnosticism was effectively a religion in its own right, which perhaps pre-dated Christianity, and later became entangled with it. Today, it is more usual to regard gnosticism as a tendency or movement that emerged *within* Christianity. It is possible that there were gnostics who did not regard themselves as Christians at all, but there is no firm evidence for this.

Some of the most important Christian teachers of the second century are thought to have been gnostics. One of the earliest was Basilides, who was teaching in Alexandria in the 130s and who wrote a huge amount, including a Gospel and a commentary on his own Gospel. Very little remains of Basilides' writings, and what there is does not appear to be very gnostic at all. It may be that Basilides himself was not a gnostic, and his followers later combined his ideas with gnostic ones.

Even more important was Valentinus. This remarkable man has a good claim to be the first systematic Christian philosopher. Only the outlines of his life are known. He was born at Phrebonis, on the delta of the Nile, probably at the start of the second century AD, and spent many years in Alexandria, where he became famous as a teacher. In the middle of the century he moved to Rome, where he spent fifteen years. He must have been one of the most prominent figures in the Roman church: we are told that he expected to be made bishop of the city, but his ambition was thwarted. As usual, however, we must take these negative accounts of his character with a pinch of salt. We are also told that he was eventually forced out of Rome

for his heretical views and died in Cyprus. He certainly did attract considerable opposition by some in Rome – notably Justin Martyr and, later, Hippolytus – although whether they really managed to drive him out is uncertain. Valentinus apparently wrote several works, which are mostly lost or exist only in fragment form, quoted by other writers. However, one of the most important Valentinian writings – *The Gospel of Truth*, one of the Nag Hammadi texts, and actually a sermon rather than a Gospel – is probably by him. It seems to represent an early form of Valentinianism and is a remarkably powerful work. It therefore seems reasonable to attribute it to the famously eloquent Valentinus himself, in which case it is that rarest of texts, a complete theological work from the pen of a major figure later regarded as a heretic.

Valentinus and his followers were part of the mainstream church and attended the normal services, but they also held meetings of their own. They seem to have considered themselves particularly advanced Christians who had come to understand the more profound elements of Christianity, lost on most Christians. The meetings continued after Valentinus' death, throughout the Roman empire: indeed there is some evidence that by the middle of the third century there were two main divisions, an eastern branch (whose leaders were called Theodotus and Mark) and a western one (led by Ptolemy and Heracleon).

highest divinity down to lower ones. Some worshipped not the highest divinity, on the grounds that he was unknowable, but some of the lesser ones. For example, the Sethians (or Barbelites) seem to have mainly worshipped the Aeon known as Barbelo, which they considered to be the greatest Aeon after the high divinity.

One of these Aeons, however, mistakenly rebelled, or tried to produce its own Aeon; this introduced discord into the divine realm, and the discord was expelled. The result was an entity which, although it originated in the divine realm, was not itself divine, and which was ignorant of its true origins. This entity, believing itself to be the highest existing thing, then created the physical world out of other remnants of discord. Many gnostics believed that the God of the Old Testament was none other than this ignorant being, the demiurge (or 'creator'), which set itself up as God but was in fact more like the devil.

There seems to have been great variety among the mythological systems of the different gnostic groups. They were all designed to explain the current situation of alienation in which the gnostics believed themselves to exist: for mingled in the stuff, cast out of the divine realm, out of which the demiurge fashioned the physical world, were some bits of uncorrupted spirit. These became the spirits of human beings (or, for the more exclusive groups, of the gnostics). This is why they find themselves mixed up in the lowly physical world today, and why they yearn to be free of it and return to the divine realm.

This leads to the second important feature of gnosticism, which is its emphasis upon secret knowledge. How is the spirit to escape the flesh and return to the divine realm? The gnostics believed it involved understanding the truth about the world, contained in esoteric teachings. For many of the gnostics, the true reason Jesus entered the world was to deliver these teachings. The Valentinians, for example, believed that Jesus was a divine Aeon who entered the world of the demiurge in disguise. He was not really human, but only appeared it – for if the physical world is basically evil, an Aeon could not really have a physical body. Thus, Valentinus is said to have taught that Jesus did not eat, drink, or go to the toilet like normal people. Other gnostics seem to have distinguished between the human Jesus and the divine Saviour who inspired or spoke through him.

The important thing, however, was Jesus' teaching. In *The Gospel of Truth*, for example, probably the work of Valentinus himself, Christ is presented as the revelation of the Father, with the striking imagery of a book:

> *The living book of the living ... is written in the Father's thought and intellect. And since the foundation of the entirety it had been among his incomprehensibles: and no one had been able to take it up, inasmuch as it was ordained that whoever should take it up would be put to death.*

Nothing would have been able to appear among those who believed in salvation, had not that book come forward.

Therefore the merciful and faithful Jesus became patient and accepted the sufferings even unto taking up that book: inasmuch as he knew that his death would mean life for many ... Jesus appeared, wrapped himself in that document, was nailed to a piece of wood, and published the father's edict upon the cross.[1]

Christ saves, in other words, by revealing divine truth. For the Valentinians, the spiritual journey is one of increasing knowledge. Those who can read the 'living book of the living' can draw closer to the Father and learn who they really are and what the world is really like. They learn, for example, that only the spiritual is truly real; the physical world is just a sort of shadow.

Christ's teaching is handed on, secretly, by those in the know; but if you are sufficiently spiritual you can also discern it in allegorical form in the Bible, hidden behind the brash words of the demiurge. In the end, the world will be separated: physical matter will be destroyed, and those who have been saved will join the 'entirety' of divinity. 'Spiritual' people will do so because it is their natural home, and merely 'psychic' people (that is, those with souls but no spirit – ordinary Christians) may also be saved, because Christ has effectively adopted them as if they were spiritual.

We do not hear so much about gnosticism after the middle of the third century or thereabouts, suggesting that the movement may have been declining somewhat. It certainly still existed after this period; the Valentinians were mentioned at the Trullan synod in AD 692. For the most part, however, the gnostics succumbed to the crackdown on Christian groups deemed heretical at the end of the fourth century. We shall see more of how that happened in chapter 11.

The rule of faith

With such an array of different views within the Christian community, how could Christians know who was right and who was wrong? Indeed, did it really matter who was right and who was wrong at all? The later second century AD saw theologians emerge who thought they had the answers to these questions. One of the most important of them was Irenaeus of Lyon.

Irenaeus and the gnostics

Irenaeus was brought up as a Christian in his native Asia Minor, and later moved to Lyon, where he became a prominent figure in the church. He was in Lyons during the famous persecution of AD 177, but he survived, and was sent to Rome with a letter for the

Christians there describing what had happened in the persecution. According to the letter, Irenaeus was a presbyter, a post he seems to have held for the rest of his life. However, after the death of the bishop of Lyons during the persecution, Irenaeus seems to have acted as bishop in at least an informal capacity, and later generations remembered him as the city's bishop.

When he arrived in Lyon, Irenaeus encountered gnostic Christianity, above all the kind taught by the disciples of Valentinus. It seems that this was the first time he had come into contact with gnostics, and he was profoundly shocked. Irenaeus' response was the longest work on Christian theology yet written: the five-volume *On the Detection and Overthrow of the So-called Gnosis*, or as it is normally known, *Against Heresies*. In this book, Irenaeus described the beliefs and practices of the gnostics that he encountered and tried to differentiate fairly between the different gnostic groups; and he explained just why he considered them mistaken. In so doing, he also described – almost incidentally – his own understanding of the Christian faith, both its contents and its sources.

According to Irenaeus, gnosticism was dangerously wrong because it split up God and his work. For example, the gnostic belief in a series of divine Aeons was really a denial of monotheism. Worse, the gnostics thought that the universe had been created by an evil or ignorant demiurge, which was not the true God of the New Testament. For Irenaeus, this view disrupted not only the divine unity but also the divine plan of salvation. Irenaeus believed passionately that God is in control of the whole of history. He believed that although human beings have free will – and that they have used that free will in ways which God did not intend – God is still in overall charge. When Adam and Eve sinned, God set in motion a plan to help them and their descendants improve morally and come to be saved. He designed the material universe in which we live as a sort of training ground: a place of tough decisions, hard choices, and difficult experiences, in which human beings would be forced to use their free will in morally responsible ways. This explains why there is suffering in the world. God could have created a sort of jolly theme park for us

Irenaeus (c. AD 130–208), bishop of Lyons.

to live in, but we would not have become morally responsible individuals if we had known only happiness.

The central part of God's salvation plan, according to Irenaeus, was the incarnation of Christ, who is the invisible God made visible. He is central to creation, and everything in creation looks towards the moment of incarnation, when God and creation are joined together. Unlike the gnostics, who believed that God could not possibly become united to evil matter, Irenaeus stresses the reality of the incarnation as God literally becoming flesh. In fact, for him, this is what brings about salvation. By infusing his own divinity into a human life in this way, God injects his own qualities of immortality and incorruptibility into human nature. The very act of incarnation itself purifies human nature – indeed, the whole of created nature. This notion of salvation coming about primarily through the incarnation would be central to most mainstream Christian theology for the next couple of centuries, and it would remain central to the theology and spirituality of the Orthodox Church for much longer.

It should be clear that Irenaeus' understanding of the Christian faith was fundamentally at odds with that of the Valentinians whom he met in Lyon. But why couldn't they just agree to disagree? After all, they were all Christians; weren't they all on the same side in the grand scheme of things? Irenaeus thought not. In the preface to *Against Heresies*, he explained why he had written his work against the gnostics:

> These men falsify the oracles of God, and prove themselves evil interpreters of the good word of revelation. They also overthrow the faith of many, by drawing them away, under a pretence of [superior] knowledge, from him who rounded and adorned the universe; as if, forsooth, they had something more excellent and sublime to reveal, than that God who created the heaven and the earth, and all things that are therein. By means of specious and plausible words, they cunningly allure the simple-minded to inquire into their system; but they nevertheless clumsily destroy them, while they initiate them into their blasphemous and impious opinions respecting the Demiurge; and these simple ones are unable, even in such a matter, to distinguish falsehood from truth.[2]

In other words, the Valentinians did not merely preach an alternative understanding of the Christian message. They preached something fundamentally opposed to that message. Those who believed their teachings were being led astray; they were believing something that was false. And those who believed these falsehoods would be damned: they were being misled away from faith in the true Christ into faith in an idol which could not save them. For a theologian like Irenaeus, those who preached gnosticism were rather like quack doctors giving ill people medicine that would not only fail to cure them, but would actually poison them all the more quickly.

But even granted that Irenaeus' readers would accept this general view – that some people were right and some wrong, and the latter were dangerous spawn of Satan leading people to damnation – why should they believe that Irenaeus' version of Christianity was right and the gnostics' wrong, rather than vice versa? What if it was Irenaeus who was misleading everyone? Irenaeus had the answer to this as well. He pointed out that the true Christian faith was what Jesus himself had taught to his disciples, and which those disciples, after Jesus' ascension, had taught in the churches they established. Those churches still existed, and were run by bishops who could trace their line back to the apostles. This was a guarantee that they taught the same faith. Moreover, anyone could examine these teachings, which were given publicly, unlike the supposed secret traditions which the gnostics claimed had been passed down in private.

Tertullian

A more thorough defence of the general position outlined by Irenaeus was provided by his contemporary Tertullian, one of the most forceful personalities of the ancient church. Perhaps a generation younger than Irenaeus, Tertullian came from Carthage and was probably the first Christian to write original works in Latin. Tertullian was the name of a prominent lawyer in Carthage at this time, and it is quite likely that he was the same person as the theologian. Much of Tertullian's writing uses legal terminology, and it is easy to hear the voice of the professional barrister in his tough rhetoric.

Unlike Irenaeus, Tertullian was brought up as a pagan but converted to Christianity in adulthood. He apparently began writing in defence of Christianity quite quickly, producing not only his famous *Apology* (modelled on those of Justin Martyr and his followers) but a host of other works. In fact, Tertullian was the first Christian theologian from whom we have a large number of treatises on different subjects. All of them are easily recognized by their strident tone, their utterly uncompromising attitude, and their often biting wit. He wrote a number of treatises attacking those he regarded as Christian heretics, including Praxeas the modalist and Marcion. He also produced denunciations of pagan practices, treatises explaining how Christians should live, and philosophical musings on aspects of Christian theology. One of these, *The Prescription against the Heretics*, sets out his take on the problem of determining the correct Christian faith. A 'prescription' was a legal term, meaning a brief or case; in this piece, then, Tertullian presents himself as a lawyer putting the case for the prosecution of those he considers heretics (and, at the same time, the defence of those he considers orthodox).

Like Irenaeus, Tertullian bases his case upon the claim that Jesus taught the true faith to his disciples and then commissioned them to go out and preach that faith to the world, founding churches as they went. So the true doctrine is whatever these churches teach, while anyone who disagrees with them must be wrong. For both Irenaeus and Tertullian, and others who took this view, the teaching of the churches itself was thus a 'canon'; the word comes from the Greek for 'measuring stick', that is, something against which other things may be tested. The 'canon', or 'rule of faith', was the body of teaching agreed by the apostolic churches. It was transmitted by tradition and incorporated the writings that would become the New Testament – for these texts, written by the apostles themselves, helped to ensure that the churches remained true to their original teachings. They also meant that anyone who was worried about the reliability of the churches could check their teachings against these texts. Irenaeus likened the apostles to rich men putting money in a bank which could be withdrawn by their successors for evermore. He summarized the 'rule of faith', upon which all apostolic churches and those in communion with them agreed, like this:

> *[We believe] in one God, the Creator of heaven and earth, and all things therein, by means of Christ Jesus, the Son of God; who, because of his surpassing love towards his creation, condescended to be born of the virgin, he himself uniting man through himself to God, and having suffered under Pontius Pilate, and rising again, and having been received up in splendour, shall come in glory, the Saviour of those who are saved, and the Judge of those who are judged, and sending into eternal fire those who transform the truth, and despise his Father and his advent.[3]*

Although Tertullian agreed with this assessment, his own career took a rather ironic course given his insistence that whatever the apostolic churches taught was the true faith. In around AD 202, he joined the Montanists. He had always been one of the most rigorist Christian writers, calling for high moral ideals and stringent discipline among the faithful, and it is likely that the similar ethical teaching of the Montanists appealed to him. He continued to write on a variety of theological subjects, but now he also lashed out at Christians who rejected the Montanist prophecies. Nevertheless, his Montanist sympathies did not stop him from remaining extremely influential within the church for many years, especially in the Latin-speaking half, and above all in Africa.

The role of the church

Clearly, the church played a very important role in the transmission and preservation of the 'rule of faith'. There were two levels at which this operated. The first was at the local level. We have already seen how a system developed here for ensuring correct belief and behaviour: it was called the episcopacy. By the end of the second century AD, in each city, one man – the bishop – was in charge of the Christian community. This 'monarchical' system ensured uniformity of belief, because the bishop was the final arbiter. Even before this time, there were methods to deal with dissent, as we saw in the case of Noetus, who was expelled from Rome by a council of presbyters. It seems that at that time Rome had not yet made the transition to the fully episcopal system.

But there was a second level in which the church was involved with the 'rule of faith', and this was the global level. It was all very well if the local bishop ensured uniformity of belief among the Christians in his city, but what if the bishop of another city disagreed with him? This was increasingly a problem for the church. Just as the second century saw the general establishment of the 'monarchical' episcopal system at the local level in each city, so the third century saw the gradual emergence of theories of the universal church, and the first church-wide mechanisms to deal with problems.

Cyprian and the unity of the church

One of the most important figures in this was Cyprian of Carthage. Cyprian was a prominent and wealthy citizen of Carthage and converted to Christianity as an adult, after which he did his best to lead as perfect a life as he could: even before being baptized he decided to devote his life to chastity, and sold his estates to give the money to the poor. Rather oddly, his friends bought the estates and gave them back to him. Cyprian became bishop of Carthage probably in AD 248 or 249.

He had hardly a moment's peace throughout his short episcopate. In AD 250, the Decian persecution broke out; many Christians were arrested for refusing to sacrifice to the pagan gods, but many others did sacrifice. Cyprian himself fled Carthage and went into hiding. Afterwards, however, many of those who had sacrificed returned, saying they had repented and wished to be readmitted to the church. Some people wanted to readmit these 'lapsed', while others believed they had lost divine grace and could not be restored. The church was divided between different factions, and Cyprian had difficulty imposing his own views. He ordered that all lapsed who wanted to return to the church must complete a long period of penance first. He wrote a treatise – *On the Lapsed* – and read it out to an assembly of Carthaginian Christians. In it, he emphasized the need for Christians to live perfect lives as far as possible, and attacked those who had argued that the lapsed should be forgiven instantly: indeed, he condemned this view as just as sinful as the sin of the lapsed themselves. He stressed that both groups of sinners must be shunned for fear that their sin might contaminate others. In other words, the church should be a society of those who are perfect, or at the very least who are trying their hardest to be perfect.

Soon after, renewed persecutions and plague put the lives of all Carthaginian Christians in danger, and Cyprian decreed that all lapsed Christians could be readmitted to the church even if they had not completed their penance. The church split again and a rival bishop to Cyprian was elected, who promised to stick to the original rigorist line. The same thing happened in Rome, where the bishop was killed in the persecutions and two rivals – Cornelius and Novatian – claimed to succeed him, representing different views on the lapsed.

The situation was a mess, unprecedented in its scale. There had certainly been rival 'bishops' in cities before. It is possible, although not certain, that the famous theologian Hippolytus of Rome had been one, a couple of decades earlier. Novatian, however, is the first figure we know of who certainly did this, making him the first known 'antipope' or rival claimant to the Roman episcopacy. He seems to have acted quickly in an attempt to have his claim recognized by other churches, writing to other bishops and even appointing his own in other cities, extending the schism beyond Rome and Carthage.

Cyprian tried to deal with all of this in another major treatise, *On the Unity of the Church*. In a famous passage, he declared:

> The episcopate is one, each part of which is held by each one for the whole. The Church also is one, which is spread abroad far and wide into a multitude by an increase of fruitfulness. As there are many rays of the sun, but one light; and many branches of a tree, but one strength based in its tenacious root; and since from one spring flow many streams, although the multiplicity seems diffused in the liberality of an overflowing abundance, yet the unity is still preserved in the source. Separate a ray of the sun from its body of light, its unity does not allow a division of light; break a branch from a tree, – when broken, it will not be able to bud; cut off the stream from its fountain, and that which is cut off dries up. Thus also the Church, shone over with the light of the Lord, sheds forth her rays over the whole world, yet it is one light which is everywhere diffused, nor is the unity of the body separated. Her fruitful abundance spreads her branches over the whole world. She broadly expands her rivers, liberally flowing, yet her head is one, her source one; and she is one mother, plentiful in the results of fruitfulness: from her womb we are born, by her milk we are nourished, by her spirit we are animated.[4]

For Cyprian, those who try to break up the church – including those who declare themselves to be 'bishops' when legitimate bishops already exist – are schismatics. They cannot be saved, even if they should be martyred, because they have rejected the church of Christ. As Cyprian puts it, 'He can no longer have God for his Father, who has not the church for his mother' (*On the unity of the church* 6). And he appeals, in particular, to the apostle Peter. Exactly what he says about Peter is uncertain, because this passage exists in two versions in the manuscript tradition, and it is unclear which one Cyprian himself wrote. In each version, Cyprian appeals to Matthew 16:18–19, where Jesus tells Peter that he is the 'rock' on which the church is built, and gives him the power of binding and

Cyprian (c. AD 200–58), bishop of Carthage, is brought before Emperor Valerian in this 14th-century fresco.

loosening. Cyprian argues that this commission is the ultimate source of the church's power and its unity, since the commission to Peter extends to the other apostles and, ultimately, to their successors, the legitimate bishops. But in one version of the text, Cyprian seems to say that the *current* bishop of Rome also has special powers. If Cyprian did believe, at least at one stage of his career, that the bishop of Rome had special primacy over other bishops, then this would show that what would later become the papacy had already begun to develop at this early stage. Certainly many Christians believed that the teachings of the church at Rome were the absolute gold standard, as it were. Irenaeus had argued that this church had the most certain and reliable version of the faith, because of its association with both Peter and Paul.

Novatian, one of the rival bishops of Rome, failed to win over most of the church there or elsewhere. He took a very rigorist line on the lapsed, thinking that they should not be readmitted to the church at all; so he and his followers split off from the church and set up their own, known as the Novatianist church. This organization became quite widespread and survived for a long time. This was an unusual schism, since the Novatianists didn't really disagree with the mainstream church on any important matter, although they tended to have a stricter moral code. But still they maintained an independent church structure, with bishops in most major cities acting as rivals to the mainstream bishop. They were still around at the end of the sixth century, over 350 years after the death of Novatian himself.

Ironically, the existence of the Novatianist church added an extra layer to the dispute, because some Novatianists soon changed their minds and decided they wanted to return to the mainstream church. Should *they* be allowed to do so? Cyprian was still arguing about this with the new bishop of Rome, Stephen, when a new bout of persecutions led to his exile in AD 257 and execution the following year.

Bishops and synods

Disputes of this kind showed that for all the idealism about a united church with a single 'rule of faith', different churches could still disagree; and their disagreements could not be resolved by simply examining the apostolic 'rule of faith' and seeing who was deviating from it. Without a system to deal with this sort of situation it could never be satisfactorily resolved. Inevitably, a system did begin to develop: the synod, or council.

'Synod' comes from the Greek word for 'assembly', and Christians had been holding such assemblies to resolve disputed matters ever since Peter, Paul, and James met at Jerusalem to decide whether Gentiles could become Christians without first having to convert to Judaism. That was certainly a fairly informal affair. More formal assemblies, involving the presence of bishops from a number of different cities, seem to have begun to be held in the first half of the third century AD. Cyprian tells us that by his day it was usual for all African bishops to meet regularly every year – a major gathering, given the number of churches in Africa. Synods such as these were still local affairs – the notion of bishops from the entire church all meeting in the same place would have to wait until the fourth century – but they were wider in scope than a single city.

These synods met so that all the bishops of an area could agree on a party line. For example, the councils under Cyprian were arranged to ensure that all the African bishops would speak with a single voice on the question of the readmittance of schismatics. But the notion soon developed that such a synod might meet in order to deal with a local bishop who had gone off-message. Such a council could operate almost as a sort of informal trial, where the bishop in question would be interrogated about his views and a decision reached on what to do about him. We saw in chapter 6 that in the first half of the third century, Origen attended a meeting that seems to have been a little like this, which was recorded in his *Dialogue with Heraclides*. A bishop was suspected of teaching something odd, and he was called to a meeting of other bishops at which Origen was invited to talk with him and assess his orthodoxy. On that occasion, Origen pronounced Heraclides' views acceptable. Quite how 'official' this meeting was, and what would have happened had Origen not been satisfied with Heraclides' answers, we don't know.

As far as we know, the first council of this kind which found against the suspected bishop was actually a series of synods, held at Antioch probably between AD 264 and 268. They were called to deal with Paul of Samosata, the bishop of that city, whose views on the Trinity were highly controversial. Many people in his own church were unhappy with them, and this concern spread to his fellow bishops. It is uncertain precisely what Paul taught, since the evidence is rather contradictory; it seems to have been some kind of Sabellianism. A series of councils was held and Paul was deposed. Unfortunately he was living in a house that belonged to the church, and he refused to vacate it. In fact he managed to stay there until AD 272, when the emperor Aurelian visited

the city and the Christians appealed to him. The emperor – who was fairly well disposed towards Christians – had Paul evicted.

So, by the end of the third century, the church had developed both a theory of its own nature and a mechanism for dealing with internal divisions. This mechanism was evidently imperfect, since if someone refused to accept the decisions of a synod the church could do little about it without calling in the help of the civil authority. But it was at least a start.

A 9th-century illumination depicting the Council of Toledo, from the Codex of the council of Albelda.

The role of Scripture

But the 'rule of faith' which rested upon the notion of the apostolic succession of bishops and their united authority rested upon something else, too – the Scriptures.

The Old Testament

The Christians believed that the Old Testament – the Jewish Scriptures – described the history of God's gracious acts towards humanity before Jesus. As we have seen, some rejected this view – the Marcionites and most of the gnostics – and were regarded as heretics because of it. For most Christians, the God of the Old Testament was identical with the Father of Jesus, and for this reason, the Old Testament should be read as a Christian text.

But the Old Testament was not a Christian text – it was a Jewish text. It was all written before Jesus lived. How, then, could it be about him? The Christians got around this problem in three main ways.

First, the Old Testament described God's activities before Jesus. Because he was the same God as Jesus' Father, this was essential background to the history of Jesus himself. As we saw in chapter 3, the church had, by the end of the first century AD, developed the notion that it (and not Israel) was the true heir to the promises that God made to Abraham and the other Jewish patriarchs. The Christian church *was* the new Israel. The history of Israel was therefore its own history.

Second, Christians believed that the Old Testament was full of prophecies concerning Jesus. For example, the passages referring to the future Messiah were interpreted as references to Jesus – not unreasonably, given that Christians believed that Jesus was that Messiah. But they also interpreted other passages as prophecies about Jesus, even passages that did not seem, on the face of it, to be prophecies at all. One prominent example is the 'suffering servant' passages in Isaiah 52–53. These speak of a servant of God who suffers, but do not specify that he will come in the future; nevertheless, Christians believed the passages to refer to Jesus. Another example is Psalm 22, which Jesus himself apparently quoted on the cross.

These two principles helped Christian exegetes to 'Christianize' the Old Testament in their interpretations of it. But there was still plenty of material that didn't seem very relevant. Some seemed dull, such as the long genealogies in the Pentateuch, and some seemed positively immoral, such as the descriptions of battles and other violent events. In response, Christians developed two major approaches to the text. These are often associated with the two schools of biblical interpretation in the eastern Roman empire: those of Alexandria and Antioch. At Alexandria, theologians typically interpreted the Bible allegorically. On this view (glanced at in chapter 4), the text had a literal meaning, but it *also* had a non-literal meaning which might be quite different. This was the technique used by Clement of Alexandria and Origen, which had been used by Philo of Alexandria before them, and which owed much to pagan commentators upon classical literature.

In Antioch, meanwhile, theologians preferred the 'typological' approach (which we met in chapter 3). On this view, the events described in the biblical text – rather than the text itself – had special meanings. For example, when Abraham prepared to sacrifice his son Isaac, he was (without realizing it) preshadowing or prefiguring the future event when God would sacrifice Jesus. To put it in technical language, Abraham and Isaac were a 'type' of God and Jesus.

There was some rivalry between the proponents of these methods. Theodore of Mopsuestia, a major Antiochene typologist of the late fourth and early fifth century, wrote a (now lost) book attacking the practice of allegory. But at the same time, one should be wary of over-stressing the differences between them. For one thing, it was not quite as geographically rigid as the terms 'Alexandrian' or 'Antiochene' might suggest; in the fourth century, one of the foremost 'allegorical' exegetes was Gregory of Nyssa, who was from Cappadocia, closer to Antioch than to Alexandria. Moreover, although the two methods may have involved different theories, they had fairly similar practical outcomes. Both a 'typological' exegete and an 'allegorical' one could agree that many passages of the Bible had a deeper meaning. The major difference was that the typologist saw the significance as resting in the event described by the text while the allegorist saw it as resting in the text itself, but for all practical purposes, that was not much of a difference.

An illumination of the beginning of the Gospel of John, taken from the Lindisfarne Gospels, c. AD 698 / 700.

The New Testament

The Old Testament was a fairly well-established, clear body of texts. All Christians read it in the Septuagint version, a translation into Greek that Jewish scholars in Alexandria had made in the second century BC. Indeed, they commonly believed that the Septuagint – and not the Hebrew original – was the inspired text. The moment of inspiration came during the translation process, not the original composition. Christians therefore treated the books contained in the Septuagint as canonical. However, the Great Bet Din, in the late first century AD, had issued a list of the books *they* considered canonical, and this list became the standard one among most Jews.

The Septuagint contained some books which were not present in the Jewish canon. So Christians sometimes regarded these books as 'deuterocanonical', or secondary, although by the fifth century they officially had the same status as the rest of the Old Testament.

The New Testament, by contrast, was far less clearly demarcated. As we have seen, there was, as yet, no generally agreed list of which books counted as distinctively Christian Scripture; that would not occur until the late fourth century AD. There was fair *de facto* agreement, however. More or less all Christians agreed that the four Gospels and the writings of Paul were central – although the Syriac-speaking churches used not the Gospels but the harmony of them known as the *Diatessaron*, compiled by the second-century theologian Tatian. The books of 1 John and 1 Peter were also accepted more or less universally by the middle of the second century. However, other books were less certain. The book of Revelation was accepted by many churches in the west, but not in the east. Conversely, the book of Hebrews was accepted by many in the east, but not in the west. Some books were widely used that would ultimately not be included in the canon, especially *1 Clement* and the *Shepherd* of Hermas. However, although these texts were certainly widely read, they are rarely referred to as Scripture during this period. The Marcionites recognized few books. The gnostics, by contrast, typically recognized far more, especially 'Acts' of the various apostles and gospels, all attributing gnostic teachings to Jesus and the apostles. The Montanists, as we have seen, wrote down the collections of their own prophecies and apparently regarded these as a continuation of the inspired writings.

Certainly by the end of the second century AD, it seems to have been common for Christians to cite the New Testament books (whichever ones they accepted) in the same way that they cited the Old Testament. In other words, even though no canon had been definitively established, and the very name 'New Testament' had not yet been coined, Christians generally believed that they possessed a second body of Scripture to go alongside the first.

Christians had two main explanations of why the New Testament books were authoritative. The first was that they were the historical records of the time of the apostles. Justin Martyr, describing Christian services in the middle of the second century AD, mentions that they would hear a reading from 'the memoirs of the apostles'. This practice would ensure that Christians remained in touch with their origins. This understanding of the New Testament was closely associated with the idea of the 'rule of faith'. Jesus taught the apostles, and the apostles taught their successors, who still govern the orthodox churches. But the apostles also wrote down what Jesus had taught them. So there are actually two lines of transmission of the same doctrines: via the apostles' successors, the bishops, and via the apostles' own writings, which could still be read directly centuries later. These two acted as the guarantee of each other, since they both derived from Christ and would thus be in perfect harmony.

The second main reason why the New Testament books were considered authoritative was that they were thought to have been written under the direct inspiration of God himself. According to 2 Peter 1:21 (a text written, perhaps, in the first half of the second century, but which was not accepted as itself canonical by most Christians until after the fourth), 'no prophecy ever came by human will, but men and women moved by the Holy Spirit spoke from God'. Christians taking this view were effectively treating the New Testament (and the Old Testament too) in the same way that many pagans treated the works of the poets, especially Homer and Hesiod.

There might seem to be some tension between these two views of Scripture. The 'historical' understanding of Scripture suggested that the text's authority derived from the authority of the apostle who wrote it; if no apostle wrote it then it had no authority, and some Christians argued that certain books were not apostolic at all and should be rejected. But the 'spiritual' understanding gave the text authority in its own right, irrespective of its human author, because it also had God as an author. However, Christians were quite capable of holding both views at the same time. In practice, they treated the texts of the New Testament – like those of the Old – as authoritative, always agreeing with each other, and always agreeing with the teachings of the church. The theory behind this did not really make much practical difference. In practice, the whole of the Bible, and each part of it, was authoritative (in conjunction with the teaching of the church) and relevant. Christians generally assumed that pretty much any part of the Bible might be relevant to whatever they were talking about. A good example comes from the Arian controversy, which we shall look at in chapter 9. Much of the argument in that controversy revolved around Proverbs 8:22, in which the divine Wisdom speaks of itself as 'created'. The Arians argued that this showed that Jesus was not divine, because he is identical with the divine Wisdom. Their opponents argued that in fact the text did not mean this; a different sense of 'created' was intended. It never seems to have occurred to them to argue that the text was not relevant at all, or that the divine Wisdom in Proverbs 8:22 should not be identified with Jesus. That was not how ancient Christians thought. For them, the scriptural text was always relevant.

8
Chapter

The Christian Empire

At the beginning of the fourth century AD, the Christian church was suffering the cruelest and most determined persecution yet at the hands of the Roman authorities. By the end of the same century, the empire was effectively Christian, the emperor was devoted to the religion, and the state was outlawing the traditional religion of Rome itself. During this century, the church changed more than it had in the whole of the preceding 200 years.

Bust of the Roman emperor Constantine, who ruled from AD 306 to 337.

The emperor Constantine

The legend

In AD 312, Constantine, son of the former emperor Constantius Chlorus, marched upon Maxentius, son of Maximian, who had seized power in Rome and declared himself emperor. Two emperors had already tried – and failed – to dislodge Maxentius from his secure position behind the walls of the capital city. But as Constantine – like Hannibal centuries earlier – marched down from the Alps and fought a series of decisive battles in Italy, Maxentius and his troops emerged from Rome to fight him at the Milvian Bridge on the River Tiber, just north of the city.

According to the Christian historian Eusebius of Caesarea, Constantine was convinced that he would require supernatural aid to defeat the wicked tyrant and usurper Maxentius. He prayed to God, asking for a sign. And Eusebius tells us that he received one:

If someone else had reported it, it would perhaps not be easy to accept; but since the victorious Emperor himself told the story to the present writer a long while after, when I was privileged with his acquaintance

*and company, and confirmed it with oaths, who could
hesitate to believe the account, especially when the time
which followed provided evidence for the truth of what
he said? About the time of the midday sun, when day
was just turning, he said he saw with his own eyes, up
in the sky and resting over the sun, a cross-shaped trophy
formed from light, and a text attached to it which said,
'By this conquer'.*[1]

Constantine therefore had a new standard made for his
army: a gold-plated cross with a banner hanging from
the crossbar. At the top was a wreath containing the
chi-rho symbol for Christ (see chapter 4, page 105), and
in the middle was a portrait of Constantine himself and
his sons. This banner was known as the *labarum*, and it
was carried at the head of Constantine's army.

The battle proved to be a rout. Constantine marched
triumphantly into Rome and was proclaimed full
emperor by the Roman senate. He then quickly acted to
overturn the previous legislation that had been enacted
against Christians. A new era was dawning.

The political context

That, at least, was the legend which was already being told within
Constantine's lifetime, and which would become the official
version for centuries. But did it really happen like that? Who was
Constantine and why did he convert to Christianity? How could the
Roman state be transformed, practically overnight, from brutally
persecuting Christians to actively promoting their religion? As usual,
the truth proves to be far more complex than later hagiography
makes it out to be.

Constantine was probably born in AD 272 at Naissus in the
Balkans, modern-day Niö in Serbia. He was the son of Constantius
Chlorus, the caesar of the emperor Maximian, who reconquered
Britain in the 290s. Constantius' power base remained Britain and
Gaul for the rest of his career, and in the early years of the fourth
century he campaigned together with his son against the Picts in
what is now Scotland.

The abdication of the emperors Diocletian and Maximian in
AD 305 was undoubtedly intended to create stability in the
government of the Roman empire: an orderly transition of power
from one generation to the next, avoiding the struggles for power
which had so marred the third century. Initially, things went
smoothly. The two caesars – Galerius and Constantius Chlorus –
became emperors. Two new caesars were appointed, Maximinus
Daia and Severus. However, not only were both of these close allies
of Galerius, but Maximian's son Maxentius and Constantius' son

Constantine is depicted in this
11th-century fresco from the Church of the
Virgin, Cappadocia, Turkey.

In the Triclinium of Pope Leo III, Christ gives keys to Pope Sylvester I and the *labarum* to Constantine the Great.

Constantine had both been expecting to be made caesar, and were extremely unhappy at being passed over. These tensions began to spiral out of control in AD 306, when Constantius Chlorus died in York after just a year as western emperor. He was succeeded, in the orderly way, by his caesar, Severus. But Constantine, also in York, was immediately hailed as the new emperor by his troops. Maxentius saw his opportunity and seized power in Rome. A period of confusion and intermittent civil war followed. The former emperor Maximian even re-entered the field and conspired against his own son before eventually being defeated by Constantine. Meanwhile Galerius appointed yet another general, Licinius, as co-emperor, with Constantine still officially as his caesar. The one person who chose to remain aloof from the whole business was the one who had once been the dominant figure of the age. Diocletian was invited to return to power but declined, stating that he was happier growing cabbages in his garden, and he was probably quite right.

The Edict of Milan

These were the tumultuous circumstances under which Constantine defeated Maxentius at the Milvian Bridge in AD 312, thereby removing him (and his allies in Africa) from the equation and leaving only Constantine himself, Licinius, and Maximinus Daia in the field as 'emperors'. Galerius had died in AD 311 and Maximinus Daia had declared himself his successor as eastern emperor. Early in AD 313 Constantine travelled to Milan and met Licinius there. Licinius married Constantine's sister, sealing the alliance between them. Here they issued a document which guaranteed the legality of Christianity. This document is traditionally known as the 'Edict of Milan', which makes it sound extremely decisive and formal. In fact, the 'Edict' took the form of a letter by Licinius addressed to the governors of the east, where Maximinus Daia, whom Licinius and Constantine regarded as a usurper, was ruling. After issuing it, Licinius headed east and defeated Maximinus in battle. During his campaign, Licinius claimed that he too had had a Christian vision: an angel appeared to him and dictated a prayer, which he had his soldiers recite on the eve of battle. So there were now only two emperors once more: Constantine in the west and Licinius in the east, and they were both claiming the patronage of the Christian God.

The Edict of Milan began like this:

> *When I, Constantine Augustus, and I, Licinius Augustus, happily met at Milan and had under consideration all matters which concerned the public advantage and safety, we thought that, among all the other things that we saw would benefit the majority of men, the arrangements which above all needed to be made were those which ensured reverence for the Divinity, so that we might grant both to Christians and to all men freedom to follow whatever religion each one wished, in order that whatever divinity there is in the seat of heaven may be appeased and made propitious towards us and towards all who have been set under our power.[2]*

The rest of the text repeats that everyone may follow whatever religion they wish, and gives instructions for any property taken from Christians during the persecutions to be restored to them. The Edict of Milan is often regarded as the turning point in the fortunes of the Christian church within the Roman empire: this was when Christians changed from being a persecuted minority to being the official religion. But in fact Christianity was already a *de facto* legal religion throughout much of the empire. Constantius Chlorus had closed down some churches but otherwise ignored the anti-Christian legislation. He had not permitted Christians to be executed in the territories he controlled. Constantine had continued the same policy from the moment he succeeded his father, six years before the Milvian Bridge. Maxentius, during the six years he had ruled Italy, had operated a similar policy. Throughout the west, then, Christianity had effectively been decriminalized since around AD 306. This was not so in the east during this period, where Galerius, the arch-enemy of Christians, reigned supreme. But he had reversed his policy towards Christians as he lay dying in AD 311. He revoked the legislation against them and asked them to pray for him. Galerius' successor and nephew, Maximinus Daia, who shared his hatred of Christians, ignored the rescript and continued the persecutions, but only for a couple of years before Licinius defeated and supplanted him as eastern emperor.

The Edict of Milan therefore made official and extended to the whole empire the legality which Christians had been enjoying in the west for several years. But it did go one step further: Constantine and Licinius ordered that the property which had been seized from

Christians during the persecutions should be paid back to them. So this was not simply a relaxation of the laws against Christianity; it was a recognition that those laws had been unjust in the first place.

Constantine the Christian

It is easy to see why the rulers of the empire might have been inclined to give up persecuting the Christians during this time. The persecutions of Diocletian and Galerius had completely failed; all that had been achieved was the creation of yet more martyrs, public sympathy for Christians, and a waste of resources. The Christians had continued to increase in numbers, representing perhaps 10 per cent of the population – a minority, but no longer a tiny one. Indeed, apart from the recent persecutions of Diocletian and Galerius, there had been none to speak of since the time of Valerian in the 250s. Seen in this way, there is nothing mysterious about the legalization of Christianity. But why did Constantine and Licinius go so far as to order the restitution of the Christians' property?

Part of the answer must be Constantine's own conversion to Christianity. As a Christian himself, he naturally wished to redress the wrongs done to Christians and to promote the religion. Many of his actions following the Edict of Milan are consistent with this explanation. The restoration of property to Christians in Constantine's territories went ahead exactly as ordered. He even ordered the proconsul of Africa to provide money to the bishop of Carthage on request. He seems to have ordered the construction of new churches and to have provided funds for the purpose, including the church of St John Lateran in Rome. Meanwhile, Christian soldiers serving Constantine were allowed to go to church on Sundays, and pagan troops were ordered to recite a monotheistic prayer at the same time. The precise dates

This 16th-century woodcut illustrates when Emperor Constantine defeated Maxentius at the battle at Milvian Bridge in AD 312.

at which all of these things happened is uncertain, but there is good reason to think that Constantine initiated at least some of them quite soon after his defeat of Maxentius. At some point he began refusing to offer the standard sacrifices to Jupiter to thank him for his victories; this may have been in AD 315 or 326, when he returned to Rome to celebrate the anniversaries of his elevation to emperor, but it could have been as early as AD 312.

But despite these apparently impeccable Christian credentials, some have argued that Constantine's conversion was not as thoroughgoing as Christian hagiography would like to make out. Before his conversion, Constantine seems to have regarded the Roman god Apollo – a sun god – as his patron. In AD 310, Constantine had a vision of Apollo, with some kind of sign in the sky that he interpreted as a prediction that he, Constantine, would enjoy a long reign. One theory is that he saw a solar halo. Whatever the case, Constantine's coins after this period frequently depicted him with Apollo, or with Sol Invictus, the deified 'unconquered sun'. They continued to do so until AD 325, years after Constantine had supposedly renounced paganism. In this context, Eusebius' story of Constantine's vision before the Battle of the Milvian Bridge seems more suspicious: how many divine symbols can one person see hovering in front of the sun? Indeed, another Christian writer, Lactantius, tells a rather different story of the emperor's conversion to Christianity. Lactantius had been a professor of rhetoric until the Great Persecution in AD 303, lost his job, and later become tutor to Constantine's son. He tells us that before the Battle of the Milvian Bridge, Constantine merely had a dream, and he reacted to it by having his soldiers make the *chi-rho* sign on their shields – a far more plausible event on the eve of a battle than the construction of an elaborate, jewel-encrusted banner. The *labarum* did exist and Constantine's troops did march under it, but it was surely not constructed until later on. In his history, Eusebius telescoped events to make the moment of conversion seem far more dramatic, and to link it more clearly to the defeat of Maxentius.

Whatever happened in AD 312, Constantine's earlier devotion to Apollo indicates that he was keen to associate himself with divine power and prone to having visions that confirmed divine favour upon him. On one interpretation, all that changed in AD 312 was that Constantine identified his divine solar patron not with Apollo but with the Christian God. In other words, Constantine was really a pagan in Christian's clothing. In the 1850s, a Swiss historian named Jacob Burckhardt argued on these grounds that Constantine was never a Christian at all. He was just a politician who recognized a good PR move when he saw one.

Most historians today reject Burckhardt's claim. Constantine certainly presented himself as a Christian even when it might have afforded little political gain. After taking control of the eastern empire in AD 324, for example, he wrote to the Persian Shah Shapur II informing the Zoroastrian Shah of his Christian faith and asking him to protect the Christians in his own domains. Some scholars have suggested that, concerned to secure the unity of the empire after years of civil war, Constantine promoted Christianity and presented himself as a Christian primarily because he recognized that the Christian church could be a powerful force for unity. But this would have been a very strange thing for Constantine to do. For one thing, while the church did have more structure throughout the empire than most other cults, it was very much a minority interest. It would have made far more sense for Constantine to try to rally everyone around his own preferred cult of Sol Invictus. Moreover, the Christians were not very united at this time anyway: quite apart from all the divisions we saw in chapter 7, such as the Marcionite and Novatianist churches, a new and serious schism – the Donatist schism – was under way in Africa. For an emperor to seek to use the church as a vehicle for general unity throughout the empire would have been an extraordinary thing to do, and in the event, he and his successors would spend much of their reigns trying to *impose* unity upon the squabbling factions within the church, not to *derive* unity from them.

Moreover, we possess a short book, very probably by Constantine himself, on Christian theology. This *Oration to the Saints* was apparently a long speech delivered by the emperor, in which he speaks of the Trinity and the divinity of Jesus, testifies to the mercy of God, cites the New Testament, and defends monotheism at some length. So the fact that Constantine's Christian faith appears to have featured many pagan elements may therefore mean not that his Christianity was insincere or barely understood, but only that he did not conceive of these elements as being inconsistent with Christianity. It would have been quite natural for a devotee of Apollo who became a Christian to think of the Christian God in similar terms to how he had thought of Apollo. In fact, as we shall see in chapter 11, it was only after Constantine that Christians really developed the notion of 'paganism' as a religion quite distinct from, and inferior to, Christianity. Christians before Constantine may have attacked the worship of pagan gods, or the actions of a state that ordered that its citizens sacrifice to them; they may have railed against a bloodthirsty government or a licentious sect; but they did not, at that time, have a notion of 'paganism' as a unified religious system. To suppose that Constantine should have dropped all the 'pagan' elements of his faith when he became a Christian is to assume that he should have had the mindset of Christians a century later.

Much of the modern literature on the transformation of the empire under Constantine has focused upon the emperor himself and the nature of his conversion. But he was hardly the only

A medallion from the period of Emperor Constantine.

person involved. What happened to the traditional pagan religion of Rome during this time? Didn't its adherents – the vast majority of Constantine's subjects – have anything to say about the sudden promotion of Christianity?

That pagan religion was still a vibrant and developing tradition. Shortly before the Edict of Milan was issued, Maximinus Daia, ruler of the eastern empire, sponsored the creation of a new pagan cult based in Antioch. Theotecnus, the treasurer of that city, was the main figure behind this cult, and he seems to have been inspired in part by the Christian church: he set up an altar to Zeus in Antioch, invented a new liturgy, and appointed priests not only in his city but throughout Maximinus Daia's territories. The cult seems to have been very popular and to have helped inspire a wave of religious zeal throughout the eastern empire. It was short-lived – after Licinius defeated Maximinus he had the leaders of the cult, including Theotecnus, executed. But it is ample evidence that traditional paganism was hardly tottering on its last legs at the time of the Edict of Milan.

Unfortunately, we know little of how Constantine's revolution was received among pagans. Perhaps the key fact to remember is that this 'revolution' was slow. While Constantine enacted plenty of pro-Christian legislation, he was much less forthcoming with anti-pagan legislation. During the decade when he ruled together with Licinius, there were no anti-pagan measures whatsoever other than the suppression of Theotecnus' new cult. As we shall see in subsequent chapters, Constantine and his immediate successors were more interested in clamping down on what they regarded as dissenting forms of Christianity than in suppressing non-Christian religion. When Constantine died, some pagans in Rome displayed banners on their houses declaring him a god, as was traditional; evidently, then, Constantine's religious policies had not alienated at least some pagans, who were perhaps prepared to overlook them in the light of his long and relatively peaceful reign.

Sole emperor

In around AD 320 relations between Constantine and Licinius deteriorated as Licinius began what seems to have been a minor persecution of Christians: they were banned from imperial service and from holding meetings. Little is known about this persecution – if indeed it was a persecution and not simply Licinius intervening in disputes within the church itself – but it provided a pretext for Constantine to begin military preparations. In AD 324, war broke out, and Licinius was defeated, imprisoned, and executed a year later. For the first time since the early years of Diocletian's rule nearly forty years earlier, the Roman empire had a single emperor.

One of Constantine's main acts upon becoming sole emperor

was the founding of a new capital at the old town of Byzantium. Constantine ordered the city to be rebuilt, with a new defensive wall, streets laid out in grids – as was standard in new Roman cities – a palace, and all the usual amenities such as bath houses, a forum, and so on. But it also featured a great mausoleum church, the church of the Holy Apostles, which contained what were believed to be the relics of Andrew and Luke. The city – renamed New Rome – was to be a Christian capital of a Christian empire. Precisely *how* Christian it was is a matter of debate, since Constantine seems to have refurbished some pagan temples there too. He also erected a statue of himself on a column in the forum, which depicted him in a similar way to Sol Invictus, with rays of light flashing out from his head. At any rate, New Rome – or Constantinople, the 'city of Constantine', as it was always known – was officially dedicated in AD 330.

As sole ruler of the empire, Constantine appears to have continued his policy of complete religious toleration: both Christians and pagans could worship as they wished. There is some evidence, however, of measures being taken against pagans during this period. A few temples were destroyed, and considerable wealth was plundered from them and redistributed to the Christians. It is possible – although unlikely – that Constantine also banned public sacrifices. But on the whole, Christianity had no officially privileged status, although it was promoted, and pagans could continue to worship as they pleased.

In AD 337, Constantine took his army east to face Shar Shapur II of Persia, who had recently deposed the Christian king of Armenia and replaced him with a puppet of his own. Constantine's journey was slow, perhaps intended to intimidate Shapur rather than attack him, and it was to include a stopover in Palestine, where Constantine planned to be baptized in the River Jordan. By the fourth century, it was increasingly common for Christians to delay baptism for as long as possible, partly on the grounds that they did not want to risk committing unforgiveable sins afterwards. But it did not go as planned. The emperor fell ill shortly after setting off, and never made it to Palestine. Eusebius of Nicomedia baptized him on his deathbed, and the emperor died soon after. His body was brought back to Constantinople and buried in the Mausoleum of the Holy Apostles.

The church and society

The status of bishops

As we saw in earlier chapters, within each Christian community, there was – at least in theory – a single bishop who was the final authority in that community. As the Christian communities swelled dramatically, the power of the bishops grew correspondingly. Instead of being the pastoral leader of a small group within a city, rather like a modern parish priest, the bishop was becoming the spiritual leader of a major faction within the city. Eventually he would be the spiritual leader of the whole city. He was in charge not of a single congregation, where he was probably on close personal terms with all or most of the members, but of many congregations within his territory, composed mostly of people he did not know and might never have met. He was like the CEO of a large organization rather than the boss of a small office. Inevitably, bishops became grander figures. It seems to have been at this time that they began to wear special vestments, or clothes, when presiding over services. The rest of the time, they dressed in the same way as traditional Roman civil administrators. They could also use the imperial postal service, previously restricted to state and military business. Also, bishops were increasingly drawn from the upper classes; they were people who, in an earlier age, might have become local governors of some kind. That meant that they were usually richer and enjoyed a higher social status than most of their flock, including their priests, who were generally less well off, often coming from the artisan classes.

Different ranks of bishops also emerged. Previously, the bishops of major cities – especially Rome, Carthage, and Alexandria – had often acted as though they had authority over neighbouring areas. The unspoken assumption seems to have been that the bishop's authority was linked to the importance of the city: the more territory a city controlled, the more churches its bishop controlled. In the fourth century, this became more formalized. By the mid-320s the position of 'metropolitan' was generally recognized, that is, the bishop of a metropolis. In AD 341, the council of Antioch decreed that all bishops living in the territory associated with the metropolis must regard the metropolitan as their senior. Thus, for example, the metropolitan of Alexandria effectively controlled the whole Egyptian church. By the end of the century, moreover, the bishops of the most important cities of all were considered to have an even higher status, that of 'patriarch'. For some time there was uncertainty over which bishops counted as patriarchs. Three were generally recognized by the end of the fourth century – those of Rome, Alexandria, and Antioch. The bishop of Constantinople would officially join their ranks some years later.

The church and the welfare system

But the new-found importance of the bishops was matched by their increased responsibilities. They had new social duties: above all, the care of the poor. It is striking just how often bishops would refer to the poor in their sermons. Augustine of Hippo, for example, told his congregation:

A French 17th-century tapestry depicting the life of Emperor Constantine contains the detail, pictured, of the foundation of Constantinople.

Now, by God's will, it is winter. Think of the poor. Think of how the naked Christ can be clothed. Pay attention to him as he lies in the portico, as he suffers hunger, as he endures the cold.[3]

He drew his imagery from Matthew 25:31–46, where Jesus says that anyone who helps the poor and destitute is helping the Son of man, and anyone who does not help them is rejecting him. The idea owed a great deal to Judaism, which also placed great emphasis upon helping the poor. Old Testament texts such as Job 29:11–16 encouraged this concern. Indeed, Christian sermons from the fourth and fifth centuries stress the need to help the poor so much that for a long time scholars believed there was a permanent social crisis during this period, with enormous numbers of destitute people wandering around begging. In fact the situation was usually not so dire as that. Christian rhetoric had created a new sort of social and moral ideal, the ideal of helping the poor as a religious duty, because Christ was present with the poor in a special and unusual way.

This was a new development in Roman society, which since antiquity had encouraged the wealthy to make donations to their cities rather than to the most vulnerable people in those cities. There

The growth of the church

It is very likely that the aftermath of Constantine's conversion saw a rapid rise in the numbers of Christians, especially in those parts of the empire that were less urbanized, such as Spain, northern Gaul, and Britain. With the ending of persecution, the church seems to have redoubled its missionary efforts beyond its core territories of Asia Minor, Africa, and the great cities of the empire. The result was that, where before Constantine the Christian presence throughout the empire had been rather patchy and concentrated in particular geographical areas, after Constantine it became more uniform. The sheer size of the church had enormously increased too, although it is uncertain to what degree; estimates vary from 40 per cent of the inhabitants of the empire now counting themselves as Christians by the time Constantine died to 50 per cent by the end of the fourth century. But this raises new problems for the historian. Just how 'Christian' were these new congregations? It is easy to imagine that many might have joined the religion because they thought it politically or socially expedient, or simply because it was fashionable. In around AD 386, the pagan rhetorician Libanius delivered a speech denouncing the many new converts to Christianity who, he claimed, were really still pagans underneath:

> *Their converts have not really been changed – they only say they have. This does not mean that they have exchanged one faith for another – only that this crew [the zealous Christians] have had the wool pulled over their eyes. They go to their ceremonies, join their crowds, go everywhere where these do, but when they adopt an attitude of prayer they either invoke no god at all or else they invoke the gods.*[1]

was virtually no provision for the poor. Now, however, the church began to provide charity on a scale hitherto unknown in the classical world. Although Jews and Christians alike had been giving to the poor for centuries, only now did the church have the resources to do it on such a large scale.

One Christian leader most famous for his work of this kind was Basil, bishop of Caesarea in Cappadocia (in what is now Turkey). Basil was a highly educated aristocrat who is probably most remembered for his work as a theologian and as a monastic founder, but in his own day, he was most prominent as a sort of social activist. Shortly before he became bishop in AD 370, there was a famine in Cappadocia, and Basil preached a fiery sermon to the wealthy landowners who refused to share their produce with the starving:

> *You miserable people! How will you answer the Great Judge? You cover your bare walls with tapestries, and do not clothe the naked. You adorn your horses with the most rich and expensive trappings, and despise your brother who wears rags. You allow the corn in your granaries to rot or be eaten by vermin, and you do not even bother to glance at those who have no bread. You hoard your wealth, and do not bother to look upon those who are worn and oppressed by necessity! You will say to me: 'How am I doing wrong if I hoard what belongs to me?' And I ask you: 'What are the things that you think belong to you? From whom did you receive them? You act like someone who goes to a theatre, and having sat in the seats that others might have taken, tries to stop everyone else from coming in, taking for himself what should have been used by everyone.' And so it is with the rich, who having been the first to gain what should be common to all, keep it for themselves and hold onto it. If everyone took only what he needed, and gave the rest to those in need, there would be neither rich nor poor.[4]*

The sermon was successful: the landowners did open their storehouses to the poor. And when he became bishop, Basil sought to put his principles into practice by organizing the building of a large complex on the edge of the city known as the 'Basileus'. This was a *xenodocheion*, a new kind of building that appeared throughout the Roman empire in the fourth century. The word means 'house for strangers', 'strangers' here having overtones of 'poor' or 'destitute'. It was a hostel for the homeless, the poor, foreigners, or other vulnerable people, as well as a hospital. *Xenodocheia* were extremely successful, and seem to have played an important role in the popularity of the church throughout this period.

Another institution which helped make the church popular was the 'episcopal audience'. Bishops had always adjudicated in disputes between members of their flock. But one of the first things Constantine did after the Edict of Milan was to make this practice official. The decision of the bishop as arbiter in disputes was to

In AD 496 or 506, the bishop of Reims baptized
Clovis I, king of the Franks, from the House of
the Merovingians c. AD 466–511.

be final, and there could be no appeals to any higher authority. We know very little about the kinds of cases that bishops heard, although it seems that it was one of the primary duties of a bishop. The audiences were generally held in a purpose-built hall near the church, in which the bishop would sit on a high throne like a secular judge. That was another factor which made bishops seem more and more important in a worldly as well as in a spiritual way. And the episcopal audience proved extremely popular, with many people apparently converting to Christianity simply so they could use it. In this way, the church came to play an increasingly vital and central role in everyday society.

Art and architecture

Christian architecture

Until the time of Constantine, Christians seem to have worshipped in one another's houses. There were buildings that were used exclusively for worship – which, for the sake of convenience, can be called 'churches' – but these were converted houses. This was quite common for minority religions at the time: synagogues and mithraea were also almost always converted from pre-existing buildings.

As far as we know, the notion of purpose-built churches, specifically designed for Christian worship, emerged in the late third century. Pagan temples were normally built following a round plan, but churches – like mithraea and synagogues – tended to follow a more rectilinear plan. This may have ultimately been inspired by the earlier house churches, which were often converted so that they contained a large room for assembly. If you want to create a larger room in a house, the simplest method is to knock down a partition wall and turn two small rooms into one long, thin room. This is exactly what happened at the earliest known house church, at Dura-Europos. A raised dais was put at one end of this long room, for the speaker to stand on, and the congregation would stand in rows facing him. The purpose-built churches of the late third century maintained the long, thin shape of the assembly rooms of the earlier house churches, but the whole building was shaped like this, not simply one room in it. But little is known of these pre-Constantine purpose-built churches, and there seem to have been few of them.

The reign of Constantine saw the appearance of a new style of church, which maintained the idea of the long, thin hall, but in a different way. This was the basilica. The word 'basilica' originally referred to the central building in any major Roman town, which functioned as a town hall and courthouse. The basilica was a long, high, relatively narrow building with a double line of pillars running up its length. These created an aisle along either side, separated from the main area or 'nave' in the middle. At one end of the nave was the

Image of the floor plan of the Basilica of San Lorenzo in Milan, whose foundations are said to date from c. AD 370.

In Ravenna in Italy, the Arian Baptistery of the 5th or 6th century displays a mosaic featuring the baptism of Christ by John the Baptist.

apse, where the magistrates would sit. Here, the administrative business of the city would be carried out, and court cases heard. The first basilica church was a partial conversion of such a building, a palace and barracks built in the basilica style, which Constantine donated to the church in AD 314. This building – the Lateran Palace – became the church of St John Lateran, and after its completion in around AD 320 it was used by the bishop of the Roman church. He would sit at the apse, just as judges did in the civil basilicas, with the congregation assembled in the nave, facing him.

There was great variation among Christian basilicas throughout the fourth century, but they all followed the basic pattern of a long hall with lines of pillars. New features were quickly invented which had not appeared on civil basilicas. One was the narthex, an entry hall immediately inside the main doors at the end opposite to the apse. Another was the transept, a hall which crossed the main hall in between the nave and the apse. St Peter's in Rome, which was built at around the same time as St John Lateran, was the first church to incorporate this element. It served as a place for the clergy during services, but also helped to emphasize the sanctity of the apse by removing it further from the congregation. This church was built over the old graveyard on Vatican Hill, where it was believed the apostle Peter had been buried in the first century AD.

Most European churches would be built in the basilica style until modern times, and later developments in ecclesiastical architecture were mostly variations on the style rather than brand-new departures from it. However, there were other architectural innovations in this period too. One was the baptistery, a place specially constructed to hold baptisms. Early house churches had featured rooms set aside for this purpose. In the fourth century, some basilica churches had extra rooms which were used as baptisteries; others did not, and the baptistery was a free-standing building nearby. They were designed in many styles, but were usually round, often in the shape of an octagon. A similar style was used for martyria, shrines built on holy places (typically somewhere where a martyr had died), or constructed to house relics. These were also built in a round or square shape, or a variation on that theme, rather like traditional pagan temples. Some were large and elaborate and had what were effectively basilica-style halls protruding from the sides.

Christian art

Most of these new Christian buildings were relatively plain and simple on the outside. On the inside, however, they offered a huge new canvas for religious artwork. We saw in chapter 4 that, before the fourth century, Christian art was quite modest. Now, however, Christian art began to flourish. Constantine himself helped to encourage this process by donating large sums of money for the renovation and decoration of churches. Not only the quantity but the quality was now generally much higher. That reflected not only the increased funding but the new function of Christian art. Before, it had been intended for viewing only by Christians. Now, however, it was highly visible and viewable by everyone. So it needed to show off the new-found social status of the church and the glory of Christ himself, to the detriment of the old gods.

183

An anchor entwined with fish, symbols of Christ and his followers, is shown in this 4th-century mosaic from the catacombs of Hermes, Sousse, Tunisia.

THE CHRISTIAN EMPIRE

New forms of Christian art appeared. Mosaics were one of the most important; a few Christian mosaics from before the time of Constantine are known, but after his reign they become much more common, mostly on the floors and ceilings of the new churches. Sculpture was also a new feature, almost exclusively in the form of reliefs – free-standing statues from this period with a Christian theme are very rare. One of the most important uses of relief sculpture was on sarcophagi. A sarcophagus (stone coffin) was a very expensive item, and only the wealthy could expect to be buried in one; the earliest known Christian sarcophagi are from the late third century AD, and many more appeared in the fourth century. The relief sculptures which appeared on them were generally of a high quality.

The subject matter of Christian art was changing too. Previously, Jesus had usually been represented as a beardless young man, dressed similarly to the people around him. He would be identifiable in most scenes only because of what he was doing – usually performing some miracle from the Gospels. But now Jesus began to appear in a more exalted way, often with a beard and halo. He might be shown sitting on a throne, handing a scroll of the law to the apostles – a representation of the principle of the apostolic succession, and one which drew a clear parallel between Jesus and the emperor. Indeed, the Jesus of post-Constantinian art is sometimes called 'imperial' in style, and it has often been thought that the style was intended to strengthen Constantine's own image as the earthly representative of Christ. Some historians have disputed this, however, and argued that the more exalted Jesus of fourth-century art represents a hijacking not of imperial pretensions but of traditional representations of pagan gods. On this view, the Jesus who is often shown exalted and glorified, with the saints worshipping him, is a Jesus who has supplanted the pagan gods.

Something similar might be true of another artistic tradition which seems to have developed during this period, of representing Jesus as quite feminine, with long hair, wide hips, and even breasts – contrasting with the much more masculine apostles around him. This was a common feature of images of Dionysus and Apollo, so it may have been that Christian artists wanted to show that Jesus had now taken their role. Perhaps they also wanted to emphasize Jesus' compassionate and merciful nature by making him seem feminine rather than masculine; perhaps they were even making a statement about how Jesus transcended masculinity and femininity, being the saviour of everyone.

At the same time, images of Jesus' passion (suffering) – previously almost completely absent – began to appear during this period. However, these images were all of Jesus' arrest, his trial before Pilate, or his carrying the cross – they never show Jesus actually on the cross. Depictions of Jesus' death would remain almost completely unknown until the fifth century, and they did not become common until the seventh. However, the cross – although without Jesus on it – did begin to appear in fourth-century art. There are some crosses in earlier Christian art, but usually they are not clearly the cross on which Jesus died: the *chi-rho* symbol sometimes looked a lot like a cross, but it was a symbol merely of the name 'Christ'. But the cross itself appears in many contexts in the later

This mosaic depicts the legend that Pope Liberius (AD 352–66) had a dream that there would be snow in Rome in August. In the snow that fell as the dream predicted, he outlined the plans for the building of the Basilica St Maria Maggiore.

fourth century onwards, as part of decorative backgrounds, or held by Jesus or the saints, or on a throne.

The new prominence of the cross in Christian art may well have been partly inspired by the discovery of the 'True Cross' (see below), which led to a rise of interest in the cross itself as a focus of Christian spirituality. This was just part of the new devotion to relics.

Relics and pilgrimages

Relics

One consequence of the legalisation of Christianity was that there were no more martyrs. From one point of view this was a good thing – Christians need not fear persecution – but it was also a problem given the way martyrs were viewed. As we saw in chapter 5, veneration of the martyrs was very important to the church; it was in their deaths that the kingdom of God could be perceived as coming closer, and their remains had miraculous powers. The end of persecution, combined with the rapid growth in church membership, created a practical problem – there was more demand for relics than there were relics to go around. But there was a more profound, theological problem too. The power of God could no longer be witnessed in the figures of those who died for their faith. Where could it be witnessed now?

Both of these problems were addressed in various ways. The martyrs were still venerated, although now it was as great men and women of the past, of a sort of golden age of the church which had produced heroes the like of which no longer existed. Their relics also continued to be venerated, and new shrines were built to showcase them. It became more common to move the relics from place to place, and such 'translations' were increasingly regarded as highly significant events. Processions were held in which the relics were paraded about, and miracles were reported. Even more dramatic was the discovery of new relics, which also happened from time to time. For example, Augustine described what happened when relics believed to be of St Stephen were discovered and brought forth:

> *At that instant the earth trembled and a smell of sweet perfume came from the place such as no man had ever known of, so much that we thought that we were standing in the sweet garden of Paradise. And at that very hour, from the smell of that perfume, seventy-three persons were healed.*[5]

The passage testifies not only to the belief that such miracles occurred at such times, but also to the expectation that they would. After all, it seems unlikely that seventy-three sick people would have been present at this exhumation if they hadn't expected some kind of miraculous healing to occur.

A 3rd-century relief form showing the miraculous multiplication of bread. As is common in early Christian art, Jesus performs the miracle using a wand, a motif taken from depictions of the Roman gods.

Sacred geography

A new feature of Christianity that emerged during Constantine's reign was the notion of sacred locations. Like the veneration of relics, this had its roots in earlier times, when Christians might consider the places where martyrs died, or where their remains were buried, to be holy. The catacombs seem to have contained small chapels or martyria where the martyrs could be honoured. This trend continued in the fourth century, with the construction of new martyria. But larger-scale geographical areas were now considered sacred too. This was the case, above all, with Palestine. The years after Constantine's defeat of Licinius in AD 324, which brought Palestine under his rule, saw enormous interest in this area as the place where Jesus had lived and where the church had begun three centuries earlier.

A key figure in this new ideology of the Holy Land was Constantine's mother, Helena. It is unknown when or how she, like her son, became a Christian. But in the mid-320s, Helena visited Palestine and travelled to the key sites in Jesus' life. In Jerusalem, she ordered a series of archaeological excavations – a very rare occurrence in antiquity – on what were believed to be these sites. Subsequently, Constantine ordered what was effectively

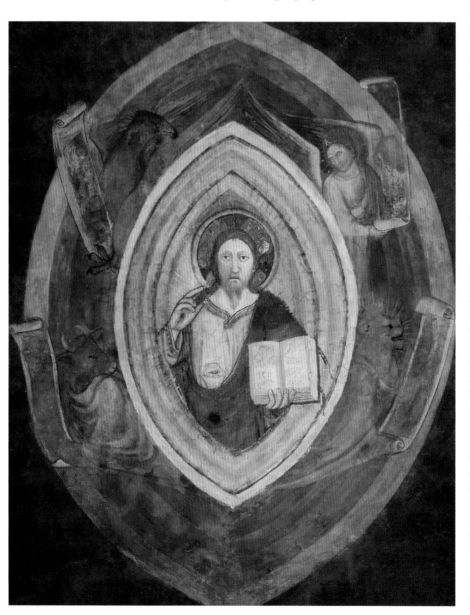

In this 14th-century fresco from the Chapel of St Laurentius, Assisi, Italy, Christ is pictured with the symbols of the four evangelists.

a Christianization of the Palestinian landscape. New churches were built at key locations, including the Church of the Nativity at Bethlehem, over the cave where Jesus was believed to have been born, and the Church of the Holy Sepulchre at Golgotha, by Jerusalem, which contained what were thought to be the sites of Jesus' crucifixion and of his tomb.

While in the Holy Land, legend tells us that Helena discovered a piece of the cross on which Jesus had died, known as the True Cross (since there were other contenders for the title). Contemporary Christian writers do not mention this discovery. The relic believed to be the True Cross was certainly being housed in the church of the Holy Sepulchre by the 340s, but the earliest known writer to attribute its discovery to Helena was the church historian Socrates, writing in the early fifth century. It seems likely, then, that the True Cross was found within a decade or two of Helena's original excavations, and some time later she was credited with its discovery. The True Cross was accompanied by the Holy Nails, by which Jesus had been attached to the cross, and which were said to have been taken back to Constantinople. This, then, marked the beginning of Christian interest in relics which were not the remains of saints, but objects associated with Jesus and especially his passion. The authenticity of relics such as these is impossible to ascertain, especially since most of them have been lost or dispersed. There are objects today that are claimed to be the True Cross, or parts of it, but it is impossible to trace their lineage with any certainty back to the object venerated under that name in the fourth century – let alone to trace *that* object's lineage back to the time of Jesus.

Simply by going to the Holy Land, Helena set a precedent. Other Christians became interested in seeing the sites of Jesus' life for themselves and began travelling there. By the end of the fourth century, this had become quite a common practice. Some Christians, however, disapproved. Gregory of Nyssa argued that it was theologically suspect, because it overemphasized the physical and overlooked the spiritual: God could be worshipped anywhere. Moreover, it was unwise, because men and women travelling together might have greater opportunity for sin. The monastic writer Evagrius Ponticus also discouraged people from going on long journeys at all, for much the same reason.

A Divided Church

The age of Constantine saw the nature of the church, and its status within the Roman empire, transformed. But it also saw the church more divided than it had ever been before. Not only that, but the combination of these divisions with the conversion of the emperor threw up a new problem. Emperors had always sought unity in their empires. Now the church was officially part of that empire. So the unity of the church was now the emperor's business. Did that give the emperor the right to impose unity upon the church whether it liked it or not? Could he tell the bishops what to do? Increasingly, throughout the fourth century AD, emperor after emperor answered these questions with a more definite affirmative.

A number of divisions from earlier periods still existed. There were still Valentinian churches throughout the empire. There were also still Marcionite and Novatianist ones, all rivals to the 'main'

Detail from a Byzantine floor mosaic, c. AD 560, illustrates Jerusalem with the buildings of Emperor Constantine in a map of Palestine.

church organization. For the sake of convenience, we can call the 'main' church the Catholic church, although using the name risks some anachronism. In this context it means all churches, in Latin-, Greek-, and Syriac-speaking regions, which were in communion with one another, and which did not recognize the smaller breakaway groups. In later centuries, this mainstream church would itself split into different churches, which remain distinct today. In a fourth-century context, however, these divisions did not exist, and we can apply the term 'Catholic' to this large, mainstream group of churches.

The Donatist schism

The Donatist schism began as another chapter in the long-running saga of the struggle between what we might call laxists and rigorists. We saw in chapter 7 how the persecutions of the third century left many Christians divided over how to deal with those who had given in to the persecutions and sacrificed to pagan gods: should they be allowed back into the church, or had they destroyed their chances of salvation for ever? This was the issue that Cyprian struggled with in Africa, and which in Rome led to the establishment of the Novatianist church.

Donatist origins

The Donatist church had a similar origin, but this time in the Great Persecution of the early fourth century. The persecution began in AD 303 when Diocletian ordered all copies of the Christian Scriptures to be handed over to the authorities. Many Christians obeyed, including a number of bishops. They became known as *traditores*, from the word meaning 'hand over' – a word which is the origin of the English 'traitor'.

Even before the persecution had ended, the familiar problem of what to do about those who had capitulated to the authorities arose, but in a new form. What about these *bishops* who had done so? There were disputes about this throughout the church, but the worst erupted in Carthage in AD 311. In that year, the local clergy elected a new bishop, Caecilian. A number of local bishops consecrated him, including one Felix of Aptonga. But other bishops, mainly from Numidia, objected. They said that Felix had been a *traditor*. The leader of this party, Secundus of Tigis, declared that Felix had lost the Spirit and with it the ability to perform the duties of a bishop. That meant that Caecilius had not been properly consecrated and was therefore not a bishop either. Secundus accordingly held a council of his own at Carthage where he and seventy other Numidian bishops consecrated their own candidate, Majorinus. There were therefore two rivals, each claiming to be bishop of Carthage, and the schism had begun.

Constantine intervenes

The emperor Constantine, fresh from his victory at the Milvian Bridge, decided that the schism could not be tolerated, and intervened. For reasons that are unknown, he decided strongly in favour of Caecilius. In fact, his first actions towards what would ultimately become the official establishment of Christianity as the Roman religion were made now as he sought to favour Caecilius over his rival. He ordered the financial officer of his African estates to donate a large sum of money to Caecilius, ordered the procurator to give any more that Caecilius required, and gave tax breaks to all Christian priests in communion with Caecilius.

The supporters of Majorinus were horrified and wrote to the emperor, asking him to rethink his position. Constantine responded by ordering Miltiades, the bishop of Rome, to hold a council on the matter. This council found in favour of Caecilius. A number of other councils were held in the following years, and they all agreed. These councils ruled that not only were the supporters of Majorinus unruly schismatics, but their theology was wrong to start with: even if a bishop were a *traditor*, that would not make any ordinations he carried out invalid.

Meanwhile, Majorinus had died and been replaced by Donatus of Casae Nigrae. Donatus, after whom the schism would be named, was a very charismatic and energetic figure, although we know little about him. He seems to have been regarded with awe by many African Christians, who, we are told, would commonly swear 'by Donatus' white hairs' for decades afterwards. He was without doubt the dominant personality in African Christianity throughout the first half of the fourth century. He travelled around the whole region raising support for his cause and was incredibly successful. Throughout Numidia, congregations and bishops came out in support of him and against Caecilius. He enjoyed especially strong support in southern Numidia, one of the few rural areas where Christianity had become successful. The inhabitants of this region, the Berbers, were culturally quite distinct from the Romanized inhabitants of Carthage and other cities, and these cultural differences helped to exacerbate the schism.

Donatus triumphant

In AD 317 Constantine tired of trying to settle the dispute by diplomatic means and ordered Donatist churches to be seized and their leaders exiled. Caecilius took control of local troops in Carthage, but the results were disastrous: a massacre of Donatists, which confirmed the views of the majority of Africans that Caecilius was beyond hope and Donatus was the true bishop of Carthage. Donatus' movement grew as his supporters came to believe that they were the only true Christians left; the others had all gone over to the emperor and the devil. In AD 321, Constantine admitted defeat and recognized the Donatists' right to exist; he was too busy with the new war against Licinius to waste any more time on the matter.

In the years that followed, the Donatist church grew by leaps and bounds. Not only did it aggressively campaign against the Catholic church, but it seems to have been far more successful than the Catholics were in winning converts from paganism throughout Africa. As a result, the Donatist church became extremely well established; it may even have been the main Christian church in much of Africa, outnumbering the Catholics. The most magnificent church buildings of the period in Africa were Donatist, testifying to the wealth as well as the vigour of the movement. Nevertheless, apart from a thriving congregation in Rome, the Donatist church had no success outside Africa. But it made this into a theological virtue; the rejection of the Donatist church by the rest of the world simply proved that it was the true church of God, which was always called to martyrdom.

More attempts to put down Donatism by force were made in the late 340s. Donatus and other Donatist leaders were exiled, imperial troops killed rioting civilians, and some Donatists were publicly tortured. One of them, Marculus, was apparently executed, making him arguably the first Christian to be executed by other Christians for heresy. Other Donatist leaders, including Donatus himself, were exiled. These measures worked for a while, and support for the Donatist church collapsed; but Donatus remained an inspiring figure in exile. When he died in around AD 355, many regarded him as a martyr.

In AD 361, on the death of Constantius II, his cousin Julian became sole Roman emperor. Julian had rejected Christianity altogether and hoped to restore traditional paganism to the empire. He did not persecute the Christians, but he did find a ready-made

The emperor Julian 'the Apostate' (ruled AD 360–63) is shown meeting the leaders of different religious and philosophical sects in this 1875 painting by Edward Armitage.

The Circumcellions

The Circumcellions, who seem to have emerged in the 340s, were rural Donatists from Numidia and Mauretania who lived an itinerant life, hanging around shrines living on handouts (hence Circumcellions, from the Latin for 'around the shrines'). They seem to have been social radicals, trying to overturn what they regarded as an oppressive social system. One practice they were known for was ambushing rich landowners as they travelled in their carriages, with their slaves running after them. The Circumcellions would pull out the landowner, install the slaves in the carriage, and let them ride off with their master running behind. They also attacked non-Donatists. The case of the bishop of Bagai was typical; he had been a Donatist, but converted to Catholicism. The Circumcellions broke into his church, smashed the altar under which the bishop was hiding, beat him up, and threw his unconscious body on a rubbish tip, where he was discovered and rescued the following day.

But they were mainly devoted to the cause of martyrdom. The cult of the martyrs was especially strong in Africa, and the Circumcellions sought to live in a way that prepared them for death or which was in itself a perpetual living martyrdom. They lived highly ascetically, being committed to chastity and fasting – although they were also noted for holding drunken dances in honour of the martyrs.

The leaders of the Donatist church considered the Circumcellions extremists, and tried to suppress the movement. In an ironic re-enactment of the imperial oppression which had spurred the growth of the Donatist church itself, they persuaded the civil authorities to clamp down on the Circumcellions. Many were killed, but the local Donatist clergy and congregations almost universally regarded them as martyrs and buried them within their church precincts. The Circumcellions were simply too popular even for the leaders of the populist Donatist church to suppress.

The most extreme Circumcellions actively sought death. They would waylay travellers and force them to choose between being killed or killing their captors. One story tells of a traveller who, captured by the Circumcellions in this way, agreed to kill them. First he tied them up, but then he just beat them up and left them by the roadside. Others simply committed suicide, and we hear of whole crowds of Circumcellions jumping off cliffs or burning themselves. This ritual suicide was considered a form of martyrdom, and those who died in this way were honoured as martyrs for Christ and for the Donatist cause.

way of causing them trouble in the internal divisions of Christianity. He decreed that all bishops who had previously been deposed or exiled could return home, but he neglected to remove their replacements first. In this way he hoped to cause as much chaos within the Christian church as possible.

In Africa, the leaders of the Donatist church returned home to a rapturous welcome. Congregations in churches across the region which had apparently been happily Catholic for years suddenly declared themselves Donatist once more. Mobs attacked Catholic bishops and priests, expelling them from their positions or even killing them, as their altars and vessels were smashed. Within an incredibly short period of time, Catholicism had been greatly weakened throughout most of Africa, and the Donatist church restored to its previous position of strength. Thus it would remain until the fifth century.

The Arian conflict

The Donatist schism was just that – a schism, that is, a split between different church organizations. On the one hand was the Catholic church, and on the other the Donatist church. The other great Christian division of the age, the Arian conflict, was not a schism, although it did inspire some local schisms. Most of the main players were within the Catholic church, but they disagreed with one another theologically. We thus cannot talk about 'Arians' on the one hand and 'Catholics' on the other – on the contrary, there was a mass of different parties, not all well defined, within the single church.

Arius

Arius was born in what is now Libya, probably in the 250s. He later studied at Antioch under the scholar Lucian, who ran a theological school there before being martyred in AD 312. Lucian seems to have believed something similar to the second-century apologists such as Justin Martyr, that Christ is to be identified with the Logos, who is subordinate to the Father. Arius thought something similar. When he moved to Alexandria, he objected to the teaching of the bishop, Alexander, that Christ – the Logos, or the Son – was eternal, and in some way equal to the Father in his divinity. In Arius' view, the Logos was *not* equal to the Father in any sense. The Logos was the greatest creation of the Father – the highest being in the universe – but not actually divine. The Logos did not have true knowledge of the Father, and did not share his divine attributes. Furthermore, the Logos was not eternal: there was a time before the Father generated the Logos.

Some earlier theologians, such as Justin Martyr or Tertullian, would have agreed with some of these views, particularly the idea that there was a point in time when the Father generated the Logos, and the notion that the Logos was subordinate to the Father (a claim that is known as 'subordinationism'). But in the third century, a number of theologians began teaching that although the Logos was subordinate to the Father, he was nevertheless eternal: the Father generated the Logos eternally, and there was never a time when he did not exist. Moreover, even though the Logos was subordinate to the Father, he was nevertheless divine. The theologians associated

A 6th-century mosaic of the Byzantine school shows the baptism of Christ, surrounded by the twelve apostles bearing crowns. To the right of Jesus is a personification of the River Jordan as an old man, carrying a rush and with horns of lobster claws. Above is the Paraclete (or Holy Spirit), personified as a dove. This cupola of the baptistery was constructed by Theodoric (c. AD 454–526).

with these views were Novatian and, especially, Origen. Arius rejected the notion of eternal generation and stressed the Logos's subordination to such a degree that he made the Logos not divine at all. So in some ways Arius seems to have been a theological conservative, although his outspoken denial of the Logos's divinity was fairly new.

So the issue over which the dispute revolved was the status of the Logos – or the Son – and his relation to the Father. Were they equal? Was the Son as divine as the Father? Or was he just a creation of the Father – the greatest such creation, but still not divine? It is important to be aware that questions such as these are about the Son, not about Jesus specifically. They are about the divine (or quasi-divine) being who became incarnate in Jesus. The issue of what that incarnation involved, and what the precise relationship was between the Son and Jesus, was a completely different issue.

The controversy widens

Arius was a popular preacher, and he also put his views into poetry that was widely circulated. The bishop of Alexandria, Alexander, condemned him in AD 318, but Arius continued to preach. In AD 320, a synod of Egyptian bishops ratified the condemnation. Arius and a group of supporters were exiled, travelling first to Nicomedia and then to Palestine. They found support with Eusebius, bishop of Nicomedia, who like Arius had once been a pupil of Lucian of Antioch. Eusebius seems to have been highly sympathetic to Arius' views and tried to gain support for his cause among other bishops. He had some success, and a number of theologians began setting out ideas much like Arius'. These were, in effect, the first Arians. It is important to note that although the term 'Arian' is generally applied to anyone who, like Arius, denies the divinity of the Son, it was a term invented by their opponents. No one in the fourth century called themselves 'Arian'. Moreover, many – perhaps most – of those dubbed 'Arians' did not hold their beliefs because of the influence of Arius; he was simply the first one to get into trouble for it. In fact later Arians would, on a number of occasions, insist that they had nothing to do with Arius and were uninterested in him.

One major supporter of Arius who was not exactly an Arian was Eusebius of Caesarea, the major church historian, Origenist scholar, and panegyrist of Constantine. Unlike his namesake from

Sand dunes at Erg Murzuk in the Sahara Desert, Libya.

Nicomedia, however, Eusebius of Caesarea seems not to have shared Arius' views. He thought that matters such as the way in which the Father generated the Son were inherently incomprehensible. Nevertheless, he wrote to Alexander of Alexandria criticizing his actions in the affair. In fact, so many bishops came out in favour of Arius that he confidently returned to Alexandria and seems to have begun setting up a rival church there.

In AD 324, Constantine defeated Licinius and took control of the eastern empire. Shortly after doing so he wrote to both Alexander and Arius, telling them that their disagreement was pointless and trivial, and instructing them to make peace with each other. Evidently, the emperor still had much to learn about the nature of theological debate, because they did nothing of the kind.

The council of Nicaea

In AD 325, Constantine decided that a line needed to be drawn under the controversy, and he summoned a general council of bishops from every part of the empire to settle it. The council was to be held at Nicaea, near Constantinople, which was still being built. Precisely why Constantine decided to summon such a large council, and preside over it himself, is uncertain. But it seems reasonable to attribute it, in part, to his belief that, as the one emperor and patron of the church, it was his duty to try to establish unity in that church. The council or synod of bishops was by now an established method of resolving local disputes. Bishops from throughout the eastern empire had been drawn into the Arius affair, so a bigger council was needed. Traditionally, 318 bishops are supposed to have attended the council of Nicaea, although it is uncertain what the precise number actually was. Most of them were from the eastern empire, although there were a few representatives of the west. The Arius affair had, so far, not had the slightest impact on any Latin-speaking region, and the proceedings of the council were conducted in Greek. Sylvester, the bishop of Rome, was not present, but he sent two presbyters to represent him.

Ossius, bishop of Cordova, Constantine's main adviser on ecclesiastical matters, presided over most of the proceedings. But Eusebius of Nicomedia – in whose territory Nicaea lay – made the opening speech of greeting to Constantine, and the emperor himself presided over the first and last sessions of the council. He spoke in Latin, through an interpreter. Although very little information has survived about the procedures of the council, it must have been a magnificent and dramatic affair: the emperor himself, enthroned in the midst of his bishops, the very symbol of the unity of the Roman empire and of the church alike, both united in his own person.

After this opening ceremony, a series of meetings was held between May and July AD 325 during which the bishops cross-examined Arius and his supporters and eventually agreed on a statement of faith. This statement of faith, known as the Symbol of Nicaea, ran as follows:

We believe in God the Father almighty,
maker of all things, visible and invisible.
And in one Lord Jesus Christ,
the only-begotten of the Father,
that is, begotten of the substance of the Father,
God from God, light from light, true God from true God,
begotten, not made,
of the same substance as the Father,
through whom all things were made, in heaven and earth;
who for us humans and our salvation came down, took flesh, and was made human,
suffered and rose again on the third day,
ascended into heaven,
and will come to judge the living and the dead.
And in the Holy Spirit.

It was followed by the following series of anathemas, or condemnations:

Wall painting of the first council of Nicaea, which took place in AD 325.

But those who say,
'There was a time when he did not exist',
and 'Before being begotten he did not exist',
and that he came into being from non-existence,
or who allege that the Son of God is of another hypostasis or ousia,
or is alterable or changeable,
these the Catholic and Apostolic Church condemns.

The creed was expressly designed to reject the teaching of Arius and his supporters. The statements which are condemned in the anathemas are all associated with Arius. The creed itself stresses that the Son was generated *from* the Father, not merely *by* the Father – another thing that Arius' supporters denied. The distinction between being 'begotten' and being 'made' attacked one of the main arguments for Arius' views, the claim that if the Son was begotten then he must be a created thing and not God at all. Also significant was the line about the Son being 'of one substance' with the Father. In Greek, this was expressed by a single word, *homoousios. Homo* means 'same' and *ousia* means 'substance'. However, at this time, both of these words were rather ambiguous. 'Same', after all, can mean either 'similar' or 'identical'. If I say that I am wearing the same hat as you, I mean that we have similar hats, not that we are both literally wearing one and the same hat. But if I say that Superman is the same person as Clark Kent, I mean they are actually one and the same individual, not merely similar to one another.

The reinvention of Christianity?

Today, there are many misconceptions about the council of Nicaea. It has been portrayed as a device of Constantine to reinvent Christianity in a form that was more politically expedient, when the old, original faith in Jesus as a human prophet was crushed to make way for a new religion featuring the divine Christ. From what we have seen so far, it is clear that such an interpretation cannot stand. The council of Nicaea did not invent the notion that Christ was divine; on the contrary, such a belief had been standard since at least the third century and can be found in plenty of Christian writings before then. Moreover, although Constantine called the council and should not be underestimated as a theologian, he did not dictate its course. His Greek was good enough to understand the findings of the bishops when they were explained to him, but not good enough for him to have participated actively in the sessions, even had he wished to. So the council was not devised to reinvent the Christian religion; rather, it was an attempt to resolve a pressing problem of disunity. The creed it issued, and the anathemas which followed that creed, were designed to address that problem. Those who issued these documents did so because they believed that they expressed the traditional faith of the church, not because they wished to change that faith to something new.

Which meaning of 'same' did the bishops of Nicaea intend? They weren't clear at all.

However, the vast majority of those present were happy with the formulation. Only two bishops refused to sign it, and they were deposed. Eusebius of Caesarea signed it, although he subsequently wrote a self-serving explanation for his congregation back home in which he stated that the anti-Arian elements meant only that the Son was superior to all other creatures. Eusebius of Nicomedia also signed it. He had had a rough time at the council: he had presented a statement of faith of his own during the early stages, which had so shocked the other bishops that he had been shouted down. No doubt he was keen to demonstrate his orthodoxy by signing the Symbol of Nicaea, but he refused to condemn Arius personally. It did him little good, at least in the short term; a couple of months after the council, Constantine exiled him and his ally Theognis of Nicaea. As for Arius himself, he was also exiled, probably to Illyria.

Arianism: the next phase

After the council, things cooled down. In fact it seems that Constantine became much more sympathetic to Arius and his supporters within just a couple of years; there is evidence that before AD 330 Arius had already been reconciled to the church and was back in Alexandria. Eusebius of Nicomedia was recalled from exile, and managed to secure the emperor's favour. And the anti-Arian party found events slipping from their control. The fate of Eustathius, bishop of Antioch, was typical. He had been a leading figure in the discussions at Nicaea and had opposed both of the Eusebii. But in around AD 330, a council at Antioch – overseen by Eusebius of Caesarea – deposed him for reasons that remain obscure, although it was certainly something to do with his outspoken opposition to Arius. He may have been denounced as a modalist or Sabellian. Sabellianism was the belief that the Father and the Son are identical with one another, and merely different names for the same individual. Those who sympathized with Arius increasingly came to regard their opponents as Sabellians, and it seems that Eustathius was the first victim of this interpretation. But he enjoyed the support of many people in Antioch, who refused to accept his deposition or recognize the authority of any of his successors. These people, known as Eustathians, set up their own church instead. Thus the Arian controversy had produced outright schism in one of the oldest and most important Christian communities.

Another prominent anti-Arian who found himself in trouble was Marcellus of Ancyra, who was deposed in the mid 330s. Marcellus had written a book against Arius' supporters in which he set out an unusual theology of his own. He believed that originally the Father was completely alone and that he generated the Son and also the Holy Spirit at a particular point in time. The Son and the Spirit are both fully divine. However, their existence as distinct entities is only temporary; there will be a time in the future when they will both be reabsorbed into the Father and he will be alone again. The supporters of Arius denounced this, and many opponents of Arius also found it objectionable. It was not exactly Sabellianism, but it did make what most people considered the mistake of denying real, individual, and permanent existence to the Son.

But a new figure was emerging on the theological scene who would dominate it for the next four decades. Athanasius became bishop of Alexandria in AD 328, upon Alexander's death. He was just as opposed to Arius as Alexander had been, and had been present at the council of Nicaea, although he had played no active part. However, the problems that plagued Athanasius soon after his election as bishop seem initially to have had nothing to do with the Arian controversy. A faction within his church accused him of malpractice, and there is some evidence that Athanasius did try to clamp down on dissent in a heavy-handed manner, arresting or imprisoning his opponents or even having them beaten up. In AD 335, a council at Tyre deposed Athanasius on a number of charges. With his usual boldness he went to Constantinople and accosted Constantine on the street, asking for the case to be heard again, but not only was his request rejected but he was exiled to Trier.

The affair of Athanasius did not distract Constantine from his aim of rehabilitating Arius. It seems that the emperor had become convinced that Nicaea had been hijacked by a group of extremists, and that the theology of people like Eusebius of Nicomedia actually represented the broadest, middle way around which to unite the church. In AD 336, he instructed the bishops to reinstate Arius as a presbyter at Alexandria. However, apparently while the bishops were deliberating about this, Arius suddenly died. According to Athanasius, his death was suitably gruesome for such a terrible heretic: he suffered an appalling haemorrhage while in a public toilet in Constantinople. The following year, Constantine himself died.

The role of the emperors

Constantine's empire was divided between his three surviving sons. Constantine II, the eldest, was given the west. The second son, Constantius II, was given the east. And the third son, the teenage Constans, received a wide strip down the middle, including Africa and Constantinople. This settlement, which seems to have been reached after some months of negotiation between the sons, the bishops, and the military, was immediately followed by a murderous purge worthy of Stalin. Imperial promotion of Christianity had never meant that the standard brutal practices of emperors ended. When Licinius defeated Maximinus in AD 313, he had Maximinus' wife and two small children killed. In AD 326, for reasons that are unknown, Constantine ordered the executions of his eldest son Crispus and of his wife Fausta – the latter being cooked to death in a bathroom. Now Constantine's surviving sons followed the usual imperial practice of eliminating potential rivals, although they did it with unusual thoroughness; relatives of all kinds, their families, prominent officials and generals, *their* families, and others were murdered, probably mostly on the orders of Constantius, who seems to have suffered pangs of guilt over it for the rest of his life.

Constantine II invaded Constans' territory, but was defeated and killed in AD 340. Constans – aged only seventeen – thus took control of Constantine's territories, which meant that the empire was once more divided into only two, under Constans in the west and Constantius II in the east. Constans was inclined towards Nicene Christianity, but Constantius was more inclined towards Arianism.

In AD 341, Julius, the bishop of Rome, called a new council to reinvestigate the Athanasius affair. He found him innocent of all charges. The council also investigated Marcellus of Ancyra, and found him to be orthodox. Julius wrote to Eusebius and his allies, accusing them of trying to overturn Nicaea. The Arian controversy, which had supposedly been ended twice – first at Nicaea with the condemnation of Arius and then ten years later by the rehabilitation of Arius – was re-emerging. The western half of the empire had so far been unaffected. Julius' intervention made it clear that most western bishops were solidly opposed to Arianism and supported even extreme Nicenes such as Marcellus of Ancyra. In the east, where the Nicene *homoousios* was fast becoming a dirty word, that intervention was decidedly unwelcome. Later in AD 341 a council was called at Antioch to respond to the Roman one, in the presence of the emperor Constantius. This council produced four creeds, mostly moderately Arian and strongly anti-Sabellian in tone. Marcellus was condemned again.

Now Constans, the western emperor, made his move. The bishops in his domains were unimpressed by the council of Antioch, and he concluded that the situation had become serious enough to warrant another council of the whole church, a new Nicaea. He secured the agreement of Constantius and called the council in Serdica, on the border between the two halves of the empire. He hoped to reconcile the two halves of the church. Unfortunately, the whole affair was a disaster. The eastern bishops refused to meet the western ones, who were accompanied by Marcellus and Athanasius. But the western bishops refused to abandon them. Eventually the easterners returned home, accusing the westerners of Sabellianism; the westerners retorted that the easterners were all Arians.

A number of small councils were called in the 340s, but to little effect. But then everything changed. In AD 350 Constans was murdered, and Constantius defeated his killer to become sole master of the empire by AD 353. As he consolidated his power over the empire, Constantius became more determined than ever to sort out the theological divisions within the church. In AD 351 he held a council at Sirmium, which produced yet another creed which represented the clearest attack yet upon Nicaea. It was followed by a council at Arles in AD 353 and another at Milan in AD 355. The locations were significant: Constantius' campaign in the early 350s had taken place in the western empire, and even after its conclusion the emperor made Milan his main centre of government. Rome, which had already been eclipsed by Constantinople, was now of very little political importance. The emperor was thus trying to impose moderately Arian views not simply upon the eastern church, which was relatively receptive to them, but upon the western church, which had hitherto been extremely opposed to them.

The council of Milan seems to have been especially fractious. One bishop, Eusebius of Vercelli, said that he was willing to condemn Athanasius – but then he pulled out a copy of the Symbol of Nicaea, and declared that everyone had to sign that first. One bishop was about to do so when another knocked the pen out of his hand. There was a scuffle and the meeting was ended. Constantius summoned the bishops to his palace, where (we are told by Athanasius, admittedly not an unbiased authority) one of them objected to the emperor that this sort of thing was not in accordance with the canon of the church, that is, the rule of faith. 'My will is the canon!' retorted Constantius. In the end almost everyone condemned Athanasius, no one signed the Symbol of Nicaea, and Eusebius of Vercelli was exiled.

The next generation

In AD 357, yet another council was held, this time at Sirmium. It issued a new creed which was more Arian than anything that had gone before. It condemned the term *homoousios* and declared that the Son was subordinate to the Father. This creed set a new standard for the controversy, and its opponents dubbed it 'the blasphemy of Sirmium'.

Now more clearly defined parties emerged from the chaos. One was the Nicene party, whose eastern representatives – although in a minority there – were still making a loud noise. The loudest was coming from Athanasius, who had refused to leave Egypt and was in hiding in Alexandria and in the nearby desert. He was working constantly to undermine George of Cappadocia, his supposed replacement, and continued to act as bishop to the majority of people in the city who were loyal to him. Somehow he also found time to write a large number of books during this period, many dealing with the Arian controversy. In them, Athanasius presented a cogent defence of Nicene theology and the *homoousios* in particular. He stressed that the eternal nature of God means that God is both eternally begetting and eternally begotten; this means that the Son is the true image of the Father. What of the Arian claim that anything that is begotten cannot be God? Athanasius replied by distinguishing between being *created* and being *begotten*. To be created would indeed be unworthy of God, but to be begotten is not. In fact, Athanasius stressed that the Son *must* be fully divine, or salvation would be ineffective. He reminded his readers that human beings are saved because God becomes human, thereby imparting the divine qualities of incorruptibility and immortality to human nature. But this could not happen if the Son were not really God. In a famous line in his book *On the Incarnation of the Word of God*, he stated: 'God became man so that man might become God.' With these arguments, Athanasius made himself the most prominent and effective opponent of the Arians.

Athanasius' defence of the theology of Nicaea was influential, especially in the west. Before AD 357, it seems that most westerners, although suspicious of those they considered Arians, knew little of the council of Nicaea. In fact Hilary, bishop of Poitiers, one of the main anti-Arian theologians of the west, later stated that he had never heard of this council *at all* until he was exiled in the east and talked to people there. But for anti-Arians in the west, the 'blasphemy of Sirmium' was so horrible that it led to new support for the Symbol of Nicaea as the best alternative. Hilary led this campaign. In AD 356 Constantius had exiled him after he had deposed the bishop of Arles for being an Arian; Hilary spent his exile, in Phrygia, speaking to eastern bishops and learning more about the background to the controversy. He wrote a number of books defending the *homoousios* and making its theology more widely known in the west.

Another party also emerged during this time which was the polar opposite of the Nicenes. The leaders of the Neo-Arians, as they are sometimes known, were Aetius and Eunomius. Aetius was apparently a former metal-worker who became prominent in Antioch in the early 350s. Where moderate Arians were prepared to accept that the Son was like the Father in many respects, but without sharing his divinity, Aetius went further and insisted that the Son was not like the Father in *any* respect. This was too much for the church in Antioch – at that time controlled by moderate Arians – and they exiled Aetius to Alexandria, where he met Eunomius, who became his secretary and later developed his ideas. This Neo-Arianism never seems to have been very popular – it was quite an extreme and intellectual position, not a popular movement. It is sometimes known as Anomoeanism, from the word for 'unlike', because its representatives believed that the Son is completely unlike the Father (or at least, this is how their opponents represented their views). It remained distinct from the main, moderate version of Arianism, which is often called Homoianism, from the word for 'like', because these theologians believed that the Son was 'like' the Father in most respects. In particular, they argued that the Son was 'like' the Father in will: they always operate together. They denied, however, that the two were 'like' in *ousia*, and denied that the Son should be considered fully divine. The effective leader of this group in the eastern church was Acacius of Caesarea.

But there was a fourth group as well, known as the Homoiousians. They were led by Basil, who had replaced Marcellus as bishop of Ancyra. Basil had apparently been a physician before becoming a priest, and was a very shrewd theologian. He tried to devise a new understanding of the Trinity which might prove acceptable to all sides. Recognizing that the Nicene *homoousios* was both ambiguous and divisive, he proposed instead the formula *homoiousios*, meaning 'similar in substance'. He believed that this captured the main thing that the defenders of Nicaea were concerned about, the similarity of the Father and the Son; but it avoided the main thing that the Homoians were worried about, the identification of Father and Son.

The emperor Constantius was impressed. It seemed to him that here was a formula which might exclude the extremists on both sides, but which everyone else could agree on. A new council was in order. This would be a joint council: the eastern bishops would meet at Seleucia, and the western ones at Ariminum. Before the councils opened in AD 359, Basil and a group of allies sat up all night drafting a document known as the 'dated creed', which they hoped would be amenable to everyone. But their efforts were in vain. At Seleucia, Acacius of Caesarea and other Homoians took control and rewrote the creed to be less conciliatory and more Arian. At Ariminum, the bishops initially refused to sign this, but eventually capitulated when Constantius refused to let them go home until they had done so. The following year, having effectively supplanted Basil as theological adviser to the emperor, Acacius presided over a follow-up council at Constantinople. That council exiled Basil of Ancyra and the other leading Homoiousians, mostly on non-theological charges.

Gregory of Nazianzus (c. AD 325–89), doctor of the church, is shown seated, writing at his desk in Constantinople.

A new solution

The middle phase of the Arian controversy ended in AD 361. In that year, Constantius died and was succeeded by his cousin, Julian. As we saw earlier, Julian immediately ordered that all exiled bishops should return home, hoping to cause chaos throughout the church.

Since most of the returning bishops were supporters of the Nicene or Homoiousian parties, this event greatly encouraged those parties at the expense of the Homoians.

In Alexandria, Athanasius returned to a hero's welcome. His replacement, George of Cappadocia, had been so unpopular he had been lynched by an angry mob even before Julian had announced the return of exiled bishops. Athanasius immediately organized a synod of local bishops, which wrote a letter to the church at Antioch calling for it to adopt the Nicene faith. The church in Antioch was still divided between two rival congregations, one loyal to Eustathius who had been deposed thirty years earlier (and was long dead), and one loyal to the current 'official' bishop, Meletius. Meletius' theological views are rather hard to pin down, but he seems to have been mostly sympathetic to Nicaea. In response to Athanasius' letter, he signed a copy of the Symbol of Nicaea. Remarkably, so did Acacius of Caesarea, apparently because he was worried about the Anomoeans and wanted to distance himself from them. But for reasons that are not well understood, Athanasius did not recognize Meletius as bishop of Antioch. Thus the schism at Antioch continued. It is usually referred to as the 'Meletian schism' – rather unfairly, given that Meletius did not cause it.

Julian died in AD 363. He was succeeded by the general Jovian – who died after a few months – and then another general, Valentinian, who appointed his brother Valens as eastern emperor. Valens was an even more committed Homoian than Constantius had been, and he ordered all the reinstated bishops to go back into exile. Athanasius was among them, but he left for only a few months; Valens was a pragmatist, and realized that keeping him out of Alexandria was more trouble than it was worth. Athanasius returned and was left in relative peace until his death in AD 373.

However, a new breed of theologians was emerging, whose work would initiate the endgame in the Arian controversy. The leader of this group was Basil of Caesarea, whose work to help the poor we saw in chapter 8. An extremely learned man, he had at an early stage become associated with the Homoiousian party of his namesake, Basil of Ancyra. But later, Basil of Caesarea became much more drawn towards the Nicene party, which he came to believe was the only effective means of combating the Arians. In the 360s he wrote a weighty book attacking the Anomoean Eunomius. In it he pioneered a new anti-Arian argument. Eunomius claimed that the nature of God was knowable, which meant that the non-divinity of the Son could be proven. Basil rejected this claim and argued that in fact God is intrinsically unknowable. He also did something that no one seems to have attempted previously, which was to define his terms carefully. Bishops had been arguing about whether the Father and Son were of one *ousia* or not, but no one knew quite what that word meant – or *hypostasis*, another term that meant something similar and which appeared in the anathemas of Nicaea as a synonym of *ousia*. Basil argued that they have the same meaning as the general to the particular. That is, *ousia* is the sort of thing that God is, and *hypostasis* is a particular thing of that kind. With this distinction in mind, he argued that there is one *ousia* in God (the divine nature itself), but that this nature is instantiated in three *hypostases* (the Father, the Son, and the Holy Spirit).

In AD 370, Basil became bishop of Caesarea and began energetically promoting the Nicene faith. He could do this, despite the anti-Nicene climate fostered by the emperor Valens, by a combination of tenacity and personal charm; Basil got on well with Valens, who was prepared to tolerate Nicenes if they were useful. In fact, at the emperor's request, he travelled to Armenia and appointed bishops there, which Valens hoped would keep the Armenians allied to Rome and not to the Persians. However, Valens did annoy Basil by reducing the size of the province of Cappadocia, which meant there were fewer bishops under the control of Caesarea. Whether he did this deliberately to annoy Basil is uncertain, but Basil responded by creating large numbers of new bishops within his remaining territory and appointing his friends and relations to the new posts. One was Basil's younger brother, Gregory, who until this point had been leading a quiet life as a teacher of rhetoric. Suddenly appointed bishop of the town of Nyssa, Gregory transformed himself into an even more able theologian than Basil. He wrote a number of works developing Basil's ideas about the Trinity. In particular, he defended the notion that the Father, the Son, and the Holy Spirit are like three things of the same kind. That sounds like tritheism – the belief that there are simply three Gods – but Gregory argued that this is not so, because they are incorporeal. They do not have any of the distinguishing features that normally tell you that things are distinct, such as being in different places. The unity of the three is therefore far greater than the unity of (say) three human beings who share human nature.

Together, Basil of Caesarea and Gregory of Nyssa – with a third theologian, Gregory of Nazianzus, whom we shall meet in more detail in chapter 11 – were developing a new understanding of the Trinity which took insights from the Homoiousian theology pioneered by Basil of Ancyra but combined them with the *homoousios* formula of Nicaea. It was a highly sophisticated interpretation of Nicaea which effectively answered the Symbol's various critics. For most of the 370s, under the anti-Nicene regime of Valens, their theology remained officially proscribed. But a dramatic political and theological turnaround at the end of the 370s would see the Cappadocian theology move decisively into the foreground.

The First Monks

The rise of monasticism was one of the most remarkable religious developments of the fourth century AD. It saw Christianity transfigured into a radically different way of life, one that took ideas from the philosophical and ascetic traditions but transformed them into a major social movement. By the end of the fourth century, the monks were a political force to be reckoned with.

Antony the Great

Towards the end of the third century AD, a young farmer was sitting in a small church in a village near the River Nile. During the service, a passage from Matthew 19 was read out, in which Jesus tells a rich young man to sell all he has and give to the poor. Struck by the command, the farmer – who owned a large estate in the area – did exactly that. He sold everything he had, gave the money to the poor, and embarked on a new life dedicated to serving Jesus.

Grotto of the Apocalypse, Patmos, where St John is said to have written the book of Revelation between AD 95 and 97.

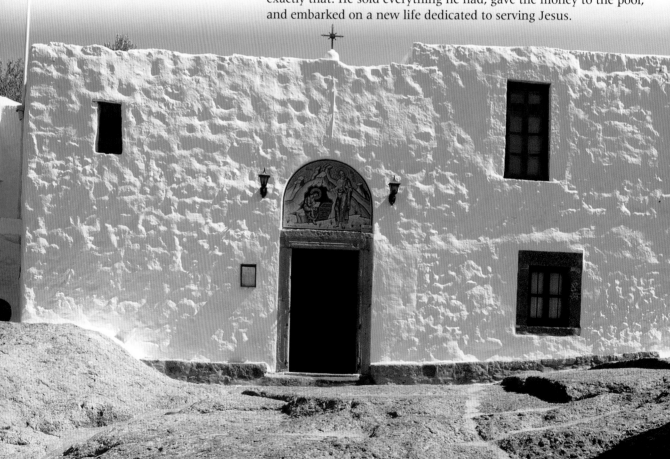

That young man was Antony, later known as Antony the Great of Egypt. He believed that if his life was to be devoted to Jesus, he had to find solitude so that he could focus completely on God. First he lived alone on the outskirts of the village, but later he moved to a nearby cemetery. After fifteen years there, he moved again, this time to an old fort in the centre of the desert. Here he remained for twenty years, completely alone, living on food that a few well-wishers threw over the wall for him.

Paradoxically, Antony's attempts to find solitude brought him fame. Would-be disciples thronged around the old fort, until eventually Antony was persuaded to come forth and set up a community. However, the desire for solitude was too strong. After a short time, he left again for Mount Colzim, near the Red Sea, where he lived alone for another forty-five years until his death in AD 356 at the age, we are told, of 105.

Antony might have been forgotten by all except his disciples, but he had had the curious fortune to become associated with a man who was in many ways as different from him as anyone could have been, despite being a fellow Egyptian Christian. That man was Athanasius, the famous bishop of Alexandria. Like many rural Copts, Antony lived in a world different from the cosmopolitan, Greek-speaking metropolis; he visited the city only twice, and that was with reluctance. The first occasion was in AD 311, to encourage the Christians there during the persecutions, and the second was in AD 338, to visit Athanasius. News of the Arian controversy had filtered to Antony's remote cell, and he wanted to pledge his support to the bishop. That may have been one of the key factors behind Athanasius' later popularity throughout Egypt, since the canny bishop recognized a good PR opportunity when he saw one. Shortly after Antony's death, Athanasius – at that time on the run, and writing tirelessly against Arianism – wrote a book telling the story of Antony's career. In it, Athanasius presented the hermit as a hero of Christianity: a man who had chosen a highly ascetic lifestyle as a route to finding God, and who had battled endless hordes of demons in the desert. The effect of the book was twofold. First, it aroused enormous interest not

The temptation of Antony is shown in this painting by Hieronymus Bosch (1450–1516).

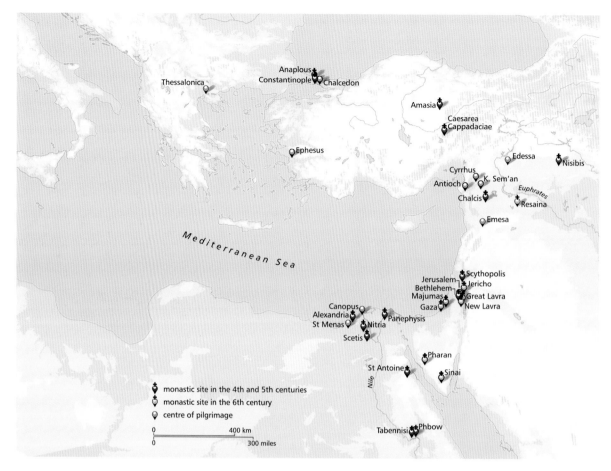

Map showing the location of principal monasteries from the 4th to 6th centuries.

only in Antony himself but in other hermits like him in Egypt. And second, it harnessed that interest to the Nicene cause, for Athanasius was careful to point out that this hero of the faith was a fervent anti-Arian.

Athanasius' *Life of Antony* would prove to be one of the most influential Christian books ever written. It was the first full-blown Christian biography of a great saint. There would be innumerable *Lives* of innumerable saints in the centuries to come, and all of them, directly or indirectly, took Athanasius' book as a model. Antony became celebrated as the first Christian hermit and the original founder of Christian monasticism. In fact he was neither. According to Athanasius himself, the young saint first made himself the disciple of an old Christian hermit living on the edge of his village. There seems to have been a common practice, in early fourth-century Egypt, of devout Christians retreating to the outskirts of settlements to live alone. Some scholars have argued recently that these 'monks' – *monachoi*, 'loners' – who lived near villages may have represented a large group of ascetic individuals who remained, to some extent, living within society. They were known as *apoktaktikoi* or 'renouncers'. But later monastic literature would tend to marginalize these pioneers, and instead celebrate the 'true' monks who renounced society altogether and moved to the desert.

The semi-communal lifestyle

By the time Antony died, even before Athanasius had written his biography, there were thousands of monks throughout Egypt. Some lived as hermits, like Antony. One of the most famous was John of Lycopolis, originally a builder from a town in the south of Egypt, who lived alone on the top of a mountain for decades. John was famed as a prophet and wise man, and we hear of other monks making long and arduous journeys to seek his advice. Hermits such as John and Antony represented one way of developing the lifestyle of the very first Christian monks. But true solitude seems to have been much less popular than the semi-communal lifestyle. On this pattern, the monks still withdrew into the desert – perhaps a few days' journey from the village or town – but they did so in a group. The monks would live apart, in their own cells (usually small huts with one or two rooms), perhaps a mile or two away from one another; they would meet up regularly for communal meals or prayers. These communities were sometimes known as *sketes*.

A rock cone in Cappadocia, Turkey, fashioned by erosion and containing caves dug by early Christians.

209

THE FIRST MONKS

The best known of these communities was Nitria, founded by a balsam-grower named Amoun. As a young man, at the beginning of the fourth century, Amoun had been pressured by his family into getting married, but he and his wife agreed to live together chastely as some Christian couples still did. They spent eighteen years like this, until they finally separated and Amoun moved to Nitria, 40 miles southeast of Alexandria, just beyond Lake Marea, on the edge of the desert. There he lived for another twenty-two years. Disciples arrived and built their own cells there, and the community of Nitria was born.

By the end of the fourth century, there were 5,000 monks on the 'mountain', as it was known (it was actually barely a low hill, but the term expressed the spiritual significance of the place). They mostly lived alone in their individual cells, coming together to eat and pray. They were served by seven bakeries, and had their own gardens for growing vegetables; the community even had its own vineyards. At the centre stood a large church, where the monks would gather on Saturdays and Sundays, and also a guesthouse. It seems that Nitria was a popular tourist destination; it was easily accessible from Alexandria (one could travel there by boat, across Lake Marea) and it boasted many famous monks. And anyone could join the community; on the first day, the other monks would help the newcomer to build his own cell, and from then on he was left to his own devices. Most would learn a trade – linen-making was especially popular – but some found other ways to contribute. We hear of one elderly monk who had been a businessman before coming to Nitria. He set up a business importing medicine and groceries from Alexandria and spent his time walking from cell to cell tending the sick and delivering goods, a trade that apparently earned him a decent profit. Nitria sounds like a bustling place, although no one could forget its purpose. One visitor described how 'about the ninth hour one can stand and hear the divine psalmody issuing forth from each cell and imagine one is high above in paradise'[1].

Some monks found Nitria too crowded, and a second community arose at Kellia in the deeper desert. Although only 12 miles from Nitria, Kellia must have been like another world. Here the desert was much harsher, and the monks would rarely meet. They came together on Saturdays and Sundays for communal worship, but otherwise Kellia was gripped by a profound silence. By the end of the fourth century, the monks of Kellia were living in small communities; each one consisted of a group of cells surrounded by a wall, and just a few monks would live there together. One of the most famous monks of Kellia was Macarius of Alexandria, a former sweet-maker, who acted as the priest of the whole community. Macarius was famous for his incredible feats of asceticism; on one occasion he killed a mosquito and was so overcome by remorse that he spent six months sitting in a swamp, allowing the mosquitoes to bite him as much as they liked. When he returned, the other monks could recognize him only by his voice.

And even beyond Kellia there was Scetis, 40 miles south of Nitria, in the real 'inner desert'. The wilderness was so vast and uniform that travellers had to navigate by the stars in order to find it. The community was founded in a valley here by another Macarius, known as Macarius the Egyptian. He had worked as a niter-smuggler before becoming a monk and as a result knew about the location, which was near niter mines. The monks lived in caves or small huts along the valley walls, and worked at manual tasks in addition to praying. During harvest time they would travel east to the Nile to seek work on farms. By the end of the fourth century, Scetis had coalesced into four distinct communities, each with its own church and priest, but the monks continued to live quite separately from one another. Macarius the Egyptian, in particular, disliked visitors so much that he apparently dug a half-mile-long tunnel from his cell to a secret cave, where he would go to escape.

Living in the desert

In some ways, life in these communities and the many others like them seems quite idyllic. The monks were living a simpler life, away from the bustle and worry of the city. But they were there not to relax but to find God. Every monk spent the vast majority of his time sitting alone in his cell, sometimes working with his hands, sometimes simply meditating, but always focusing upon

Evagrius Ponticus

Evagrius was from Pontus, on the coast of the Black Sea, and as a young man had been a disciple of Basil of Caesarea and Gregory of Nazianzus. However, an affair with a married woman in Constantinople had led him to flee his homeland and eventually end up in Kellia, where he attached himself to Macarius of Alexandria and became famous for his own asceticism. Evagrius was an accomplished theologian, strongly influenced by Origen, but the numerous works he produced in the desert were mostly written in the style of the oral tradition he found there: short, gnomic sayings which forced the reader to meditate upon them to extract their full meaning. Evagrius encouraged his readers to focus upon God and work hard at achieving the state of mind which would allow them to see him. Evagrius called this state of mind *apatheia* or 'passionlessness', an idea that came ultimately from Stoic philosophy. Only by becoming completely serene, without any passions, could the mind be still and undisturbed enough to see God. This was not an easy state to achieve, and Evagrius predicted that the monk who sought it would be plagued by unwanted thoughts which would arouse his passions. Evagrius categorized these thoughts into eight kinds: gluttony, fornication, avarice, sadness, anger, listlessness, vainglory, and pride. Each kind, he believed, was associated with a demon. As the monk tried to pray, the demon would agitate his mind, bringing up one of these eight thoughts, and the monk would be overwhelmed by emotion.

God. They believed that God was to be found only in withdrawal: both a physical withdrawal from 'the world' into the desert, but also a spiritual withdrawal into the self. They were convinced that God could be found within the human heart if only one could learn to see him there.

Evagrius Ponticus, one of the most important writers of the Egyptian desert, described the vision that awaited the most disciplined monk: an experience of his own soul, shining blue like a sapphire or the midday sky, illuminated by God. In such a state, it could be hard to tell where the soul stopped and God began. Indeed, Evagrius himself was so unsure that he made the eighteen-day journey to visit John of Lycopolis to ask him what he thought. John could give him no certain answer.

The demons of temptation

All of the desert fathers seem to have regarded themselves as engaged in spiritual warfare. Tales of demonic attacks are common. Sometimes we hear of demons appearing to monks in visions and dreams; at other times, miraculous events are reported. There are healings and exorcisms. Even the defeat of one demon may provide another with the opportunity to attack, as the victorious monk becomes proud of his achievement. One story tells of a monk who suffered three defeats in a row. He became famous for his ascetic lifestyle, and grew proud of himself. That was the first defeat. Then he met a young woman in the desert who asked for shelter, and he allowed her into her cell, where, during the night, he became overpowered with lust. That was the second defeat. She transformed into a demon and disappeared, and he realized he had been tricked. Overcome with shame, he believed that his soul must be lost, and he gave up the monastic life and returned to the city. That was his third and worst defeat, for the monks regarded despair as another temptation to be resisted.

Evagrius comments that greed is usually the first demon to attack, opening the door to the others, and many monks seem to have been tormented by thoughts of fruit, hard to obtain in the desert. A more pervasive temptation was sheer boredom. Evagrius listed *acedia*, a kind of nervous listlessness, among the eight sinful thoughts. Anyone who has tried to focus upon a boring or lengthy task might recognize the symptoms of acedia:

> When he reads, the one afflicted with acedia yawns a lot and readily drifts off into sleep; he rubs his eyes and stretches his arms; turning his eyes away from the book, he stares at the wall and again goes back to reading for awhile; leafing through the pages, he looks curiously for the end of texts, he counts the folios and calculates the number of gatherings. Later, he closes the book and puts it under his head and falls asleep, but not a very deep sleep, for hunger then rouses his soul and has him show concern for its needs.[2]

The cure for acedia, according to Evagrius, was simple: just stick at it and do not leave the cell. The monks believed that all of the attacks of the demons could be repelled one way or another. The most important technique was discipline. The monk was to focus upon his work and, above all else, not give in to his own inherent weaknesses. Women were always to be avoided at all costs; we hear of monks who pledged never to look upon a woman having to talk to female visitors through the window. One elderly monk, Pion, visited his sister when she asked to see him after fifty years apart; he stood outside her house with his eyes shut, so that she could see him but he would not see her. The impression one gets from the monastic literature is of a world so male-dominated that women were almost invisible, and were to be excluded as much as possible. That is not entirely accurate. Rather, the sexes were to be kept apart as much as possible for fear of giving sin a foothold. There were female ascetics, many of whom were praised rather misogynistically as being so virtuous that they were like men. Nevertheless, male ascetics certainly greatly outnumbered the female ones. Even though female ascetics were praised, it must have been much harder for women who wished to leave normal society and take up the ascetic lifestyle than it was for men. Virtually all the women we hear of becoming ascetics were widows, single women, married women whose husbands also wished to live as ascetics, or even (in the case of Mary of Egypt, a famous female hermit) prostitutes. In other words, they were mostly women who did not have to answer to men and who were relatively free to do as they wished. But as we have seen, in Roman society, such women were very unusual.

Discipline

In addition to avoiding people of the opposite sex, the monk who was determined to master himself or herself had to discipline the body. Most monks ate, drank, and slept very little; one meal a day was the most common practice, although some are said to have eaten even less. Water, hard to come by as it was, was restricted as well; many monks believed that drinking too much water encouraged demonic attack. And it was usual for monks to sleep only a little during the night, seeking to remain watchful for the Lord. Indeed, it may be that the meditative trances in which they spent much of their time allowed some to go without proper sleep for long periods. Moses the Ethiopian (actually probably a Nubian) was said to have spent six years standing in his cell, never closing his eyes, in an unsuccessful attempt to still the thoughts that plagued his mind. Particularly dedicated ascetics sometimes avoided lying down or even sitting. It became common for cells to feature alcoves in the wall, where tired monks could prop themselves up while remaining standing. Evagrius reported a conversation with Macarius of Alexandria, in which the older man told him:

> Take courage, my child! For all of twenty years I have not taken my fill either of bread or water or sleep. I ate my bread by weight, drank water by measure, and I have snatched some little portion of sleep by leaning against the wall.[3]

But for those who persevered, the rewards could be great. The monks believed that, hard as their task was, it was easier than trying to find God in society. They were not proud of their lifestyle (although pride was another demon that could always strike) – rather, they are often presented in contemporary literature as rather embarrassed by the fact that they were not strong enough to live as Christians in the city. They felt lucky to be able to follow God in this way, and many others envied them. There is a story of the emperor himself (we are not told which one) visiting a monk incognito. After the monk has shared his bread with the emperor and talked to him, the emperor declares:

> You are truly blessed because you do not have the cares of this world. I was born to kingship, and the affairs of my empire are a constant concern to me. Each day I dine on the richest meats and cakes and the finest wines are poured into my goblet. And yet, today mere bread and water have satisfied me as no sumptuous feast ever has.[4]

Pachomius and the first monasteries

The hermits and the sketes were the most well-known forms of monasticism in the fourth century, but there was a third variety as well: the cenobites. Where, in sketes, the monks mostly live by themselves but come together for communal activites, in a cenobitic community, they live together all the time.

The man most associated with the first Christian cenobitic communities is Pachomius, who set up a number of them in the 320s and 330s. Pachomius was a native Egyptian, born in around AD 290, and brought up as a pagan. He was conscripted into the Roman army and stationed in Thebes, where he met local Christians and was impressed by their charity. Upon his release from the army he joined the 'renouncers', who lived as hermits but without withdrawing to the desert. After a couple of years, he began building cells to allow other monks to join him. Some were other desert hermits, but others seem to have been local villagers who simply lived in the complex that Pachomius was building, and for whom Pachomius acted as a servant. One way or the other, after a few years Pachomius had effectively founded a monastery. It was based upon the principles of mutual help and support, but also upon Pachomius' belief that one could see God most clearly not in private visions but in the character of other human beings.

The monastery had about 300 monks, who were divided into a number of 'houses', each of which contained about twenty monks. Each monk had his own cell, where he slept and performed private prayer. Communal prayers were held at dawn, including readings from the Bible and periods of silence. For most of the day the monks would work at trades – mainly basket-making – in order to support the community. As they worked they were encouraged to meditate silently upon the biblical passages they had heard earlier in the morning. They ate a meal in the middle of the day and another in the evening – also in silence, each monk in the seat assigned to him – after which Pachomius would preach to them; they then returned to their houses to pray, discuss the sermon, or read. Pachomius believed that learning was important; illiterate monks were taught to read, and the monastery maintained a library.

Pachomius began founding other monasteries. By the time he died in AD 346, he had founded a total of nine throughout the region, with some 3,000 monks living under the rules that he wrote to govern them. Each monastery had a high wall around it, with a single gatehouse manned by a monk. The compound contained the large communal church, refectory, bakery, kitchens, and meeting halls, as well as the houses in which the monks lived. The network of monasteries was known as the *Koinonia*, or 'fellowship' or 'community', and the largest was at Phbow, with over 1,000 monks. There were also monasteries for women, which operated along much the same lines; the men and women never met, apart from the priests, who would visit the women once a week. It is likely that some of the monasteries were not completely new foundations, but that Pachomius found a group of monks already living together and drew them into his organization.

It has been suggested that Pachomius was inspired, in part, by his time in the army, living together with other soldiers in barracks. The monasteries that he built were also barracks, in a sense, where monks would be trained in spiritual combat. Pachomius believed that communal discipline would help avoid the discouragement that claimed many who lived as hermits or in the sketes. The monks wore the same outfits – sleeveless habits marked with a purple cross – and were expected to obey those in authority without question. Pachomius also conceived of his monasteries as self-sufficient little communities, and after his death they diversified their economic activities. Some monks worked as tailors, others as metal-workers, carpenters, or camel-drivers, and the monasteries even owned their own ships on the Nile to deliver their goods. For some in the later years, the success of Pachomius' movement was itself a sort of failure. We are told that Theodore – a disciple of Pachomius who later governed the community – came to believe that the range of possessions controlled by the monasteries compromised their spiritual integrity. He would regularly pray and weep before Pachomius' tomb. Perhaps he was right to do so: shortly before he took over, the monastery at Thmousons had actually broken away from the Koinonia because its leader had wanted to expand the monastery's agricultural business beyond what the network would allow.

For most of this period, the cenobitic style of monasticism was less popular than the sketes. It was mainly found in southern Egypt, where Pachomius was active. Indeed, communal monastic life seems to have developed in other, even more striking contexts in this region. The city of Oxyrhynchus was said to contain almost as many monks and nuns as lay people: some 30,000 of them altogether, so many that one could hear their chanting throughout the city. Whether the city was really as monastic as this suggests is uncertain, but it does seem likely that, despite the fame of the 'desert fathers', there were always just as many hermits and monks in the towns and cities as there were in the desert itself.

Syrian monasticism

Although the Egyptian desert fathers were the most famous, there were parallel movements elsewhere at this time. Probably the most important of these was in Syria. It seems that the church here had always had a particularly strong ascetic streak. Tatian, the most famous figure of the second-century Syrian church, had been known for his encratatic views (we met this position in chapter 4):

he believed marriage to be sinful, and such views were probably common among Syrian Christians.

Ephrem the Syrian

In the fourth century, the most prominent Syrian Christian was Ephrem (or Ephraim), who spent most of his life in Nisibis, one of the frontier cities of the Roman empire. In AD 363, Nisibis fell into Persian hands, and most of its Christians left; Ephrem settled in Edessa, where he remained until his death in the 370s.

Ephrem was probably a deacon; he is said to have feigned madness to avoid being made a bishop. He wrote an enormous amount, including commentaries on the Bible, sermons, hymns, and poems. Many of these were intended to reinforce the Nicene faith, for Ephrem was a fervent anti-Arian, but many were also intended to extol the virtues of the ascetic life. For Ephrem, the ascetic life was the 'angelic life' led by 'watchers' who kept a vigil for Christ and would not be found sleeping when he returned.

Ephrem testifies to an asceticism rather like that of Origen in the third century: a highly rigorous lifestyle, but one lived within normal Christian society. There is no celebration of 'withdrawal' from the world in his works as there is in the sayings of the Egyptian desert fathers. In the second half of the fourth century, however, such withdrawal was becoming more common in the area. A good example of this is the early career of John Chrysostom, later to become the patriarch of Constantinople and one of the most prominent churchmen of the age.

John Chrysostom

John was born in Antioch in around AD 349; he studied rhetoric under the famous pagan teacher Libanius and by all accounts was a star student. The nickname 'Chrysostom', which he would later acquire, means 'golden mouth' and was sometimes given to outstanding orators. However, in his early twenties, he became associated with an ascetic school in the city that was run by a pair of well-known ascetics, Diodore and Carterius. Very little is known of what form this school took, but it attests to the popularity of the ascetic lifestyle among Antioch's Christians at this time; John persuaded some of his friends to attend it as well. One of them was Theodore, later bishop of Mopsuestia and one of the most famous theologians of the fifth century.

Later, John moved out Antioch altogether and retreated to the nearby Mount Silpius, determined to live there as a hermit. There were already many hermits in this area, and it seems likely that Silpius was rather like one of the sketes of the Egyptian desert. After four years here, John left the community and retreated to a cave by himself in a more remote region of the mountain, where he lived

Messalianism

By the fifth century, Syrian hermiticism had reached even more dramatic forms. It had spawned the movement known as Messalianism, about which little is known. The Messalians seem to have had a very holistic understanding of human nature: they believed that the body and soul were identical to such an extent that both sin and grace could exist in physical form in the body. Only by unceasing prayer could a person obtain sufficient grace from God to squeeze sinfulness out of their bodies. One of their characteristic ideas was that a person could actually feel this; therefore, if you were not conscious of divine grace working within you, it was not. Many Messalians were itinerant, and we hear of groups of Messalian monks or hermits wandering the Syrian countryside, their voices calling out in unending prayer. Although they were condemned at Ephesus in AD 431, the Messalians made their mark on Syrian spirituality. There is a series of writings attributed to the desert father Macarius the Egyptian, but which were actually written in Syria in around AD 400, and they seem to come from a similar context to that of Messalianism – although whether these homilies are themselves moderately Messalian, or actually intended to correct what their author perceived as the excesses of Messalianism, is uncertain. The writings of 'Pseudo-Macarius', as this corpus is known, stress the need to pray in order to obtain God's grace (although not literally all the time), and they focus on the heart, the spiritual centre of a person's being.

an even more ascetic lifestyle: never lying down, eating whatever he could gather from the surrounding area, and studying the Bible intensively until he had memorized the entire text. Such a move seems to have been quite common among Syrian ascetics of the time, who might often regard the communal life of Mount Silpius as just a sort of training for the really severe, completely solitary life of the hermit. In John's case, the lifestyle proved too extreme. He permanently ruined his health and was forced to leave the mountain after two years. He would later become patriarch of Constantinople, but he retained his admiration for the monks all his life, together with his conviction that their lifestyle was the ideal for all Christians to emulate. In his eyes, there was no real distinction between ordinary Christians on the one hand and monks on the other. All Christians were called to practise perfect lives, although it didn't necessarily mean living in a cave alone; and conversely, monks and hermits were part of the wider church, and retained responsibilities in it.

The monks and the wider world

The first Christian monks were also pioneering not only a new lifestyle, but a new religious ideal, that of the ascetic as exemplary. Many hermits became famous, and others would come to them seeking instruction, or simply hoping to emulate them. We are told, for example, of a famous hermit named Apollo:

The saint quickly became famous as a new prophet and apostle who had been raised up for our generation. As his reputation grew, large numbers of monks who lived round about in scattered hermitages kept coming to join him, making gifts of their own souls to him as if to a true father. Some of these he invited to contemplation; others he commanded to apply themselves to practical virtue, showing first by deed what he exhorted them to do by word.[5]

The sayings and deeds of Apollo and other hermits like him were remembered and repeated, and eventually written down. There are a number of texts from the fourth and early fifth centuries preserving them, which proved extremely popular throughout the empire. They helped to transform the Egyptian desert, in the popular Christian imagination, into a second Holy Land: a landscape of monks and hermits who not only sought God but whose emaciated forms proclaimed his power.

It has often been suggested that one of the reasons the monks were so popular throughout the Christian world was that they effectively replaced martyrs. By withdrawing from the world, the monks were effectively dying to the world. Their ascetic lifestyles were, in some important sense, perpetual deaths. That was certainly not the original inspiration for the monastic movement (Antony of Egypt, for one, took up this lifestyle at around the time of the Great Persecution) but it quickly became an important element of its appeal.

Consecrated in AD 386 by Ambrose, St Ambrose's Church in Milan has seen different buildings added to its original complex right up to the 16th century. In AD 739, a monastery for Benedictine monks was added.

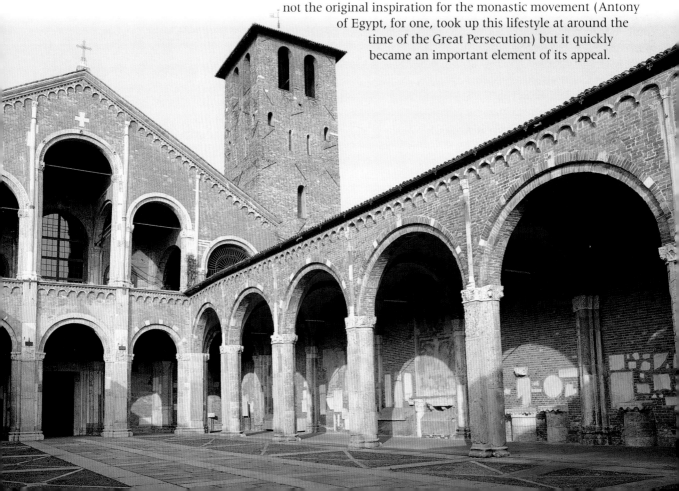

The philosophical ideal

But there were other elements to the appeal of monasticism too, which tapped into traditions that had already been part of classical culture for centuries. These were apparent in the attempts of many Christians to emulate the monks without travelling at all. Throughout the Roman empire, in the second half of the fourth century, we hear of Christians trying to live ascetic lifestyles or even set up their own monasteries in imitation of the Egyptian hermits. The Spanish Priscillianists, whom we shall meet in the next chapter, were an example of this. Another example, also from Spain, was an aristocrat named Paulinus, who in the 380s and 390s decided to dedicate himself to chastity, together with his wife, after their son died. Eventually they sold their property, moved to Nola in Campania, and set up a monastery that became quite famous.

And a whole series of monastic experiments was put into practice by a group of friends and relations from Cappadocia. In the 350s, shortly after completing their studies at Athens, Basil of Caesarea and his close friend Gregory of Nazianzus set up a retreat at Pontus, where they hoped to spend their time in contemplation. It never really worked out, but the rules that Basil drew up for the community would later be extremely influential, especially in eastern monasticism. Basil's brother Naucratis attempted a similar idea. He and a servant set up a small hermitage in a remote part of his family's estate, where they divided their time between contemplation and fishing and hunting, giving much of the game they caught to the local poor. Unfortunately, both hermits drowned in a fishing accident after five years. Finally, their sister, Macrina, also set up a community which proved more successful. Macrina had been devoted to an ascetic lifestyle since the age of twelve, and she eventually persuaded her mother to join her. They transformed the household into a sort of commune, where they and their servants lived as equals. Other ascetically inclined women joined, and within a couple of decades it was a new nunnery.

Basil's family was one of wealthy landowners. In an earlier age, they might have spent their time reading the classical poets or engaging in the cut and thrust of imperial politics. In a Christian age, however, such families were increasingly likely to use their leisure and money pursuing what they felt were nobler aims. In fact, the new monastic ideal took on some of the qualities of the older pursuits. Its adherents often called it the life of 'philosophy'. In antiquity, philosophy sought to address issues of life and death just as religion did, and many – especially among the elite classes – devoted themselves to it. This meant not simply sitting about reading books but actually living a life inspired by the ideals in those books. Alcinous, a second-century pagan philosopher, defined his subject like this:

Philosophy is a striving for wisdom, or the freeing and turning around
of the soul from the body, when we turn towards the intelligible and
what truly is; and wisdom is the science of things divine and human.[6]

This was a real and important endeavour for many people. Many
believed it to be the most valuable thing one could try to do. The
great Roman orator of the first century BC, Cicero, reported a friend
as telling him:

for my own part I adopt the great pursuit of philosophy in its entirety
both (so far as I am able) as a guiding principle of life and as an
intellectual pleasure, and I agree with the dictum of Plato that no
greater and better gift has been bestowed by the gods upon mankind.[7]

In the fourth century, this traditional philosophical lifestyle merged
quite naturally with the new monastic ideal. For some Christian
writers, the term 'philosophy' itself – without any qualifiers –
became a technical term, referring to the Christian contemplation
of God. Gregory of Nazianzus used it frequently in this sense, while
John Chrysostom called the monastic lifestyle 'the true philosophy'.

Augustine of Hippo

One figure who sought to put this new 'philosophy' into practice was
the young Augustine of Hippo. Augustine's life story has been told
repeatedly, not least by himself, in his classic *Confessions*, a book in
which he effectively invented the genre of spiritual autobiography.
Augustine was born in AD 354 in Tagaste, a small town in Africa.
His mother, Monica, was a devout Christian who later converted his
father to the religion. Augustine was educated in Carthage, where
he was an outstanding student at rhetoric and philosophy, being
especially fond of the works of Cicero. He became a scholar and
teacher in Carthage, and also joined the Manichaeans, a sect similar
to the gnostics.

In AD 383, Augustine moved to Rome, apparently because he
hoped the students there would be better behaved. They proved
no better than the African ones, but Augustine secured a very
prestigious post teaching rhetoric in Milan, where the imperial court
was based. Here he attended the sermons of the bishop, Ambrose,
hoping to pick up rhetorical tricks from the famous preacher. But he
found himself far more impressed with the bishop's teachings than
he had anticipated, which together with a general disillusionment
with Manichaeanism led to something of a spiritual crisis. In a
famous incident, Augustine found himself sitting in his garden in
anguish, when he overheard a child's voice next door singing, 'Take
up and read.' Taking this to be a divine sign, Augustine picked up
Paul's letter to the Romans, read a passage at random, and from then
on counted himself a Christian.

Although the story of Augustine's conversion is well known, it is less often appreciated that he seems, both at the time and in his subsequent analysis of the event, to have considered himself a convert not so much to Christianity as to the 'philosophical' lifestyle. Immediately before the incident in the garden, Augustine had been speaking with a Christian acquaintance who had told him about Antony of Egypt and the monks, and explained that Ambrose had recently established a monastery right there in Milan. It was his amazement at hearing this that led Augustine to wander into the garden in something of a daze. When he read Paul's text, it convinced him not so much that Christianity was true as that it was time to act upon its call, just as Antony and the other hermits had done. He gave up his teaching duties and retired to a friend's villa at Cassiciacum. Here, Augustine hoped to devote himself to contemplation. Together with a group of friends and relations – including his mother and his son – he spent his time in a blend of the traditional 'philosophical' lifestyle as espoused by the likes of Cicero and worship of God as practised by Antony. The group would pray together in the mornings and study together (reading even pagan writers, such as Virgil). In their spare time they would discuss philosophical and religious matters. Here, Augustine wrote his earliest surviving works, on mainly philosophical topics.

Joos van Gent's 1460 portrait of Augustine of Hippo (AD 354–430).

After two years, Augustine visited the monastery at Milan, which enormously impressed him. He decided to return to Africa and set one up of his own. He arrived at Tagaste in AD 389 and founded a new community rather like that of Cassiciacum. A major feature of this monastery was the emphasis upon study and learning. As we saw, Pachomius had stressed the need to study the Bible, and taught illiterate monks to read, but Augustine believed that this should be central to the monastic life.

In AD 391, Augustine visited the city of Hippo, where during a service in the church he was unexpectedly grabbed by the congregation and ordained as a priest. This sort of ordination 'by acclamation' was fairly common at the time. Augustine moved to Hippo, but he set up a new monastic community in the garden of one of the churches. He decided that this community would be modelled on the life of the first Christians as described in Acts, holding all property in common. The monastery proved popular and grew quickly, and Augustine – like Pachomius and Basil before him – wrote a rule to govern it. The monks lived highly regulated lives, with strict hours prescribed for the various tasks of labour, study, prayer, and eating. Each person worked for the good of the community, never for himself. There was little emphasis upon asceticism. Augustine believed that if the monks had too little to eat, hunger would distract them from their true purpose. In this garden monastery, the characteristic features of western monasticism – as opposed to the more ascetic forms of eastern monasticism – were already taking shape.

Augustine remained closely involved with his monasteries throughout his career. After becoming bishop of Hippo in AD 395, he left the garden monastery, for fear of disrupting the community's life with his hectic schedule, but he set up a sort of quasi-monastic existence in own house, by establishing a household with other priests of the city who wanted to live together. This community, too, was based around the notion of common ownership of property. They ate their simple meals together, and all wore the same habits – in an age when bishops were dressing as civil governors, Augustine always dressed as a monk. He emphasized the need for kindness and love: critical gossip was forbidden, and needy guests were always welcome – unless they were women, whom Augustine would not allow in the house, mainly for fear of inciting gossip.

John Cassian

The second half of the fourth century saw monasticism spreading into Gaul. One of the first monks in this region was Martin, who established a monastery near Poitiers in around AD 360, shortly before becoming bishop of Tours. But the man who wielded the most influence over monasticism not just in Gaul but throughout the west was John Cassian. Surprisingly little is known of his life. He may have been born in what is now Romania, or perhaps in Gaul. He was, at least, a Latin-speaking westerner. He and a friend named Germanus spent many years travelling through the eastern empire, staying in monasteries in Palestine and Egypt, and also becoming associated with John Chrysostom in Constantinople. In around AD 415, after Germanus' death, Cassian founded a monastery for men and another for women in Marseilles, in southern Gaul, where he wrote the books that made him famous: the *Institutes* and the *Conferences*.

The *Institutes* describes in some detail the monastic lifestyle and its meaning, and provides a detailed description of the eight sinful 'thoughts' that Evagrius had written so much about. The *Conferences*, meanwhile, describes what purport to be lengthy discussions that Cassian and Germanus had with the desert fathers in Egypt. They depict the perfect Christian life as involving three great renunciations. First, the Christian renounces the immoral life, above all wealth, and begins to live ethically. Second, he renounces his attachment to the world, and withdraws to the monastic life, to live in community with others. But third, he renounces all visible things, even the cenobitic life, and withdraws completely to contemplate God alone. The life of the hermit thus represents a higher stage of perfection than the life of the cenobitic monk.

The *Conferences* was extremely popular – after Cassian published the first part, his readers persuaded him to write far more than he had originally intended – and it played a major role in presenting the lives and teachings of the desert fathers to the west. In the sixth century, Cassian's works would be a major influence upon Benedict of Nursia, whose rule for his own monasteries would become the most commonly used in the Middle Ages, and who recommended Cassian to all his monks.

Palestine

As we saw in chapter 8, the age of Constantine saw a reinvention of Palestine as the Holy Land, where the physical landscape where Jesus had once walked took on a special spiritual significance, and where the key locations of his life became centres of pilgrimage. Some of these pilgrims remained and became hermits or founded monasteries. Thus, unlike the Syrian and Egyptian monastic movements, the Palestinian one was mainly not indigenous but developed by outsiders, who were influenced by movements in their home regions or by the reports of Egypt. One of the earliest of these was Chariton, from Iconium in what is now Turkey. He is said to have visited the Holy Land in the early fourth century and to have founded three *lauras* near Jerusalem. These lauras were a distinctive kind of Palestinian monastery. Like the Egyptian sketes, the monks lived in separate cells, but they lived near a group of communal buildings and were all subject to a single abbot. So it was more organized than a skete, but less communal than a cenobitic monastery.

But the two most famous figures in fourth-century Palestinian monasticism were Rufinus and Jerome. They were both probably born in the early 340s, in Aquileia and Dalmatia respectively. Jerome later moved to Aquileia, where he became good friends with Rufinus.

The two of them set up an ascetic retreat there, together with a group of other friends, where they sought to live the kind of lifestyle they were hearing about from Egypt. But they fell out, although only temporarily. They both left Aquileia and travelled east. Rufinus spent some time in Alexandria, where he knew the great scholar and Origenist theologian Didymus the Blind. Jerome, meanwhile, seems to have had difficulty finding anyone to get on with at all. First he lived as a hermit in the desert of Chalcis, but fell out with the other hermits; then he moved to Rome and became the secretary of the bishop, Damasus, but fell out with many people in the church there. When Damasus died, Jerome travelled to Palestine with two aristocratic Roman women whom he had converted to an ascetic lifestyle, Paula and her daughter Eustochium. They set up a monastery in Bethlehem.

There seem to have been many women like these who were attracted to asceticism, more than there were among the desert hermits. During this period, the Virgin Mary, Jesus' mother, was increasingly regarded as a model for them to follow. It was around now that many Christians came to believe not only that Mary had been a virgin when she conceived Jesus, but that she remained a virgin all her life, and even preserved her virginity 'in parturition', meaning that she gave birth to Jesus in a miraculous way that did not damage her physically. Christian women sought to emulate this perpetual virginity in their own ascetic lifestyles.

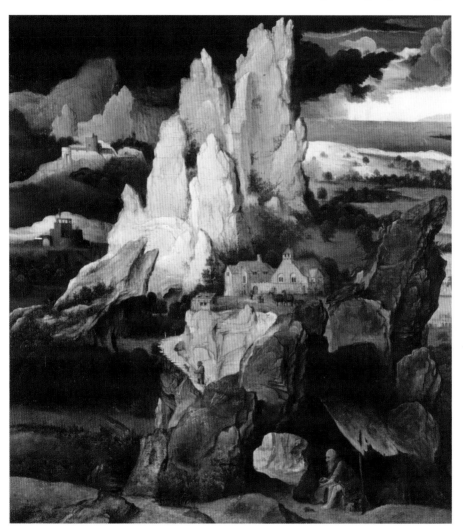

Jerome (c. AD 347–420) is pictured in a rocky landscape in Joachim Patenier's painting, c. 1520.

Rufinus had also set up a monastery at the Mount of Olives by Jerusalem together with Melania, another noble Roman Christian woman. His monastery and Jerome's became well known throughout the Christian world and seem to have inspired many imitations. Augustine of Hippo, in particular, did his best to cultivate a friendship with Jerome, and references to their monasteries are frequent in their correspondence.

Both Jerome and Rufinus were formidable scholars. Jerome wrote a number of historical works, including *On Illustrious Men*, describing the lives and writings of all Christian writers to date. The longest and most impressive entry is the last, on Jerome himself, listing his own works in exhaustive detail. To be fair, Jerome *had* achieved a huge amount. Damasus had commissioned him to translate the Bible into Latin; a number of translations were already available, but they were fragmentary and not considered authoritative. Jerome continued to work on this monumental project in the Holy Land; he consulted Origen's *Hexapla* (see chapter 6), which was still in Caesarea, and attracted controversy by his decision to translate from the original Hebrew and not from the Greek Septuagint. He also wrote many commentaries on the Bible and translated others. Throughout, he relied heavily on the work of Origen; he translated some of Origen's works, and his own commentaries often incorporated many ideas or even passages from the famous theologian. Rufinus also translated much of Origen's work into Latin, as well as other works by Greek-speaking theologians.

However, Jerome's fiery temper, which had got him into plenty of trouble before, continued to cause havoc. Rufinus and Jerome eventually had an extremely public argument over Origen. Jerome became convinced that Origen had been a heretic, and denied that he had ever admired him; Rufinus argued that Origen's works were spiritually useful, and resented his former friend's attempt to distance himself from his earlier work. Rufinus died in around AD 410, but Jerome continued to attack him repeatedly in the most abusive language for many years.

The Official Church

The first half of the fourth century AD had seen Christianity not only legalised but promoted by a succession of Christian emperors. In the second half, the process accelerated. Christianity was absorbing many elements of traditional Roman culture: not only were traditional feast days being reinterpreted as Christian celebrations, but philosophical ideals were being transformed into the monastic lifestyle. Traditional religion was being squeezed out. The process was becoming increasingly antagonistic.

Christianity outside the empire

Moreover, Christianity's triumph within the Roman empire coincided with a period of growth beyond its borders.

The Sassanid empire

In the early third century AD, the Sassanids, a new dynasty from Iran, defeated the Parthians, took over most of the Persian empire, and became the new major rival to Rome in the Middle East. In AD 260, the Sassanid Shah Shapur I captured Antioch and the surrounding region, and deported large numbers of Roman citizens. Many of these people were Christians. These unwilling immigrants were joined in the same period by willing ones, as many Christians fled the persecutions of Decius and, later, Diocletian. The result was a large Christian population throughout the Sassanid empire, but one which did not mix with the earlier, native Christian communities. The new Christians spoke Greek and held their own, separate church services. Many were forcibly housed in new towns, such as Gondeshapur, founded by Shapur I in the third century, and settled with captured Roman Christians. This helped Christianity to spread into new areas, especially Iran, far more effectively than it had done before. In fact southwestern Iran became a particular stronghold of Christianity.

A Zoroastrian fire temple of the Sassanian period (3rd–7th centuries AD) located at Firuzabad, in modern-day Iran.

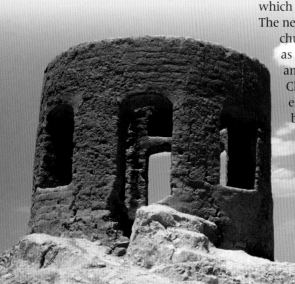

Another major Christian centre in this region was Nisibis, near the border with Rome. The city had been swapped between the two great empires more than once; in AD 297 it passed from Persia to Rome, and in AD 363 it passed back again, triggering a mass exodus of Christians who did not want to live under the Sassanids. But it remained an important centre of Christianity. In the early fourth century, the energetic bishop, Jacob, identified a nearby mountain as having been the place where Noah's ark had come to rest. A monastery was built upon the spot. Indeed this whole area was renowned for its monasticism. Jacob had lived as an ascetic before taking office, and many monasteries were founded in the nearby Isla Mountains during this period.

Prat de Maishan – modern-day Basra, in southern Iraq – became a metropolitan see in the early fourth century, indicating that there was a thriving Christian population in the area. This period seems to have seen a general restructuring of the Persian church, with the establishment of new sees (or dioceses), episcopal and metropolitan. It was around now that Papa, the first known bishop of the capital, Seleucia-Ctesiphon, sought to have his own authority accepted over the whole eastern church. He is often considered the first catholicos, or head of the Church of the East, although this title was not used until later.

The Zoroastrian complex of Amir Chakmak, Yazd, Iran.

The Persian church seems to have avoided the schisms and theological controversies, including Arianism, which so disrupted Roman Christianity during the fourth century. But it faced worse problems of its own. The Sassanids were keen to encourage traditional Persian religion as part of their programme to revitalize the empire and ward off the threat from Rome. To that end, they promoted Zoroastrianism, making it the state religion. In the second half of the third century, Herpad Kartir – a powerful statesman known as 'judge of all the empire' – was the main figure associated with the policy. In the 270s he restructured Zoroastrianism and began persecuting the Manichaeans. In the 280s, he ordered the persecution of Christians too.

Kartir lost his influence or died in the early fourth century, and the persecutions eased for a couple of decades. But Constantine's conversion in AD 312 meant that the authorities became far more suspicious of Christians, who now shared the religion of the Sassanids' greatest rival. Shah Shapur II did little about them to begin with, but in around AD 340 he lost his patience after the Christians refused to take part in his war against Rome. He therefore placed a special tax on Christians and ordered Shimun, bishop of Seleucia-Ctesiphon, to collect it. Shimun refused. Shapur ordered the destruction of all churches and monasteries, executed 100

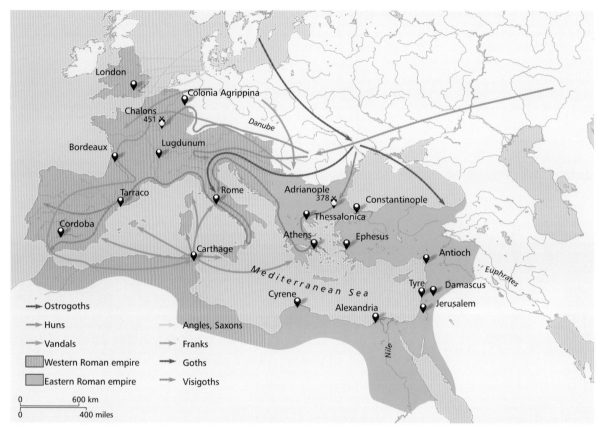

Map of the empire's borders in the 5th century AD, showing the movement of tribes and non-Roman people.

Christian priests before Shimun's eyes, and killed Shimun last of all. A persecution of Christians then followed which dwarfed anything that had been seen in the Roman empire, as troops destroyed Christian buildings and simply massacred all the Christians they could find, without bothering to arrest them. We are told that in some places, such as Kirkuk, there were too many Christians for the soldiers to kill them all, so they released criminals from the prisons, gave them weapons, and told them to join in. The violence was so reckless that non-Christians, including many Zoroastrians in regions where that religion was in a minority, were killed as well. Shapur therefore ordered the general persecution to be scaled down, and from then on it was confined to Christian priests and converts from Zoroastrianism. Over the next forty years hundreds of Christians were killed, often in especially sadistic ways: we hear of Christians being trampled to death by elephants, slowly dismembered over the course of several days, or eaten alive by rats.

The persecutions continued under Shapur's successor, Ardashir II, until AD 383, when Shapur III ascended the throne. He pursued a more peaceful policy with Rome, and accordingly treated the Christians far better. However, Christians were still subject to unofficial mob violence during this period, in which thousands of people are said to have died. In AD 410, Yazdgerd I officially legalized Christianity (although converting to the religion from Zoroastrianism was still a capital crime). In the same year, Isaac of Seleucia-Ctesiphon held the first major council of the eastern church. This council sought to unify the eastern church by ensuring that there was to be only one ecclesiastical structure – the Greek-speaking Christians were still meeting separately – and everyone should use the same dates for Easter and other festivals. It also endorsed the creed and canons of the council of Nicaea.

That was not the end of Persian persecution. In the 440s and 450s, Shah Yazdgerd II would order another exceptionally bloody purge of Christians, in which many tens of thousands more were slaughtered. Apart from this, however, the Christians now enjoyed a mostly peaceful existence within the Sassanid empire, and the religion spread as missionaries travelled throughout the region.

The barbarians

'Barbarian' was the name given by Greeks and Romans to all people who did not speak Greek or Latin. It did not necessarily have pejorative overtones, although often it did. This was especially the case when referring to the 'barbarians' of northern Europe, whom many Romans regarded as semi-civilized nomads. In fact these people lived just as sedentary a lifestyle as the Romans. Many lived within the Roman empire; they included the Celts of Gaul and Britain, conquered in the days of Julius Caesar, as well as the inhabitants of Lesser Germania, to the west and south of the Rhine, which was a Roman province. Probably few if any of these people converted to Christianity before the days of Constantine.

The fourth century saw this situation begin to change. Martin, bishop of Tours in Gaul, devoted much of his time to trying to convert pagans, and he seems to have directed his energies towards Celtic pagan religion as well as Roman pagan religion. We hear of him destroying sacred trees – a feature of Celtic religion – as well as temples. He seems to have been quite successful.

By this stage, there were far more barbarians living in the Roman empire. In a series of events that are still not well understood, Germanic tribes began migrating and crossing the border into the empire in the middle of the third century AD. In particular, the Goths conquered and occupied Dacia, roughly where Romania is today, which had previously been part of the Roman empire. A series of Roman emperors solved the immediate military threat from the Germans by negotiating treaties allowing some of them to live within their borders. Many Germanic mercenaries were hired as Roman soldiers, until by the end of the fourth century most Roman armies were composed mostly of barbarians.

This meant that the barbarians were increasingly familiar with Roman culture, and with it, Christianity. The fourth century saw

The Armenian church

There were also important developments in the Caucasus during this period. Here, the kingdom of Armenia clung on to a precarious independence, caught between the two superpowers of the region. Christianity seems to have arrived in Armenia by the third century, when we hear of bishops in the kingdom. But we know nothing about the Armenian church during this period, and it must have been very small.

Things changed at the beginning of the fourth century, when Gregory – later known as the Illuminator – arrived in the kingdom. Gregory was the son of an Armenian nobleman who had assassinated the king of Armenia, allowing the country to become controlled by the Sassanids. To escape the purge of his family which followed, Gregory and his brother were raised and educated in Caesarea in Cappadocia. Tiridates III, the son of the assassinated king, was also raised in exile, in Rome. In AD 287 he defeated the Sassanids with Roman help and took control of the country. Gregory returned to Armenia as well, although it is uncertain when.

Upon taking possession of his kingdom, Tiridates began trying to eradicate Christianity. A number of Christians were martyred in Armenia, and Gregory was imprisoned for many years – perhaps as much for what his father had done as

for the Christian faith which he now proclaimed. But the king fell ill; Gregory was brought from his cell and healed him; and Tiridates converted to Christianity. That, at least, is the version of events found in later accounts, but precisely how it happened is uncertain. What is certain is that Tiridates did convert to Christianity, probably in around AD 301, meaning that Armenians have a claim to belong to the first nation that still survives today to have adopted Christianity.

Gregory became bishop of Akhtishad and travelled around the country building churches and cathedrals, ordaining priests and converting bishops, and also closing down temples and smashing their idols. Despite these often heavy-handed techniques, Gregory was remarkably successful. By the time he died in AD 325, Christianity had become quite well established. Gregory's son, Aristarces, succeeded him as bishop of Akhtishad and attended the council of Nicaea. The links to Cappadocia were maintained: in the 370s, Basil of Caesarea appointed a number of bishops throughout Armenia.

In the Armavir Province, in the Republic of Armenia, stands a memorial to the conversion of King Tiridates III (285–339) to Christianity helped by Gregory the Illuminator.

many of them converting to Christianity for the first time. We know little about the details of the process; the first we hear of it is a mention of one Theophilus, bishop of the Goths, attending the council of Nicaea in AD 325, but we know nothing about him. We do, however, know of one major figure, who in his own person epitomized the new mingling of Roman and Germanic cultures. Ulfilas was born to Cappadocian parents, who had been captured by Gothic marauders and taken to Dacia. They must have become culturally assimilated to their captors, since they gave their son a Gothic name. He was later educated in Constantinople. Eusebius of Nicomedia consecrated him as a bishop in AD 341, during the council of Antioch, and sent him to take charge of the church in Dacia. Evidently there were already Christians in this area, but they had not been there long. Ulfilas spent seven years there, during which time he seems to have preached to pagan Goths as well. He seems to have had considerable success – although intermittent wars with the Romans meant that the Gothic leaders often persecuted Christians, just as the Sassanids did. This was a difficult time for the Goths; they were being invaded from the north and east by the Huns, a people originally from central Asia, against whom the Germanic peoples were unable to muster effective resistance. Little wonder that they were so keen to cross the River Danube and find safety within the Roman empire.

But they were divided among themselves too. In AD 376, one of the Gothic leaders, Fritigern, managed to make an alliance with the emperor Valens. Together they defeated Fritigern's Gothic rival, Athanaric. Fritigern became a Christian, apparently out of a sense of obligation to his imperial benefactor. Many of his people did the same thing; Athanaric had been a persecutor of Christians. Fritigern's Goths (later known as the Visigoths) were allowed to settle within the borders of the Roman empire. However, they were ill-treated by the Roman authorities, and lacked enough food; in AD 378 Fritigern and Valens went to war, and Valens was killed.

A couple of years later, Valens' successor as eastern emperor, Theodosius, established a more stable peace. He fought and defeated the Ostrogoths, who were outside the empire, while allying with the Visigoths and allowing them once again to settle within the empire, retaining their own social and political structures. Many more now became Christians. For the Goths, conversion involved literacy, since until this point they had no written form of their language. Ulfilas therefore devised one and translated the Bible into it; the remaining fragments of this work suggest that he was an extremely able translator.

However, Ulfilas was a Homoian Arian. So too was Fritigern. In fact, we hear of no non-Arian missionaries to the Goths at all during this period. The vast majority of Gothic Christians were therefore Arian as well. However, the Goths do not seem to have played any role in the debates over Arianism that dominated Roman Christianity during the fourth century. Nicene Christians seem to have devoted all their energy to attacking Arianism among their fellow citizens, not among the barbarians. This situation would change in the fifth century, especially under the Vandals, who invaded north Africa and persecuted non-Arians. Not until the sixth century would most of the barbarian Christians convert to Nicene Christianity.

Christianity and paganism

We saw in chapter 8 that Constantine seems to have maintained religious freedom for everyone, both pagan and Christian, and if he did enact measures against paganism, they were slight. But within a decade of his death, things began to change. Constans and Constantius II, who ruled the western and eastern halves of the empire respectively, were far less tolerant of paganism. Within a few years of beginning their rule, they seem to have increasingly adopted a quite different understanding of the relationship between church and state from that of their father. This showed itself in their greater interference in the Arian crisis. But it was also evident in their attitudes towards paganism. If the emperor was to rule over the church as well as the state, what room was there for rival religions?

The 340s accordingly saw the two imperial brothers moving against paganism in a way in which their father had never done. First Constans banned sacrifices, apparently presenting this law as simply a reinforcement of one his father has passed. Later, in AD 346, a law was issued banning worship in any pagan temple. The law was obeyed, more or less, in towns, where it was enforceable; but it was ignored in many places, especially in the countryside.

The rebellion of Magnentius

In early AD 350, a Roman officer named Magnentius declared himself emperor and had Constans killed. Magnentius was a pagan, and it seems that many people joined his cause specifically to make a stand against the attempted Christianization of the empire. He found a lot of support in Rome, where paganism remained very strong. The leading families and priests there had been suffering one snub after another since the days of Constantine, who had refused to sacrifice to Jupiter and founded a new capital of his own. By the end of the year, Magnentius had established himself as emperor of the west, and throughout his territories, the temples were officially reopened. He then made overtures to Constantius, hoping to secure an alliance with him, but Constantius would not ally with a pagan usurper. He wrote to the Arian Christian Germanic tribes who were, at that time, invading Gaul, telling them that they could keep any territory they captured there. Thus he hoped to distract Magnentius in both military and religious terms; better barbarian Christians than pagan Romans.

So civil war broke out again, in which Constantius had the upper hand. His victory was slow, though, and he had to fight his way westwards over a couple of years. As Constantius advanced, he closed the temples once more and ordered that all sacrifices cease, on pain of death. It is easy to believe that, this time, the orders were largely obeyed. Constantius was a violent, paranoid man even by the standards of Roman emperors, and had been so ever since ordering, or at least tolerating, the massacre of his relations after his father's death. He seems, moreover, to have suffered constant emotional strain, and to have had a chronic problem with nightmares. After defeating Magnentius, Constantius came to suspect that his cousin and caesar, Gallus, who had commanded his forces in the east, had been planning a coup. Despite the fact that Gallus seems never to have planned any such thing, he and his family were killed.

Constantius and the pagans

Constantius maintained the heightened clampdown on pagan practices for the rest of his reign. In AD 357 he visited Rome and ordered the altar to Victory removed from the Senate. At around the same time, new laws were issued outlawing all divinatory practices, and cruel new punishments introduced for those found guilty of them. Even so, pagan practices continued, especially in Rome. In AD 359, the prefect there performed sacrifices to ensure that the grain ships reached the city.

However, there is good reason to think that although pagan practices and folk beliefs remained strong throughout the empire, the old ceremonial system – and above all the priesthood – was much weaker than it had been before Constantine. Pagan priests had less of a role in society and were accorded much less respect than they once had been. The Christian priests and bishops had succeeded in supplanting them at a social level, something they had achieved above all by their support for the poor and needy.

But it is also important to recognize that Christianity did not simply supplant paganism within the empire as a result of imperial patronage, natural growth, and its own positive qualities. It took sustained, deliberate effort on the part of the Christians, directed specifically against any non-Christian religious expression. Christian bishops and writers spurred the emperors on, telling them that it was their religious duty to eradicate wicked and blasphemous rites.

Not all bishops thought like this. We hear of Pagasius, bishop of Ilion – the ancient site of Troy – wishing to preserve the ancient temples in his city in the 350s, despite Constantius' laws against them. The bishop removed a few token stones from the temples so that he could say he had complied with the imperial directives, without doing any real harm. And he kept the fires burning on the altars as a sign of respect to the heroes of the past.

However, Pagasius seems to have been an unusual bishop.

Most Christian bishops during this period were increasingly viewing traditional religion as something wholly incompatible with Christianity, and urging their congregations not only to shun pagan practices but to act against pagan images or institutions near their homes. These grassroots, low-level campaigns may have been even more significant than the decrees of Constantius and the other anti-pagan emperors. Throughout most of the fourth century, there is little evidence that the imperial prohibitions against pagan practices were enforced, at least in most places. And where they were enforced, it was generally because local bishops or other Christian leaders took it upon themselves to do so. Often, this meant whipping up a mob. Nowhere were the results of this more evident than in Alexandria in the fourth and early fifth centuries, where we hear of an endless succession of mobs of all religions looting one another's holy places and lynching one another's leaders. The war of sermons, pamphlets, and governmental decrees which are preserved in the literary remains were just part of a wider social and religious struggle which could always erupt into violence. During the fourth century, at least, that violence was generally not officially sanctioned. The Christians did not yet do to the pagans what the pagans had once done to the Christians, and execute them for their faith. Moreover, paganism would continue to survive for decades, even centuries, to come. But all of the factors now counting against it did take their toll.

Julian and the pagan revival

In AD 360, Julian, Gallus' half-brother, the cousin of the emperor Constantius, and a military commander in the west, was hailed as emperor by his troops in Gaul. Julian accepted the title, and prepared for war against Constantius. But Constantius unexpectedly fell seriously ill as he travelled to meet his cousin in battle. He had the good grace to acknowledge Julian as his heir before dying, leaving Julian the undisputed sole ruler of the Roman empire.

Julian was a complex figure who has fascinated many in modern times. He was born in AD 332, the son of Constantine's half-brother. Five years later, in the aftermath of Constantine's death, Julian and Gallus were the only male family members to survive the massacre of their relatives. He seems to have blamed his cousins – and above all Constantius – for the deaths of his father and other relations when he was a child.

This resentment against the Christian dynasty was one of the factors that led Julian – who had been brought up as a Christian – to renounce the religion secretly at the age of twenty, and convert to paganism. Another factor was his great love of classical literature and philosophy; as a young

Solidus coin of Julian 'the Apostate' draped, cuirassed and wearing a diadem.

man, sidelined from the political action, he spent most of his time studying. Upon arriving in Constantinople as emperor in late AD 361, Julian now 'came out' as a pagan. The funeral of Constantius in the city was the last time he ever set foot in a Christian church. From that time on, his aim was to reverse the religious policies of the preceding twenty years: to restore paganism as the official religion of the empire, and to eliminate Christianity as far as possible. For this, he would be dubbed by later generations 'the Apostate', that is, the one who converted away from Christianity.

Julian immediately repealed all the anti-pagan laws and ordered the temples to be rebuilt and reopened. He specified that anyone who had destroyed a temple was responsible for paying for its restoration, which caused enormous problems for the Christian church, since many bishops or their congregations were thereby liable. Julian did not proscribe Christianity or seek to persecute Christians. He had no desire to create more Christian martyrs, and it would have been at odds with the philosophical style of government that Julian wanted to achieve. But he did try to cause the Christians as much trouble as he could of another kind. This is why he ordered complete religious toleration, including toleration of all Christian schismatics or heretics, which, as we saw in chapter 9, reignited the Donatist schism and the Arian controversy.

Shortly afterwards, Julian issued a series of more clearly anti-Christian laws. First he banned Christians from teaching classical literature. Since all education revolved around the study of classical literature, this meant that Christians could no longer teach at all. Julian was a passionate believer in the importance of education and of the Greek classics in particular, and his law seems to have been motivated by a desire to improve education throughout the empire, since he believed that most Christians were basically stupid and not to be entrusted with something so important. But the move also drove a wedge between Christianity and classical culture, precisely at the moment that the two were beginning to merge. Next, Julian banned Christians from practising the law.

At the same time, Julian tried to rejuvenate paganism. He recognized the enormous success that Christianity had had at a social level, above all with its provision of social security for the poor and vulnerable. He restored the post of high priest that Maximinus Daia had created decades earlier, and put him in charge of the pagan religion throughout the empire. In so doing he hoped to reform the priesthood, restore the status of priests, and begin charity work to imitate that of the Christians. In particular, a pagan system of *xenodocheia* (see chapter 8) was to be created. Julian wrote:

> *Don't we see that nothing fostered atheism [ie, Christianity] more than kindness with foreigners, attention to burials, false respectability in their way of life? ... Set up, town after town, a network of homes for guests, so*

that foreigners enjoy our attention, not only those who share our beliefs, but any of them.[1]

But in the middle of AD 363, only eighteen months after becoming emperor, Julian was killed in battle against the Persians. He had been the last surviving member of Constantine's family; he had no children, and so the remarkable Constantinian dynasty came to an end. One of his leading generals, Jovian, became emperor in his place. But Jovian died after just a few months – apparently killed by smoke in his tent – and was replaced by another general, Valentinian.

Julian's attempts at religious reform collapsed with his death. They had proven too shallow and ephemeral. Julian's reformed paganism was not really a return to the old-style religion of Rome. It was a reinvented paganism, the sort of paganism that an intellectual, raised in a Christian atmosphere, imagined might have once existed in an idyllic classical age. It fared no better than most attempts to create a religion artificially.

Paganism after Julian

Julian's failure left many pagans dispirited. Libanius of Antioch, a famous pagan rhetorician who had known Julian personally, wrote a year after his death:

> *[Christianity] has quenched the sacred flame; it has stopped the joyful sacrifices, it has set them on to spurn and overthrow your altars; it has closed, demolished or profaned your temples and sanctuaries are given to harlots to live in. It has utterly undone the reverence that was yours and has established in your inheritance a dead man's tomb.*[2]

Things were indeed gloomy from a pagan point of view, but there was no return to the anti-pagan drive of Constantius. Jovian did not interfere in religious matters, leaving in place Julian's official toleration of all religions. Valentinian, likewise, was uninterested in religious matters, being far more concerned with fighting the barbarians in the west. He appointed his brother, Valens, as eastern emperor. Valens *was* interested in religious matters, being not only a Christian but an Arian; but his interference in religious matters was restricted to the Arian controversy, and he did not act against paganism. Indeed, just as Libanius bemoaned the decline in paganism, Christians complained about the strength of paganism under Valens.

However, some pagan cults seem to have dwindled during this time, such as Mithraism, which appears to have been declining even before Constantine. Paganism also seems to have become more marginalized within society in the later fourth century. The very name 'pagan' first emerged during this period. *Paganus* had originally meant someone of inferior social standing. The Christians now applied it to their religious opponents. Orosius of Braga, a Spanish Christian who wrote a major religious history in the early fifth century, connected the word to *pagani*, peasants. 'Pagans' were thus not only invented as an identifiable group, but sneered at as second-class, rustic fools.

But some forms of pagan religion were thriving, above all in Rome. There was a revival of paganism in the old capital, where throughout the 360s, 370s, and even 380s new altars to traditional gods were erected, especially in the temple of the Great Mother on Vatican Hill. One of the most significant figures in this revival was Vettius Agorius Praetextatus, a Mithraist priest who was also a major political figure in the city and who encouraged a revival of Mithraism.

The age of Theodosius

In AD 375, Valentinian died, dividing the western empire between his sons, the teenage Gratian and the infant Valentinian II. Gratian was a Nicene Christian. Three years later, the eastern emperor, Valens, was killed by the Visigoths, and Gratian appointed the general Theodosius emperor in his place. Theodosius was also a Nicene Christian. Moreover, both Gratian and Theodosius were – or would become – much less inclined to tolerate paganism than their predecessors had been.

Ambrose of Milan

The most prominent churchman in the west at this time was Ambrose, who had become bishop of Milan in one of those odd ways that seem to have been not uncommon at the time. Ambrose was raised as a Christian, given an excellent education in Rome, and rose to become governor of Aemilia-Liguria, which he administered from Milan, now the administrative capital of the western empire. In AD 374, Auxentius, the bishop of Milan, died. He had been one of the most prominent Arians in the west, appointed by Constantius II two decades earlier, and a popular figure. Crowds gathered at the basilica where his successor was to be elected. Fearing trouble, Ambrose went along as well, only to find himself unexpectedly being nominated. According to later historians, a child in the crowd shouted, 'Ambrose for bishop!' and the crowd took up the chant. Ambrose tried to escape, but the people were having none of it, and he was duly consecrated.

Gratian, whose court was in Milan, came under Ambrose's spell. Historians have not usually been kind to Gratian, generally portraying him as a weak-willed, rather feeble young man who allowed the more charismatic bishop to boss him around. That is not entirely fair, since Gratian does seem to have had some backbone when it came to paganism. He did not legislate against paganism, but he did stop hiring new pagan priests or paying the wages of the existing ones. When a group of senators complained, Gratian refused to receive them, and dropped the title of *pontifex maximus*, which every emperor – pagan or Christian – had adopted since the time of Caesar Augustus (see chapter 5). With that act, he in theory disestablished paganism.

In AD 378, the nineteen-year-old emperor commissioned Ambrose to write an introduction to theology for him. The result was *On the Faith*, in which Ambrose, who was an enthusiastic Nicene, set out the Nicene version of Christianity and promised Gratian success if he adhered to it. But while Ambrose was writing it, the eastern emperor, Valens, was killed. Refugees from the eastern empire flooded into the west. Many of these refugees were Arians. Gratian commandeered one of the basilicas in Milan and handed it over to the Arians for their use. Ambrose was outraged, and was at loggerheads with the court for some years. However, Gratian never lost his admiration for the bishop. In AD 381, the emperor called a council at Aquileia, but Ambrose persuaded him not to bother inviting any eastern bishops; the result was a grand victory for the Nicene party.

In AD 383, a general named Magnus Maximus seized power in Gaul, had Gratian assassinated, and installed himself as emperor of the western half of the west, alongside Valentinian II, still officially emperor of the eastern half of the west. Valentinian was still a child, and his mother, Justina, was now the effective ruler of the court. She was quite pro-Arian and disliked Ambrose, but in AD 386 the bishop produced a masterstroke in the struggle for the loyalty of Milanese Christians. He had already spent some years building new churches throughout Milan; he knew that if the Nicene party had more impressive architecture, that would send out a powerful signal. During the ceremony to dedicate one of these – the Basilica Ambrosiana – Ambrose announced that he wanted a sign of divine favour in the form of the relics of martyrs. At that point, he later claimed, divine inspiration entered him. He marched to a particular spot within the basilica and ordered his men to dig. Before the watching congregation, the bones of two men were discovered.

Ambrose (c. AD 337–97), bishop of Milan.

He announced that these were the relics of two ancient martyrs and had them solemnly transferred to a chapel, where there were many reports of miraculous healings.

Historians have, perhaps naturally, been suspicious of Ambrose's claim that all this happened under divine inspiration; it seems like a too perfectly stage-managed event. But it certainly had the desired effect. In the eyes of the Christians of Milan, the Nicene party, which Ambrose represented, clearly enjoyed the favour of God and of the blessed martyrs of ancient times. Arianism fell in popularity.

Theodosius I and Gregory of Nazianzus

In the east, meanwhile, things were looking even worse for the Arians. The appointment of Theodosius as eastern emperor must have been as much of a surprise to him as it was to others. Aged only thirty-one at the time of his appointment, he was a soldier, the son of a general, with whom he campaigned under Valentinian I. In AD 375, Theodosius' father was disgraced and executed for reasons that remain obscure. Theodosius retired to his estates in Spain, where he no doubt expected to live out his life in safe obscurity. But in AD 378 Gratian plucked Theodosius from his estate and installed him as the new eastern emperor, charging him to deal with the Gothic crisis which had killed Valens. Gratian's choice of co-emperor proved astute. Theodosius spent his first two years as emperor waging a difficult campaign against the Ostrogoths; he had few troops, and none who was loyal to him. But he succeeded in his campaign and negotiated peace with the Visigoths. In AD 380, Theodosius finally entered Constantinople.

He found it in a state of religious agitation. The Homoian and Nicene parties were bitterly contesting the city. The bishop, Demophilus, was a Homoian, but the Nicenes refused to acknowledge him. The leading figure in the Nicene community was Gregory of Nazianzus, one of the most brilliant theologians of the age. Gregory had been the closest friend of Basil of Caesarea, like him a highly educated, aristocratic Cappadocian. In AD 372, Basil made Gregory bishop of a small village called Sasima. This was part of his plan to increase his own influence by creating new bishops within his territory. Gregory of Nazianzus loathed Sasima, which he refused even to visit, and remained in his home town of Nazianzus.

Shortly after Basil's death in AD 379, the Nicene community in Constantinople invited Gregory to come and help administer it. The job was tough, especially for a retiring, bookish theologian who claimed to want only peace and quiet. During the Easter vigil, an Arian mob invaded Gregory's church; he was injured and another man was killed. But during this time Gregory preached a series of

Gregory of Nazianzus (c. AD 325–389), as depicted in *The Homolies* AD 867–86.

sermons which have become known as the 'Theological Orations'. They are 'theological' in the sense of teaching the divinity of all three persons of the Trinity – Father, Son, and Holy Spirit – and for this reason Gregory is often known as Gregory the Theologian. In these lectures, Gregory presented what is generally taken to be the definitive version of the Cappadocian doctrine of the Trinity, in which the full divinity and equality of the Father, the Son, and the Holy Spirit are of central importance. Gregory argued that the names 'Father', 'Son', and 'Spirit' refer not to different substances (as the Homoians believed) or to the same person (as Sabellius had once held), but to relations within God. Within the one divine *ousia* (nature), there are three distinct *hypostases* (individuals), but these are not simply a collection of three things co-existing – they are defined in relation to one another and cannot exist without one another.

Clearly, the Nicene doctrine of the Trinity had reached a level of sophistication previously unknown to Christian theology. It is hard to imagine that this sort of advanced theology had much effect on the Christian in the street, as it were. But Gregory of Nyssa, who visited Constantinople at around this time too, gives a vivid picture of just how obsessed ordinary people were with this kind of thing:

> *Every place in the city is full of them: the alleys, the crossroads, the forums, the squares. Garment sellers, money changers, food vendors – they are all at it. If you ask for change, they philosophize for you about generate and ingenerate natures. If you inquire about the price of bread, the answer is that the Father is greater and the Son inferior. If you speak about whether the bath is ready, they express the opinion that the Son was made out of nothing.[3]*

The emperor Theodosius made it clear that he was interested in this too; and that, despite being appointed to tackle a military crisis, he was going to take a very close interest in ecclesiastical matters. Early in AD 380, he issued a joint proclamation with Gratian in which they declared that all their subjects should profess Nicene Christianity. For the first time since the 330s, then, the faith of Nicaea was once again the official doctrine of the church, at least as far as the state was concerned. And when he arrived in Constantinople, Theodosius showed that he was determined to enforce this edict. Within two days he had deposed the bishop, Demophilus, for refusing to sign the Symbol of Nicaea, and replaced him with Gregory of Nazianzus.

The council of Constantinople

The following year, Theodosius convened a new council to address the Arian conflict. Meletius, bishop of Antioch, presided over it. The schism in Antioch was still going on, even though by this time both factions there were Nicene. Theodosius strongly supported Meletius, putting him in charge of the new council at Constantinople, and those who opposed him lost considerable support. Unfortunately Meletius died during the council and the factions at Antioch split apart again; but the anti-Meletian groups were smaller than they had been before, and the schism was finally ended completely in AD 415.

Gregory of Nazianzus took over as president of the council. Around 150 bishops were present, all from the eastern half of the empire. Most were of the Nicene party, although there were some Homoians present. They immediately pointed out that the canons of Nicaea had forbidden the movement of bishops from one see to another. Gregory of Nazianzus had been bishop of Sasima, so he shouldn't now be bishop of Constantinople. He was therefore deposed and sent back off to Nazianzus, where he retired with an almost audible sigh of relief tinged with regret, to live out his life writing cultured but rather miserable poetry.

The council, meanwhile, ratified the Symbol of Nicaea as the true statement of Christian faith. Oddly, the decrees of the council have not survived. But the later council of Chalcedon, held in AD 451, published a creed which it attributed to the council of Constantinople. This creed was basically a new version of the Symbol of Nicaea. It contained the *homoousios*, but it also stated that the Son's kingdom would have no end, a rejection of the doctrine of Marcellus of Ancyra. The creed also featured a new statement about the Holy Spirit, stressing that he too was divine, just as the Cappadocian theologians had argued.

The council of Constantinople was the last of the great councils on the Arian controversy, and would later be recognized as the second ecumenical council, after Nicaea. The creed which it issued is still recited in churches around the world today, under the not quite accurate name of the Nicene Creed. Theodosius convened a series of meetings over the next couple of years in which he tried to find a way to get the Homoians to agree to its decisions, but by AD 383 he had lost patience and simply banned Arianism as well as other movements such as the Manichaeans. It seems that these laws were not rigorously enforced, but they were certainly quite effective. It was during this period that Christian groups that were considered heretical – and which had, in some cases, existed for centuries – entered a terminal decline.

As we saw earlier, Maximus Magnus deposed the pro-Nicene western emperor, Gratian, in AD 383 as Theodosius was enacting his anti-heretical legislation. In AD 387, Maximus invaded Italy, seeking to depose Valentinian II, who still ruled that region. Theodosius gathered his forces, headed west, and defeated Maximus. Once again, there were just two emperors, Theodosius in the east and Valentinian II in the west. But in reality, the teenage Valentinian was almost completely sidelined. Theodosius was the real power, which meant that the Nicene faith, as promulgated by the council of Constantinople, was imposed upon the whole empire. The Arian controversy was, finally, at an end – at least, within the empire. We hear virtually no more from Latin- or Greek-speaking Arians after this time. But the barbarians were still Arians, and they would remain Arians for a long time. Theodosius seems to have been prepared to tolerate this state of affairs, perhaps recognizing that his alliance with the Visigoths was simply too important and precarious to risk. In AD 383 he allowed Ulfilas to have a magnificent funeral in Constantinople, despite his Homoianism.

Paganism in the age of Theodosius

Theodosius seems to have been quite tolerant of paganism in the early years of his rule, when he was more concerned about Arianism. In AD 384, his close ally, Cynegius, the prefect of the east, began closing temples and banning sacrifices in Egypt. Two years later he provided troops to Marcellus, the bishop of Apamea, to destroy the temple of Zeus in that city. Theodosius neither condoned nor condemned these measures, and in AD 388 replaced Cynegius with a pagan, Tatianus – although Cynegius remained a close ally.

Things changed in the 390s, although it is not certain why. One reason may have been the increasing influence that Ambrose of Milan held over Theodosius, who was resident in the western empire during this period. In AD 388 a group of monks burned the synagogue in Callinicum. Theodosius would have ordered that the Jews there be paid compensation, but Ambrose persuaded him not to, on the grounds that burning down synagogues was a reasonable thing for Christians to do. Two years later, Theodosius ordered a massacre in the city of Thessalonica to punish the people for a riot. Some 7,000 people died. Ambrose of Milan denounced the emperor for this, and refused to admit him to the cathedral to take part in the Eucharist. Theodosius duly did penance, and the two were soon reconciled. Events such as these powerfully illustrated a new theory that Ambrose was developing of the relationship between church and state. The successors of Constantine had increasingly assumed that the church was just another organ of the state, subject to the emperor. Ambrose insisted upon the reverse. He believed that all people – no matter what their status – had a duty to lead a moral life. But morality is the business of the church. Where immorality occurs, the church may therefore intervene. In theory, this makes the whole of the state – including the emperor – subject to the church.

Apart from Ambrose's influence, other factors may have helped prompt Theodosius to move against paganism. One was the fading away of the pagan revival in Rome, which seems to have petered out after AD 384, when Agorius, its main leader, died. The year AD 389 saw the first of the series that would later be known as the 'Theodosian decrees', as the emperor ordered that all pagan feast days that had not yet been Christianized were to be abolished and become ordinary working days. In AD 391, he ordered the flame on the altar of Vesta in Rome – which had burned, uninterrupted, for centuries – to be extinguished. Sacrificing to the gods and divination were again banned. Attendance at temples was banned, as was 'raising the eyes' to statues. Many temples were now converted into churches, and many others were destroyed. It was during this period that Theophilus, bishop of Alexandria, inspired a Christian mob to destroy the great temple of Serapis in that city. Afterwards, Theophilus invited Pachomian monks to build a new monastery where it had once stood.

In AD 393, the last ancient Olympic Games were held. It is not certain whether Theodosius ordered the games to cease, but if he did it may have been because of their pagan associations. In effect, the Theodosian decrees meant the proscription of paganism and the elevation of Christianity to the status of the official religion of the empire. But it is uncertain whether this was Theodosius' conscious aim, or whether it was simply the net effect of a series of edicts that were issued for particular and distinct reasons.

A 5th-century Greek amphora shows a foot race.

Morality in an official church

We have seen in previous chapters how disagreement over moral principles was a particular problem in the early church. In particular, different Christians disagreed over how strict moral principles needed to be, and how those who transgressed them should be treated. With a huge influx of new members into the movement in the late fourth and early fifth centuries, these problems now took on a new and more urgent form.

Jovinianism

There was a series of disputes which, in different ways, revolved around the question 'How stringent should Christian morality be?' One dispute concerned the views of Jovinian, who argued that it should not be very stringent at all. Jovinian seems to have been a monk before giving up on the lifestyle and criticizing it. He moved to Rome, where he wrote a book attacking ascetic practices in the church in general, and particularly those recommended by Jerome. In particular, he insisted that it is no better to be a virgin than to be married – he denied that Jesus' mother had preserved her virginity 'in parturition' – and no better to starve yourself than to eat normally. But he also taught that all sins are equally serious, and that God rewards all the faithful equally too.

Many people in Rome agreed with Jovinian. Jerome, whose personality was abrasive to say the least, was unpopular in the city, and there were concerns that he stressed the need for asceticism, especially the preservation of virginity, to such an extreme that he was in danger of crossing over into encratitism. Nevertheless, Jovinian was also perceived as too extreme in the opposite direction, and in AD 390 he was condemned in Rome.

In other words, most Christians agreed that ascetic practices, and austere morality, *were* important. But how important?

Priscillianism

One figure who argued that they were *very* important was Priscillian, a nobleman from southern Spain who, in the 370s, began calling for higher moral standards in the church. For example, he encouraged all Christians to commit themselves to celibacy. He also encouraged them to go on fortnight-long retreats into the mountains before major Christian festivals to practise solitude and asceticism. In effect, Priscillian wanted all Christians to live – at least some of the time – as monks. His message proved popular, and spread throughout Spain and into southern Gaul. Many bishops in the area were unhappy, not simply because they disagreed with Priscillian's ascetic message but because of the magical practices that he seems to have encouraged. In fact Priscillian himself had a strong interest in the occult, especially number mysticism. His opponents accused him of controlling the weather by magical means.

However, in AD 381 Priscillian became bishop of Avila. His election was controversial. In AD 384, a council was called at Bordeaux to investigate him, but Priscillian refused to attend. Instead he travelled to Trier to appeal to the court of Magnus Maximus, the general who had killed Gratian and declared himself emperor. It was an unwise move. Maximus was keen to secure the support of the bishops in his domains, who mistrusted him after his treatment of Gratian. Priscillian was hauled before Maximus' praetorian prefect on a charge of sorcery, found guilty, and executed together with a group of supporters. However, Maximus' attempt to placate the bishops by removing Priscillian did not work: Ambrose of Milan, Siricius of Rome, and Martin of Tours all condemned what had happened.

Priscillian is usually cited as the first Christian to be executed for heresy, although he was executed as a sorcerer rather than as a heretic, and some of the Donatist martyrs probably have a better claim to the title. Priscillianism survived his death; it had something of a revival after Theodosius defeated Maximus in AD 388 and declared all his decrees null and void, but a series of councils in the early fifth century condemned the movement and it lost most of its support.

Donatism

The major legacy of the earlier conflicts between rigorists and laxists was the Donatist church, still the dominant Christian organization in Africa. Not until the end of the fourth century did things begin to change, and that was due in large part to the efforts of Augustine. From his church in Hippo, Augustine could

hear the hymns being sung by the much larger congregation at
the nearby Donatist church. Little wonder that, for the twenty
years or so after becoming bishop of Hippo in AD 391, Augustine
devoted most of his spare time and energy to working against the
Donatists. He met with every leader of the Donatist church who
would agree to see him, and tried to persuade them to rejoin the
Catholic church. When that didn't work, he wrote a long series of
sermons, letters, and books attacking Donatist theology. In them,
he undermined the basic belief which had led to the establishment
of the Donatist church: the belief that a bishop who had sinned was
unable to act *as* a bishop, and that the consecrations performed by
traditores were therefore invalid. Augustine argued that, in fact, the
sacraments performed by Christian priests – including consecration,
baptism, and the Eucharist – are all performed by Christ *through*
the priest. The moral worth of the priest himself is irrelevant. So
even if *traditores* had consecrated bishops, those were real and valid
consecrations. There was therefore no justification for the Donatists
to maintain their schism.

Augustine did not have huge success converting Donatists to
Catholicism. Nevertheless, he did succeed in repositioning the
dispute as a theological one. The argument was difficult, because
Cyprian of Carthage – universally revered throughout Africa – had
argued the exact opposite. Augustine had to engage in fancy verbal
footwork to convince his readers that the famous saint was on his
side and not on that of the Donatists.

Nevertheless, after the beginning of the fifth century, the Donatist
church seems to have waned somewhat in north Africa, as it was
counted among the heretical movements that were officially banned.
In AD 411, a council known as the conference of Carthage was held
to tackle the problem. Since both the Catholics and the Donatists
sent all the bishops they could muster, this was one of the largest
church councils of antiquity, so big it had to meet in the public bath
complex. Augustine was the main defender of the Catholic position,
of course, while the Donatist case was made by their leading thinker,
Petilian of Constantine. But given the attitude of the civil authorities,
there was little doubt about the outcome. The Donatists lost the
argument and were condemned once more.

The Donatist church continued to exist in parts of Africa,
although it never again enjoyed the dominance it had had for much
of the fourth century. Indeed, the schism was finally ended only
in the seventh century, when the Arabs invaded and all forms of
Christianity found themselves dominated by Islam. However, the
decrees of the conference of Carthage were significant quite apart
from their effect on the north African church. The Donatists had
argued that the church had to be morally spotless. If a Christian
sinned, the Holy Spirit could not dwell in him or her. But Augustine
had argued that matters were not so clear-cut. The church contained
both sinners and saints, and God's grace extended to them all. The

conference of Carthage, and the Catholic church as a whole, agreed with Augustine.

Pelagianism

Augustine also played a central role in the biggest debate about Christian morality in this period, which revolved around the teaching of Pelagius. Pelagius came from Britain, although it is not known where precisely (there is no evidence for the common claim that he was Welsh), and he became prominent in Rome in the early fifth century. He lived a highly ascetic lifestyle, had a number of disciples, and acted as a spiritual adviser to many Christians in the city. He also wrote a number of books, including a commentary on the letters of Paul, which survives, making him the earliest British author whose writings are extant.

But Pelagius was shocked by what he considered to be the laxity of Roman morality. Perhaps this was one of the results of the growth of the church, and the anti-pagan measures, over the past few decades. The church was no longer a small group of dedicated believers, but an organization to which most people belonged without necessarily being very committed to its ideals. But what was worse in Pelagius' view was the fact that some people justified their moral sloppiness theologically. They argued that human nature had been warped ever since Adam and Eve had sinned and been cast out of Eden. Human beings are incapable of doing good by their own efforts; they can manage it only if God steps in and gives them the ability.

These ideas were associated with Augustine of Hippo. On one occasion Pelagius attended a public reading of Augustine's *Confessions*, an event which itself indicates how influential the African theologian had become. At one point in this book, Augustine says to God: 'Command what you will, and give what you command' – in other words, God not only commands human beings but makes them follow his commands. When the reader reached that sentence, Pelagius stood up and protested. He believed that this view made human beings mere puppets of God. Instead, he argued, neither original sin nor God can force human beings to act one way or the other. Human beings always retain free will and are capable, in theory, of avoiding sin altogether if they wish to. It is even possible to lead a perfect life. He did not deny that God's grace helps Christians to do so, but he felt that this grace consists of the teaching of Jesus and other things that help them from the outside, as it were. God does not reach inside and tinker with human beings' hearts and minds, as Augustine seemed to think.

In modern times, Pelagius has often been viewed very sympathetically as a defender of human freedom. However, it is worth remembering that he stressed not human beings' *ability* to act freely but their *responsibility* to act rightly. He believed that because it is possible to lead a perfect life, anyone who does not do so is guilty of sin and subject to God's judgment. In effect, he felt, like Priscillian, that all Christians were called to live as ascetics or monks.

Pelagius had a disciple named Caelestius who seems to have been far more outspoken than Pelagius himself was. In AD 411 he was in Carthage, where a synod condemned his views. Pelagius wrote a book defending his ideas, to which Augustine replied with a book of his own. He believed that Pelagius' views left no room for divine grace at all. He seemed to say that human beings save themselves by living moral lives. But in that case, what role would there be for Jesus except as a moral teacher? What of his saving death?

The other African bishops agreed, and pushed for the condemnation of Pelagius and Caelestius. A series of councils followed, which finally ended in AD 418 with a major council at Carthage, an encyclical (or letter to be read throughout the church) by Zosimus, bishop of Rome, condemning Pelagianism, and even an order from the emperor Honorius expelling all of Pelagius' followers from Italy. Pelagius himself seems to have submitted to this with dignity and lived out his years in exile.

Pelagianism, as a movement, did not end with this. Many people, especially in the west, felt that Augustine, not Pelagius, was the extremist. The debates over Pelagianism would continue for centuries, especially in Gaul. They tended to focus upon questions of the nature of divine grace and how it interacts with the human will. But there was more consensus regarding the question of morality which had inspired Pelagius' original teachings as well as the other disputes we have looked at. From those disputes had emerged the notion that Christians are indeed called to a higher standard of living than other people, and that some are called to a still higher standard, one of advanced asceticism. But not everyone is called in that way. It is better to be a monk than a lay person, better to be a virgin than to be married, and better to fast than to feast. But that does not mean that the less ascetical lifestyle is wrong or inadequate – merely that it is less good. The story of Mary and Martha became the standard illustration of this. According to Luke 10:38-42, these were two sisters with whom Jesus stayed. Mary sat at Jesus' feet listening to him, while Martha did the housework. Eventually Martha got annoyed and complained that Mary was doing nothing useful; Jesus replied that Mary had chosen 'the better part'. Christians took Martha to represent life in the world, and Mary to represent monastic or philosophical contemplation of God. Mary's lifestyle was 'better', but Martha's was still good. In this way, a middle course was found between Jovinianism and Pelagianism.

Epilogue

In AD 392, the young and marginalized emperor of the west, Valentinian II, was found dead, hanged in his room. He was succeeded by Eugenius, who was a Christian but had the support of a powerful pagan faction who persuaded him to endorse the traditional religion and restore temples in Rome. That did not go down well with Ambrose, who refused to attend Eugenius' court when it arrived in Milan, or with Theodosius, who grudgingly recognized Eugenius but began preparations to remove him as soon as possible. The clash came in AD 394 at the battle of the River Frigidus. Not only was Eugenius' power base largely pagan, but most of his troops were pagan barbarians. Theodosius, by contrast, led an officially Christian army, although much of it, too, was barbarian. Helped by a lucky wind, which blew dust directly into the faces of Eugenius' troops on the second day of the battle, Theodosius' army was victorious, and Eugenius was captured and executed. Theodosius' victory meant that he was now the sole ruler of the Roman empire – the last man who would ever enjoy that position. But more significantly, both sides regarded the encounter as symbolic of the struggle between Christianity and paganism. In Rome, the aristocratic pagans simply gave up resisting the new political and religious reality; we hear of no more attempts to restore the old religion. The Christians, meanwhile, were overjoyed at the overthrow of the pagan usurpers – just as they had been over the defeat of Magnentius forty years earlier, and over the defeat of Maxentius forty years before that. The difference this time was that the victory was more or less final, making the River Frigidus as significant, in its own way, as the Milvian Bridge. In around AD 420, Isidore, a Christian priest from Pelusium in Egypt, could write that paganism had completely vanished.

Historians often like to compartmentalize history – to distinguish between one period and the next, and identify the great turning points where one age ends and another begins. That is part of the natural human desire to see patterns in reality and categorize things to make them easier to understand. In reality, history is complex, changes come gradually and the great 'turning points' are mostly just convenient markers rather than moments when the world really changed. Theodosius' victory at the River Frigidus, together with his anti-pagan legislation and the collapse of organized pagan resistance to the Christianizing of the empire, was a genuinely pivotal moment, and one that makes a fitting end to our survey of how Christianity emerged from an obscure Jewish movement in Galilee and became the religion of empires. After this point, not only was the Roman empire officially Christian for the next thousand years, but the Germanic peoples with whom Theodosius had negotiated peace were also devoted to the religion. When Rome fell within the next century, these Christian barbarians would fill the power vacuum and lay the foundations for a Christian Europe.

But at the same time, significant though it was, Theodosius' apparent victory over paganism did not change the world overnight. After the battle at the River Frigidus, he ruled a united empire for less than a year until his death in early AD 395, a few days after his forty-eighth birthday. And the transformation of a pagan world into a Christian one, although accelerated by Theodosius' reign, was still far from complete. Frigidus saw the end of organized resistance by paganism, but paganism still existed. There were still pagans even in the top levels of government well into the fifth century. Edessa was still celebrating its traditional pagan spring festival at the end of the fifth century. Even in the sixth century, the emperor Justinian devoted considerable resources to the destruction of pagan temples and images, and the forcible conversion of pagans. This purge – two and a half centuries after the conversion of Constantine – would be the first really thorough attempt on the part of the Roman authorities to stamp out paganism, and the first time that the various laws against paganism were seriously enforced. It would also see a development that had not occurred even under Theodosius or his immediate successors: capital punishment for pagans. The wheel had come full circle: where once pagan authorities had tortured and killed Christians, the Christian authorities hunted down and killed the lingering devotees of the old religions.

The story of later Christian history, with both its triumphs and its tragedies, lies beyond the scope of this book. But in this chapter we have seen how even the close of one story – the struggle between the old paganism and the new Christianity for the soul of the Roman empire – is just the beginning of a new story, or rather, the continuation and transformation of the same story. As one problem is settled, the seeds of a new one are sown. In the century that followed the death of Theodosius, not only would Christians face new moral problems of the kind outlined in the previous section; they would also find their religion splintering in ways even more drastic than had occurred in the fourth century, with the first great division of Christendom, between the Greek- and Latin-speaking churches of the west and the Coptic- and Syriac-speaking ones of Africa and the Middle East. That division, like much of subsequent Christian history, had its roots in the doctrinal and other developments that were forged in the first four centuries of the church.

Notes

3 Opposition and Persecution

1 Quoted in H. Maccoby, *Judaism in the First Century* (London: Sheldon, 1989), p. 131

2 Quoted in D. Boyarin, *Dying for God: Martyrdom and the Making of Christianity and Judaism* (Stanford, CA: Stanford University Press, 1999), p. 23

4 The Church in the Empire

1 Tertullian, *On the Crown* 11

2 In H. Musurillo, ed., *The Acts of the Christian Martyrs* (Oxford: Clarendon, 1972), p. 247

3. In W. Schneemelcher, ed., *New Testament Apocrypha* (Cambridge: James Clark, 1992), vol. 2, p. 344

4 In *New Testament Apocrypha*, vol. 2, p. 344

Alexandria

1 C. Haas, *Alexandria in Late Antiquity* (Baltimore, MD: John Hopkins University Press, 1997), p. 148

5 Christians in a Hostile World

1 *Nat. D. 2.8*, quoted in R. Wilken, *The Christians as the Romans Saw Them* (New Haven, CT: Yale University Press, 2003), p. 57

2. *On the True Doctrine* 1, in R. Hoffmann, ed., *Celsus: On the True Doctrine* (Oxford: OUP, 1987), p. 53

3 *Octavius* 8.4, in G. Clarke, ed., *The Octavius of Marcus Minucius Felix* (New York: Paulist, 1974), p. 63

4 *Octavius* 10.2, *The Octavius of Marcus Minucius Felix*, p. 66

5. In R. Walzer, *Galen on Jews and Christians* (London: OUP, 1949), p. 14

6 *On the True Doctrine* 8, in *Celsus: On the*

True Doctrine, p. 103

7 In *The Christians as the Romans Saw Them* (New Haven, CT: Yale University Press, 2003), p. 156

8 In *The Acts of the Christian Martyrs*, p. 63

9 In *The Acts of the Christian Martyrs*, pp. 72–73

10 In, *The Acts of the Christian Martyrs*, pp. 158–159

11 *Epistle to the Romans* 4–5, in M. Staniforth, ed., *Early Christian Writings* (London: Penguin, 1987), pp. 86–87

12 In *The Acts of the Christian Martyrs*, pp. 15–17

Christians on trial

1 In *The Acts of the Christian Martyrs*, pp. 87–89

6 Christian Philosophy

1 Justin, *Second Apology* 13

2 Justin, *Dialogue with Trypho* 128

3 Origen, *On Song of Songs* III 8

4 Origen, *Homilies on Song of Songs* I 7

7 Heresy and Orthodoxy

1 B. Layton, ed., *The Gnostic Scriptures* (London: SCM, 1987), p. 255

2 Irenaus, *Against Heresies* preface 1

3 *Against Heresies* III 4 2

4 Cyprian, *On the Unity of the Church* 5

8 The Christian Empire

1 In A. Cameron and S. Hall, eds., *Life of Constantine* (Oxford: Clarendon, 1999), p. 81

2 In J. L. Creed, ed., *De mortibus persecutorum* (Oxford: Clarendon, 1984), p. 71

3 *Sermon* 25.8.8, in P. Brown, *Poverty and Leadership in the Later Roman Empire* (Hanover, NH: University Press of New England, 2002), p. 64

4 Basil, *Against the Rich*

5 In J. Salisbury, *The Blood of Martyrs: Unintended Consequences of Ancient Violence* (London: Routledge, 2004), pp. 63–64

The growth of the church

1 In R. MacMullen and E. Lane, eds., *Paganism and Christianity 100–425 CE: A Sourcebook* (Minneapolis, MN: Fortress, 1992), p. 284

10 The First Monks

1 *Lausiac History* 7.5, in R. Meyer, ed., *The Lausiac History* [Westminster, MD: Newman, 1965], p. 41

2 *Eight Thoughts* 6.15, in R. Sinkewicz, *Evagrius of Pontus: The Greek Ascetic Corpus* (Oxford: OUP, 2003), p. 84

3 *Praktikos* 94, in R. Sinkewicz, *Evagrius of Pontus: The Greek Ascetic Corpus* (Oxford: OUP, 2003), p. 113

4 *Praktikos* 94, p. 113

5 In N. Russell, ed., *The Lives of the Desert Fathers* (Kalamazoo, MI: Cistercian, 1981), p. 71

6 *Didaskalikos* 1.1, in J. Dillon, ed., *Alcinous: The Handbook of Platonism* (Oxford: Clarendon, 1993), p. 3

7 *Academica* I.2, ed. R. Rackham (London: Heinemann; New York: Putnam's, 1933), p. 417

11 The Official Church

1 *Letter 84*, in P. Chuvin, *A Chronicle of the Last Pagans* (Cambridge, MA: Harvard University Press, 1990), p. 47

2 Oration 17.7, in A. Murdoch, *The Last Pagan: Julian the Apostate and the Death of the Ancient World* (Stroud: Sutton, 2003), p. 209

3 'Oration on the Deity of the Son and the Holy Spirit', in W. Placher, *A History of Christian Theology* (Louisville: Westminster John Knox, 1983), p. 68

Further Reading

Anatolios, K., *Athanasius*, Abingdon: Routledge, 2004

Ashwin-Siejkowski, P. *Clement of Alexandria: A Project of Christian Perfection*, London: New York: T. & T. Clark, 2008

Ayres, L., *Nicaea and Its Legacy: An Approach to Fourth-Century Trinitarian Theology*, Oxford: OUP, 2004

Barnes, T., *Athanasius and Constantius: Theology and Politics in the Constantinian Empire*, Cambridge, MA: Harvard University Press, 1993

Barrett, C. K., *Paul: An Introduction to His Thought*, London: Continuum, 2001

Baum, W., & Winkler, D., *The Church of the East: A Concise History*, London: RoutledgeCurzon, 2003

Baumer, C., *The Church of the East: An Illustrated History of Assyrian Christianity*, London: Tauris, 2006

Bentley-Taylor, D., *The Apostle from Africa: The Life and Thought of Augustine of Hippo*, Fearn: Christian Focus, 2002

Boyarin, D., *Dying for God: Martyrdom and the Making of Christianity and Judaism* Stanford, CA: Stanford University Press, 1999

Bradshaw, P., *Eucharistic Origins*, London: SPCK, 2004

Brakke, D. *Demons and the Making of the Monk: Spiritual Combat in Early Christianity*, Cambridge, MA; London: Harvard University Press, 2006

Brent, A., *Ignatius of Antioch: A Martyr Bishop and the Origin of Monarchial Episcopacy*, London: Continuum, 2007

Brown, P., *Augustine of Hippo*, London: Faber & Faber, 2000

Brown, R., & Moloney, F., *An Introduction to the Gospel of John*, New York: Doubleday, 2003

Burkett, D., *An Introduction to the New Testament and the Origins of Christianity*, Cambridge: Cambridge University Press, 2002

Campbell, W., *Paul and the Creation of Christian Identity*, London: Clark, 2006

Carroll, J., ed., *The Return of Jesus in Early Christianity*, Peabody, MA: Hendrickson, 2000

Chadwick, H., *The Church in Ancient Society: From Galilee to Gregory the Great*, Oxford: OUP, 2001

——*The Early Church*, London: Penguin, 1993

Chilton, B., & Neusner, J., eds., *The Brother of Jesus: James the Just and His Mission*, Louisville, KY: Westminster John Knox Press, 2001

Clark, G., *Christianity and Roman Society*, New York; Cambridge: Cambridge University Press, 2004

Clauss, M., *The Roman Cult of Mithras: The God and His Mysteries*, Edinburgh: Edinburgh University Press, 2000

Crossan, J., & Reed, J., *In Search of Paul: How Jesus' Apostle Opposed Rome's Empire with God's Kingdom*, London: SPCK, 2005

Curran, J., *Pagan City and Christian Capital: Rome in the Fourth Century*, Oxford: Clarendon, 2000

Daley, B., *Gregory of Nazianzus*, London; New York: Routledge, 2006

Davidson, I., *The Birth of the Church: From Jesus to Constantine, AD 30–312*, Oxford: Monarch, 2005

DeSilva, D., *An Introduction to the New Testament: Contexts, Methods, and Ministry Formation*, Downers Grove, IL: InterVarsity; Leicester: Apollos, 2004

Donfried, K., *Paul, Thessalonica, and Early Christianity*, Grand Rapids, MI: Eerdmans, 2002

Donovan, M., *One Right Reading? A Guide to Irenaeus*, Collegeville, MN: Liturgical Press, 1997

Drake, H., *Constantine and the Bishops: The Politics of Intolerance*, Baltimore, MD; London: Johns Hopkins University Press, 2000

Dunderberg, I., *Beyond Gnosticism: Myth, Lifestyle, and Society in the School of Valentinus*, New York: Columbia University Press, 2008

Dunn, G., *Tertullian*, London: Routledge, 2004

Ehrman, B., ed., *The Apostolic Fathers*, Cambridge, MA: Harvard University Press, 2003

—— *Lost Christianities: The Battle for Scripture and the Faiths We Never Knew*, New York; Oxford: OUP, 2003

—— *The New Testament: A Historical Introduction to the Early Christian Writings*, New York; Oxford: OUP, 2004

Ehrman, B., & Jacobs, A., eds., *Christianity in Late Antiquity, 300–450 CE: a reader*, New York; Oxford: OUP, 2004

Elliott, T., *The Christianity of Constantine the Great*, Scranton, PA: University of Scranton Press, 1996

Esler, P., ed., *The Early Christian World*, London: Routledge, 2000

Evans, G., ed., *The First Christian Theologians: An Introduction to Theology in the Early Church*, Oxford: Blackwell, 2004

Ferguson, E., ed., *Christianity in Relation to Jews, Greeks and Romans*, New York; London: Garland, 1999

Ferguson, J., *Pelagius: A Historical and Theological Study*, New York: AMS, 1978

Freeman, C., *AD 381: Heretics, Pagans and the Christian State*, London: Pimlico, 2008

Frend, W. H. C., *The Donatist Church: A Movement of Protest in Roman North Africa*, Oxford: Clarendon, 2000

—— *The Early Church: From the Beginnings to 461*, London: SCM Press, 2003

Goehring, J., *Ascetics, Society, and the Desert: Studies in Egyptian Monasticism*, Harrisburg, PA: Trinity, 1999

Grabbe, L., *An Introduction to First-Century Judaism*, Edinburgh: Clark, 1996

Grant, R., *Irenaeus of Lyons*, London: Routledge, 1997

—— *Paul in the Roman world: The Conflict at Corinth*, Louisville, KY, and London: Westminster John Knox Press, 2001

Gregory, A., & Tuckett, C., eds., *Trajectories through the New Testament and the Apostolic Fathers*, Oxford: OUP, 2005

Griggs, C., *Early Egyptian Christianity: From its Origins to 451 CE*, Leiden; Boston, MA: Brill, 2000

Guy, L., *Introducing Early Christianity: A Topical Survey of Its Life, Beliefs and Practices*, Downers Grove, IL: InterVarsity, 2004

Hanson, R. P. C., *The Search for the Christian Doctrine of God: The Arian Controversy 318–381*, Edinburgh: T. & T. Clark, 1988

Hargis, J., *Against the Christians: The Rise of Early Anti-Christian Polemic*, New York: Lang, 2001

Harmless, W., *Desert Christians: An Introduction to the Literature of Early Monasticism*, Oxford: OUP, 2004

Harvey, S., & Hunter, D., eds., *The Oxford Handbook of Early Christian Studies*, Oxford: OUP, 2008

Hinson, E., *The Early Church: Origins to the Dawn of the Middle Ages*, Nashville, TN: Abingdon Press, 1996

Holmes, M., ed., *The Apostolic Fathers*, Grand Rapids, MI: Baker, 2007

Hunter, D., *Marriage, Celibacy, and Heresy in Ancient Christianity: The Jovinianist Controversy*, Oxford: OUP, 2004

Hurtado, L., *Lord Jesus Christ: Devotion to Jesus in Earliest Christianity*, Grand Rapids, MI: Eerdmans, 2003

Hyldahl, N., *The History of Early Christianity*, Frankfurt am Main: Lang, 1997

Jensen, R., *Understanding Early Christian Art*, London: Routledge, 2000

Kelly, J., *Golden Mouth: The Story of John Chrysostom – Ascetic, Preacher, Bishop*, London: Duckworth, 1995

Kelly, J. N. D., *Jerome: His Life, Writings and Controversies*, London: Duckworth, 1975

Klauck, H. J., *The Religious Context of Early Christianity: A Guide to Graeco-Roman Religions*, Edinburgh: T. & T. Clark, 2003

Lampe, P., *From Paul to Valentinus: Christians at Rome in the First Two Centuries*, London: T. & T. Clark, 2003

Lapham, F., *An Introduction to the New Testament Apocrypha*, London: T. & T. Clark, 2003

Layton, B., ed., *The Gnostic Scriptures: A New Translation with Annotations and Introductions*, Garden City, NY: Doubleday, 1995

Lenski, N., ed., *The Cambridge Companion to the Age of Constantine*, Cambridge: Cambridge University Press, 2006

Lieu, S., & Montserrat, D., eds., *Constantine: History, Historiography and Legend*, London: Routledge, 1998

McLynn, N., *Ambrose of Milan: Church and Court in a Christian Capital*, Berkeley, CA; London: University of California Press, 1994

Marjanen, A., & Luomanen, P., eds., *A Companion to Second-Century Christian 'Heretics'*, Leiden and Boston, MA: Brill, 2005

Markschies, C., *Gnosis: An Introduction*, London: T. & T. Clark, 2003

Matthews, G., *Augustine*, Oxford: Blackwell, 2005

Meredith, A., *Gregory of Nyssa*, London; New York: Routledge, 2003

—— *The Cappadocians*, London: Geoffrey Chapman, 1995

Mitchell, M., & Young, F., eds., *The Cambridge History of Christianity, 1: Origins to Constantine*, Cambridge and New York: Cambridge University Press, 2006

Moorhead, J., *Ambrose: Church and State in the Late Roman World*, London: Longman, 1999

Nanos, M., *The Irony of Galatians: Paul's Letter in First-Century Context*, Minneapolis, MN: Fortress, 2001

—— *The Mystery of Romans: The Jewish Context of Paul's Letter*, Minneapolis, MN: Fortress, 1996

Neusner, J., *Judaism and Christianity in the Age of Constantine*, Chicago, IL: University of Chicago Press, 2007

O'Donnell, J., *Augustine: A New Biography*, New York: Ecco, 2005

Odahl, C., *Constantine and the Christian Empire*, London; New York: Routledge, 2004

Osborn, E. *Clement of Alexandria*, Cambridge: Cambridge University Press, 2005

—— *Irenaeus of Lyons*, Cambridge: Cambridge University Press, 2001

—— *Tertullian: First Theologian of the West*, Cambridge: Cambridge University Press, 1997

Pagels, E., *The Gnostic Gospels*, London: Penguin, 1990

Painter, J., *Just James: The Brother of Jesus in History and Tradition*, Minneapolis, MN: Fortress, and Columbia, SC: University of South Carolina Press, 1999

Patzia, A., *The Emergence of the Church: Context, Growth, Leadership and Worship*, Downers Grove, IL: InterVarsity, 2001

Pearson, B., *Ancient Gnosticism: Traditions and Literature*, Minneapolis, MN: Fortress, 2007

Pelikan, J., *The Christian Tradition: A History of the Development of Doctrine, 1: The Emergence of the Catholic Tradition (100–600)*, Chicago, IL, and London: University of Chicago Press, 1971

—— *Christianity and Classical Culture*, New Haven, CT, and London: Yale University Press, 1993

Perkins, P., *Peter: Apostle for the Whole Church*, Minneapolis, MN: Fortress, 2000

Pettersen, A., *Athanasius*, London: Geoffrey Chapman, 1995

Pohlsander, H., *The Emperor Constantine*, London: Routledge, 2004

Ramsey, B., *Ambrose*, London: Routledge, 1997

Rankin, D., *Tertullian and the Church*, Cambridge and New York: Cambridge University Press, 1995

Rapp, C., *Holy Bishops in Late Antiquity: The Nature of Christian Leadership in an Age of Transition*, Berkeley, CA: University of California Press, 2005

Rebenich, S., *Jerome*, London: Routledge, 2001

Rees, B., *Pelagius: Life and Letters*, Rochester, NY: Boydell, 1998

Ross, S., *Roman Edessa*, London: Routledge, 2001

Roukema, R., *Gnosis and Faith in Early Christianity: An Introduction to Gnosticism*, London: SCM, 1999

Rousseau, P., *The Early Christian Centuries*, London: Pearson, 2002

—— *Pachomius: The Making of a Community in Fourth-Century Egypt*, Berkeley, CA; London: University of California Press, 1999

Rowland, C., *Christian Origins*, London: SPCK, 2002

Rubenstein, R., *When Jesus Became God: The Struggle to Define Christianity During the Last Days of Rome*, San Diego, CA; London: Harcourt, 1999

Rutgers, L., *Subterranean Rome: In Search of the Roots of Christianity in the Catacombs of the Eternal City*, Leuven: Peeters, 2000

Salisbury, J., *The Blood of Martyrs: Unintended Consequences of Ancient Violence*, New York; London: Routledge, 2004

Sanders, E., *The Historical Figure of Jesus*, London: Penguin, 1993

—— *Paul*, Oxford: OUP, 1991

Shanks, H., ed., *Christianity and Rabbinic Judaism: A Parallel History of Their Origins and Early Development*, Washington, DC: Biblical Archaeology Society, 1992

Skarsaune, O., *In the Shadow of the Temple: Jewish Influences on Early Christianity*, Downers Grove, IL: InterVarsity, 2002

Slee, M., *The Church in Antioch in the First Century CE: Communion and Conflict*, London; New York: Sheffield Academic Press, 2003

Stark, R., *The Rise of Christianity: A Sociologist Reconsiders History*, Princeton, NJ: Princeton University Press, 1996

Stegemann, E., & Stegemann, W., *The Jesus Movement: A Social History of its First Century*, Edinburgh: T. & T. Clark, 1999

Stump, E., & Kretzmann, N., eds., *The Cambridge Companion to Augustine*, Cambridge: Cambridge University Press, 2001

Theissen, G., *Fortress Introduction to the New Testament*, Minneapolis, MN: Fortress, 2003

—— *The Religion of the Earliest Churches: Creating a Symbolic World*, Minneapolis, MN: Fortress, 1999

Tomkins, S., *Paul and His World*, Oxford: Lion, 2004

Trevett, C., *Montanism: Gender, Authority and the New Prophecy*, Cambridge: Cambridge University Press, 1996

Trigg, J., *Origen*, London: Routledge, 1998

van Dam, R., *The Roman Revolution of Constantine*, Cambridge: Cambridge University Press, 2007

Vermès, G., *The Changing Faces of Jesus*, New York; London: Penguin, 2002

White, J., *Evidence and Paul's Journeys: An Historical Investigation into the Travels of the Apostle Paul*, Hilliard, OH: Parsagard, 2001

Wilken, R., *The Christians as the Romans Saw Them*, New Haven, CT: Yale University Press, 2003

Williams, D., *Ambrose of Milan and the End of the Arian–Nicene Conflicts*, Oxford: Clarendon, 1995

Williams, R., *Arius: Heresy and Tradition*, London: SCM, 2001

Wright, N. T., *The Resurrection of the Son of God*, London: SPCK, 2003

Young, F., Ayres, L., & Louth, A., eds., *The Cambridge History of Early Christian Literature*, Cambridge: Cambridge University Press, 2004

CHRISTIANITY

Index

Biblical books

Acknowledgments

Picture research by Zooid Pictures Limited

All maps and the diagram of basilica (p182) by Richard Watts at Total Media Services

pp8/9 Oleg Popov/Reuters/Corbis UK Ltd., 9t Hanan Isachar/Alamy, 12 Reproduced by courtesy of the Librarian and Director, The John Rylands University Library, The University of Manchester, 15 akg-images, 21 Bibliothèque Municipale Rouen/Dagli Orti/Art Archive, 24 akg-images, 26/27 Jon Arnold Images Ltd/Alamy, 27t Erich Lessing/akg-images, 29 Niedersachsisches Museum/Art Archive, 30 Dagli Orti/Art Archive, 34/35 Edgar Romer/Associated Press/Press Association Images, 36 Caro/Alamy, 37 PhotoStock-Israel/Alamy, 39 Tetra Images/Alamy, 41 Thomas Hartwell/Corbis UK Ltd., 42 C.M.Dixon/Ancient Art & Architecture Collection, 43t Dagli Orti/Baptistery of Orthodox Ravenna/Art Archive, 43b Joseph Martin/akg-images, 45 Candido Alves/AFP/ Getty Images, 46t Cameraphoto /akg-images, 47b The Granger Collection/TopFoto, 52 PA/Universitatsbibliothek Tuebingen, 53 Musee d'Art et d'Archeologie, Moulins, France/Lauros/Giraudon/Bridgeman Art Library, 56 Museum voor Schone Kunsten, Ghent/Giraudon/ Bridgeman Art Library, 58t Israel images/Alamy, 58 Noortman, Maastricht, Netherlands/Bridgeman Art Library, 59b Nathan Benn/Alamy, 60 Kharbine-Tapabor/ Art Archive, 64 Roger-Viollet/TopFoto, 66 Mary Evans Picture Library/Alamy, 68 Scala/Photo Scala, Florence, 69 Mary Evans Picture Library/Alamy, 70 Ann Ronon/ HIP/Photo Scala, Florence, 72 Delaware Art Museum, Wilmington, USA/Gift of Mrs Richard C. DuPont/ Bridgeman Art Library, 73t akg-images, 73b Private Collection/Bridgeman Art Library, 75 Photolibrary Group, 76 Dagli Orti/Accademia Venice/Art Archive, 78 Cameraphoto/akg-images, 81 akg-images, 84 Poodlesrock/Corbis UK Ltd., 86 Adam Woolfitt/Corbis UK Ltd., 87 akg-images, 88 Bibliotheque Nationale, Paris, France/Bridgeman Art Library, 91 Silvio Fiore/TopFoto, 97 akg-images, 99 Erich Lessing/akg-images, 100 akg-images, 102 Dagli Orti/Museo della Civilta Romana Rome/Art Archive, 105 Ancient Art & Architecture Collection, 106 Dagli Orti/Museo della Civilta Romana Rome/Art Archive, 107 Israel Images/Alamy, 108 Luciano Romano/Photo Scala, Florence, 109 Dagli Orti/ Provinciaal Museum G M Kam Nijmegen Netherlands/ Art Archive, 110 British Museum/Harper Collins Publishers/Art Archive, 113 Bibliotheque Nationale, Paris, France/Giraudon/Bridgeman Art Library, 113 Coll.

Archiv f.Kunst & Geschichte/akg-images, 114 Erich Lessing/akg-images, 116 Dagli Orti/Museo del Prado Madrid/Art Archive, 121 Ann Ronan/HIP/Photo Scala, Florence, 122 Dagli Orti/Galleria Borghese Rome/Art Archive, 124 Stapleton Collection/Corbis UK Ltd., 126 Biblioteca Nazionale, Turin, Italy/Bridgeman Art Library, 129 joel zatz/Alamy, 130 Bibliothèque Nationale Paris/ Art Archive, 135 akg-images, 136 Mary Evans Picture Library/Alamy, 142 Carmelite Collection Clamart/Dagli Orti/Art Archive, 144 akg-images, 150 The Institute for Antiquity and Christianity, 155 Dagli Orti/Art Archive, 161 Museo Episcopal de Vic, Osona, Catalonia, Spain/ Index/Bridgeman Art Library, 163 Erich Lessing/akg-images, 165 British Library/akg-images, 168 Alfredo Dagli Orti/Museo Capitolino Rome/Art Archive, 169 Dagli Orti/ Goreme Cappadoccia Turkey/Art Archive, 170 Andrea Jemolo/akg-images, 172 Paris, Bibliotheque Nationale./ akg-images, 174 Art Archive, 178 Gianni Dagli Orti/ Château de Chambord/Art Archive, 180 Bibliotheque Nationale/akg-images, 182 Erich Lessing/akg-images, 183 Dagli Orti/Archaeological Museum Sousse Tunisia/ Art Archive, 184 Andrea Jemolo/akg-images, 185 Erich Lessing/akg-images, 186 Gerhard Ruf/akg-images, 188 Erich Lessing/akg-images, 191 © Walker Art Gallery, National Museums Liverpool/Bridgeman Art Library, 193 Giraudon/Bridgeman Art Library, 194/195 Photolibrary Group, 196 Prisma/Ancient Art & Architecture Collection, 203 Monastery of Saint Catherine Sinai Egypt/Dagli Orti/Art Archive, 206 Dagli Orti/Art Archive, 207 Erich Lessing/akg-images, 209 Maynard Owen Williams/NGS Image Collection/Art Archive, 218 Electa/akg-images, 224 Eileen Tweedy/National Gallery London/Art Archive, 226 Julian Chichester/Bridgeman Art Library, 227 Jon Arnold Images Ltd/Alamy, 230 akg-images, 234 Bridgeman Art Library, 238 Stefan Diller/akg-images, 239 Oasis/Photo12. com, 243 Musee Municipal Antoine Vivenel, Compiegne, France/Lauros/Giraudon/Bridgeman Art Library

Lion Hudson

Commissioning editor: Paul Clifford
Project editor: Miranda Powell
Proofreader: Rachel Ashley-Pain
Designer: Emma DeBanks
Production manager: Kylie Ord